Smoke & Spice

Smoke & Spice

Cheryl Alters Jamison
and Bill Jamison

Foreword by Chris Schlesinger

THE HARVARD COMMON PRESS
Boston, Massachusetts

The Harvard Common Press
535 Albany Street
Boston, Massachusetts 02118

© 1994 by Cheryl Alters Jamison and Bill Jamison
Illustrations © 1994 by Paul Hoffman

The kettle grill silhouette (page 15) is a registered trademark ® of the Weber-Stephen Products Company, Palatine, Illinois, U.S.A.

Printed in the United States of America

Library of Congress Cataloging-in-Publication Data

Jamison, Cheryl Alters.
    Smoke & Spice : cooking with smoke — the real way to barbecue / Cheryl Alters Jamison and Bill Jamison ; foreword by Chris Schlesinger.
      p. cm.
  ISBN 1-55832-060-1 (cloth). — ISBN 1-55832-061-X (paper)
  1. Barbecue cookery. 2. Smoked foods. 3. Spices. I. Jamison, Bill. II. Title. III. Title: Smoke and spice.
  TX840.B3J36 1994
  641.7'6—dc20

Special bulk-order discounts are available on this and other Harvard Common Press books. Companies and organizations may purchase books for premiums or for resale, or may arrange a custom edition, by contacting the Marketing Director at the address above.

Text design by Joyce C. Weston
Illustrations by Paul Hoffman
Cover design by Joyce C. Weston
Cover photographs by Lois Ellen Frank

10 9 8 7 6

Dedication

To that merry band of barbecue fanatics
who've done so much over the last
couple of decades to bring an old
American craft back to its homegrown
roots—especially to Jim and Donna
Quessenberry and Wayne and PJ
Whitworth.

Contents

☆ Foreword ☆
by Chris Schlesinger

Nine years ago, when I opened the East Coast Grill in Cambridge, Massachusetts, I realized a dream conceived almost a decade earlier, just after I completed my first year as a cook. Now, finally, I was the chef. I could cook anything I wanted.

Given this new freedom, I decided to make the kind of food I like to eat. This meant a relentless reliance on grilled food—food with the spicy, loud flavors that I had discovered in places like Mexico, Central America, and the West Indies; and, of course, the beloved barbecue of my childhood.

I grew up in Williamsburg, Virginia. Although my folks were transported Northerners, eating barbecue was a cherished family tradition. In my part of Virginia, going out for barbecue meant driving twenty minutes out of town to a little joint called Pierce's Pitt Bar-B-Que.

On Pierce's menu was only one thing—shredded pork sandwiches. About twenty yards behind the restaurant was a second, smaller building where the pork shoulders were cooked in a simple concrete block pit covered with corrugated tin. The pork was slow-smoked directly over hardwood coals until it was very tender and smoky with a crisp exterior. It was then shredded, combined with vinegar and some hot sauce, and served on a cheap, spongy bun with creamy, sweet coleslaw on top. This was the barbecue I remembered, and this was the barbecue I wanted to recreate for my restaurant.

But, to my total surprise, I had no idea how to make it. I tried slow grilling, smoking, and everything in between, but I couldn't get close. At no time during all my years of professional training, including two years at the Culinary Institute of America and stints in some of New England's best restaurants, had I encountered anything like what I had in mind. Barbecue, a technique that was not listed among the leading culinary operations as defined by Escoffier, the father of classic French cuisine, was apparently not considered a fit subject for serious study.

My frustration ignited a fire in me that has burned ever since. I became determined to gain a firm culinary understanding of barbecue. One of the waitresses at the East Coast Grill, who was from Memphis, told me about the annual international barbecue competition held there every spring, known as Memphis in May. So I said, "What the hell, let's enter," and—reconfigured as Dr. Smoke and the Professors of BBQ in honor of the academic nature of our adopted hometown—I and two staff members sent in an application. No doubt humored because we were the first and only team from Massachusetts, we were accepted as contestants.

After a thirty-hour drive in a truck with an eighteen-foot smoker attached to the back, three tired Yankees and a one-eyed dog arrived at Tom Lee Park on the banks of the Mississippi in Memphis for a 72-hour intensive schooling in the technique, style, and good fellowship of that fine old tradition that both epitomizes and is nurtured by the culture of the South. Despite my lack of sleep and heavy beer consumption (or maybe because of it), I was able to exponentially increase my knowledge of barbecue by staggering through the grounds of the contest, continually posing questions to the pitmasters, who were more than willing to share their expertise with that funny Yankee fellow from Massachusetts.

What I discovered in those hazy hours in the swamp heat of Memphis May nights was that barbecue is a unique American foodway. It is defined in the voice and terms not of professional cooks, but of firemen, plumbers, airline pilots, and people for whom staying up all night cooking pork is a favorite way to spend time off. "You can't heat too hot too quick, or the meat she'll seize up on you," one told me. "If it gets too hot, the juices gonna steam off," said another. "Thermometers don't do no good; it's how the meat pulls that tells you when it's done," insisted a third.

As I got answers to my barrage of questions, it started to come to me: low temperatures, long periods of time, making tough cuts of meat tender, cooking through the point of doneness. Hey, we're talking about braising principles here. I started to piece together a definition of barbecue in culinary terms: "A process whereby a large cut of tough meat is cooked by the smoke of a hardwood fire at low temperatures (210 degrees or less) for a long period of time, with doneness determined by the meat's tenderness."

More important, I began to view barbecue from a new perspective, seeing it as an important part of American culture, like the luau in Hawaii or the *charrascuria* of Brazil. The people who taught me this are neither academics nor professional cooks, but their knowledge was honed in experience and shared with joy. For them barbecue means getting dirty, drinking beer, and talking while cooking great food with no trace of pretension. For, next to survival, fellowship is the main purpose of cooking and eating. People spending time together while preparing food and eating—this is the essence of barbecue, and this essence is captured here in Cheryl and Bill's book.

Even though barbecue typifies the expression "an inexact art," the Jamisons prepare the cook for all eventualities. Here you will find the basics of barbecue technique, with particular focus on the three key principles of heat, time, and fuel. Having provided a solid base of knowledge, the Jamisons show barbecue in its various guises, giving recipes for everything from the barbecue classics like rubs and sauces to dishes containing a whole range of ingredients and flavors, such as Jamaican Jerked Salmon or South-of-the-Border Garlic Soup.

But my favorite parts of *Smoke & Spice* (and the sure sign that true believers wrote it) are the tales, generously sprinkled throughout the book, of the real people who created the barbecue tradition. These tales will acquaint you with some of the more notorious barbecue events and traditions in this country.

So grab a beer, dust off the smoker, and get ready to barbecue everything from the classic whole hog (the recipe here includes the advice of one of the true masters of barbecue, the Arkansas Trav'ler) to exotic things like Soused Swordfish. *Smoke & Spice* is informative, creative, and packed with outstanding food.

Chris Schlesinger, a chef and restaurateur in Cambridge, Massachusetts, is the co-author of The Thrill of the Grill.

A Passion, a Pastime, ☆ and a Party ☆

It's time to graduate from grilling. American cooks have been enrolled in "Introductory Barbecue" for a half century now, since the days when we all liked Ike. We've enjoyed cooking outdoors, but we're weary of wieners and charred chicken, yearning more and more for the full flavor of old-time, real barbecue, the kind popularly known as "Bar-B-Q," food that dances on your senses and gets your lips to rejoicing.

This is a complete guide to the genuine article, where we move beyond searing and sizzling into really smoking. Some of the dozens of books on barbecue grilling acknowledge and applaud this advanced art, but they usually suggest that a home cook can't hope to match the results of a professional pitmaster in the Carolinas, Kansas City, Memphis, or Texas. At best, they may say, you can add a few wood chips to a conventional grill or slather a smoky sauce over food. Bunk.

In the last decade there's been an unheralded revolution in home smoking equipment and supplies, the subject of the first two chapters. The new developments allow anyone to make great barbecue—real, honest-to-goodness 'Q'—in their backyard, on their balcony, or even inside, often in ways that avoid the potential health hazards of grilling. All you need to succeed are the right resources and a little learnin' about the barbecue craft and its delightful, part-and-parcel culture. The cooking isn't more complex than grilling—just the taste—and it's actually much more fun.

Let's Join the Party

Today we use the term "barbecue" in a multitude of ways, but in the American past, it mainly meant a big, festive community

1

gathering. An English visitor in the eighteenth century described the custom to friends back home, saying that Americans were "extremely fond of an entertainment they call a Barbacue," which was "a large party" that "generally ended in intoxication." George Washington probably even slept at one. In his diary, the first president noted that he once went to Alexandria, Virginia, for a "barbicue" that lasted three days.

When workers laid the cornerstone for the nation's capitol in 1793, the leaders of the new republic celebrated with a huge barbecue. Right before the outbreak of the Civil War, Scarlett O'Hara met Rhett Butler at a barbecue in *Gone with the Wind*. Throughout American history, when churches wanted to lure the less devoted, when politicians needed to attract a crowd for a campaign speech, when folks had any cause for festivity, they held a barbecue and invited everyone.

The cooks didn't grill hamburgers at these affairs. They dug a long, deep pit in the ground, filled this trench with logs, burned the wood down to low-temperature coals, and then slow-roasted whole animals and fish suspended above the smoky fire. That was barbecue then, and it's still the essence of the art. To get real with barbecue, you have to return to the roots, and that means *celebrating* a meal with friends and family by *smoking food slow and low over smoldering wood.*

That's been a grand tradition in the United States from the beginning, but many Americans lost touch with the legacy about the time they discovered frozen vegetables and TV dinners. We were moving to cities and suburbs in droves then and couldn't tear up our streets and backyards to build underground pits. Only the predominantly rural regions of the South, Southwest, and Midwest maintained the memory of real barbecue. The rest of us learned to make do with high-heat charcoal grilling and began calling it barbecue simply because it was done outdoors.

Grilling is a fine method of cooking, but it doesn't produce food with the hearty, woodsy resonance of slow-smoked fare. Those who have tasted true barbecue know the difference, and they are almost certain to be passionate about the distinction.

For them, smoked ribs are as superior to a grilled pork chop as a lottery win is to taxes.

In the same vein, anyone who has spent an afternoon barbecuing with children or friends understands why Americans made that their traditional party of preference. It's a national pastime older than baseball and just as spirited. When you add the fun to the flavor of the food, you don't need a diploma to tell you that you've reached a new level of barbecue bliss.

Part One

Honest-to-Goodness Barbecue

The Secrets of
☆ Success ☆

Real barbecue is bragging food. Maybe it's the great smoky flavor or maybe it's the adulation of the eaters, but somehow all pitmasters develop into natural boasters, cocky enough to milk a bull. They learn to tell tall tales, wear odd clothes, act in wacky ways, and otherwise promote their aura as magicians of meat.

When asked about their secrets, experienced pitmasters prance around the answer like Elvis in concert, hinting of mysterious ingredients in their special dry rub, marinade, or sauce. It's all part of the fun of barbecue, but beginners shouldn't be deceived about the main secret of success. While everything you do makes some difference in your results, the only critical consideration is your smoking equipment and how you use it.

A lot of devices will work, including your old kettle grill, homemade contraptions, inexpensive water smokers, and sure-fire metal pits. We cover the various options in this chapter, focusing on the strengths and limitations of each. Specific information about using the equipment—and other barbecuing advice—is scattered throughout the recipe chapters in a range of "BBQ Tips." As long as you know your equipment and understand some barbecue basics, you're just a little practice short of your own bragging rights.

Barbecue Basics

The two essentials of real barbecue are a low cooking temperature and a cloud of wood smoke. You need sufficient heat to cook the food—the main difference from smoke curing—but you want to keep the temperature just above the level that meat will register inside when done. Since pork needs to be cooked

7

to an internal temperature of 160° F to 170° F, you barbecue it at 180° F to 220° F, a good range for other food as well.

In smoke curing, by contrast, a combination of salt and smoke is used to preserve food rather than cook it and temperatures are held below 100° F. That's what makes a barbecued pork shoulder an entirely different animal than a cured country ham. Both processes are likely to reduce the moisture content of meat—concentrating flavor—but barbecuing does little or nothing for preservation. If you find yourself with leftovers, they must be refrigerated like anything else you cook.

Grilling goes in the opposite direction with heat. Much of the time you want the highest temperature possible in grilling because the goal is to sear meat on the outside and hold the juices inside. The method works best with tender cuts, like a good steak or chop, which are relatively free of connective tissue. Traditional barbecue meat, on the other hand, is as tough as John Wayne's boots. Spareribs, beef brisket, and the like require slow cooking at a low temperature to break down their stubborn tissues, the reason they were ideal for barbecue from the beginning. When you barbecue steaks, fish, or vegetables, as we do in many of our recipes, you do it to add smoky flavor, not because the slow cooking is needed for tenderness.

The rich smokiness you want in all barbecue should come from smoldering wood, not from fat or oil dripping on coals or hot metal. The difference is enormous, both in taste and in health risks. The smoke produced by burning fat contains benzopyrene, a carcinogen that sticks to food. The effect is almost unavoidable in grilling, but it isn't a problem in barbecuing if you have a water reservoir or pan beneath the meat, an option with much of the equipment.

The use of water or other liquids is a bit controversial in barbecue circles. People in the past didn't add water to their pits in any fashion, and many pitmasters disdain the idea today, contending that barbecuing must be a dry cooking process. In truth, though, most methods of barbecuing have always involved the circulation of moisture-laden air over food, making the process much "wetter" than cooking in a conventional oven. We think water has a proper place in barbecuing, depending on how it's used and what you're cooking. Traditional barbecue meats benefit from losing moisture as they cook, shrinking their size, but many nontraditional foods benefit from bumping up the humidity inside the smoker. As long as you avoid cooking the food with steam instead of smoke—potentially a problem when the water boils—the extra moisture helps to prevent lean meat and fish from getting too dry.

Cooking Times and Temperatures

Though critical in barbecuing, a low cooking temperature isn't always easy to measure or maintain. Equipment manufacturers are still oriented to grilling, where you need only minimal control over the cooking temperature. Even major companies often fail to put useful thermometers on their smokers, telling complainers like us that barbecuing is an "inexact art." There's a lot of truth in that statement, but the art isn't as inexact as their thinking. As with any other cooking process, if you can gauge the cooking temperature and control fluctuations, you can make a reasonably reliable estimate of the time required for barbecuing anything.

That's exactly what we do in our recipes. We provide an approximate cooking time based on optimum barbecuing temperatures around 200° F, allowing for some variations in factors such as weather and altitude. Cooking times are important information in recipes, but they won't be fully useful unless you've got a good thermometer and a way to control the heat level of your smoker.

Industrial-quality thermometers are built into the best smokers, but the thermometers that are sometimes included with other kinds of barbecue equipment may not be adequate. Any type of gauge that reads something like "warm," "ideal," and "hot" isn't worth much more than the beer concession at a Baptist picnic. Replace it with a true thermometer fitted in the same opening or get an oven or grill thermometer that sits on the grate next to the food, basically the same options that are available to people without any form of temperature gauge on their smoker.

The most practical solution, if your equipment has a vent or other opening on the lid, is to use a portable candy thermometer that has a head facing outward, such as Taylor's model 5972. Insert the probe into the opening, placing the tip as close as possible to the cooking area without touching the food, and position the head so that it's not blocking all air circulation and is clearly visible. You can check the temperature without lifting the lid, a major advantage over an oven and grill thermometer inside the smoker. If you have to remove the cover to see your thermometer, you release substantial heat and slow the cooking process beyond the time projected in a recipe.

A thermometer is most useful when you have the means to fine-tune the cooking temperature—with air vents or the amount of fuel you're burning—but it's a valuable tool even when you lack much control. In that situation, common with water smokers, you can at least add or subtract cooking time based on whether the internal temperature is higher or lower than the range suggested in a recipe.

A thermometer is particularly important when you're first getting the feel of new equipment or making the transition from grilling to smoking on old equipment. With a season or two of experience, you may be able to gauge the cooking temperature in other ways. You'll learn how much flame you want in your log pit, or how much heat your electric water smoker is generating under normal conditions in your climate with your extension cord. If you're burning charcoal, and tracking the cooking temperature over time, you'll develop a good sense of how many briquettes or hardwood lumps are needed to produce and maintain a 200° F fire in your size and type of smoker.

However you manage it, you need to make sure you're cooking slow and low. The principle is vital in barbecue, and however inexact the art may be, measurements of your success are as useful as in any other form of cooking. If you can confirm that you're smoking steady between 180° F and 220° F, you can count on the approximate cooking times in our recipes. More important, you can count on great 'Q' from a wide range of equipment.

Log-Burning Pits

The best way to barbecue is with a log fire, which is how it all began. In the early years the only equipment Americans needed was an ax and a shovel. They cleared trees along a stretch of open land, cut the branches into logs, and loaded the wood into a long pit several feet deep. They burned the logs down to smoldering coals and cooked their food over the smoky fire for a full night or longer, adding wood as necessary to maintain a steady, low temperature.

Originally the pits were open on top and the meat was hung above the fire or placed on a ground-level grate. Many people still barbecue in a similar style, but around the turn of the century, the country's first commercial Bar-B-Q joints introduced important changes in the technology.

You can see how pits evolved by visiting some of the oldest joints, such as Kreuz Market in Lockhart, Texas. When German immigrants founded Kreuz's in 1900 as a meat market, the clever butchers adopted American barbecuing as a way to tenderize and sell tough cuts of meat. They built a brick pit in the back of the shop, just like the one that's there today. It doesn't look a bit modern anymore, but it still offers many advantages over an open underground trench. The brick walls elevated the working level enough to keep the cooks out of the chiropractor's office and the newfangled metal lid trapped heat and smoke inside to make the cooking process more efficient and even. The home-spun inventors also placed the fire farther from the food, moving the burning logs from directly underneath the meat to the far end of the long pit opposite an outside vent.

Hundreds of other Bar-B-Q joints created their own similar closed pits, simple but ingenious contraptions that carried an old legacy into a new age. No one has really improved on the design in the century since, and just recently it has become the model for a big breakthrough in home barbecue equipment.

About a decade ago, several small but dynamic companies started manufacturing log-burning metal pits with an offset fire-box at one end and a chimney at the other, just like that ancient brick pit at Kreuz Market. You can keep the fire well away from the meat, get good smoke circulation, and maintain a constant low temperature for extended periods, regulating the heat with damper controls on the firebox and chimney. You check the temperature every twenty to thirty minutes and add wood as needed, maybe once an hour.

The advantage of burning logs is the density of wood smoke they produce. Like the lava rocks in a gas or electrical grill, most charcoal doesn't generate smoke unless fat or food falls on it. So a major part of the heat source in any kind of charcoal, gas, or electrical device cooks food without smoking it, regardless of how many wood chips or chunks you use. You can barbecue many things well with this kind of equipment, as our recipes show, but you can never quite match the smokiness of the meat at a great Bar-B-Q joint.

Prime Log Pits

Top-of-the-line log pits do produce that full flavor from traditional barbecue meats, and they do it to perfection. If you are set on making the best pork shoulder or beef brisket in town, this is the way to go. The premier pits, made by custom fabricators, weigh a minimum of several hundred pounds and start in price around five to six hundred dollars, comparable to the cost of a quality gas grill. The weight and the expense come from the use of thick, heavy-gauge metal that's capable of standing up to serious log fires for a lifetime of use.

When we went shopping for a log pit a few years ago, our choice ultimately was the Pitt's & Spitt's model that's pictured, a genuine gem. On all of the Houston company's products, the craftsmanship is outstanding in looks, durability, and capability. The pits feature an offset firebox with ¼-inch plate

12

walls, a grilling area above the firebox, stainless steel parts, an accurate industrial thermometer, a water reservoir with a drain, and superior smoke drafting. Call 800-521-2947 for more information, or visit the Houston showroom.

Other leading manufacturers in the young and booming field include Oklahoma Joe's (405-336-3080), JR Enterprises (800-432-8187), and Smokemaster (512-345-7563), all worth checking out. Among the companies, Oklahoma Joe's probably has the widest distribution, at least in the Midwest and Southwest, and competitive prices.

When you compare the range of options among companies and among models, be sure to look at all the features, not just the cost. Consider the heft of the firebox and the lightness of the lid. Decide the value of a water reservoir, which helps to keep meat juicy and eliminates the possible carcinogenic effects of fat dripping on hot metal. Examine the quality of the metal fabrication, even the sturdiness of the wheels. All the details matter because a prime log pit should provide a lifetime of barbecue bliss.

Popular Value Pits

One of the few liabilities of the top log pits is their size. The heavy-duty construction is an asset in barbecuing, but it makes the pits fairly expensive and bulky. If your bank account or outdoor space is limited, you might want to look at other ways to cook with wood.

The best alternatives are the moderately priced, lighter-weight pits that are becoming widely available in discount stores, warehouse clubs, hardware stores, and mail-order catalogs. They look similar to their big brothers and function much the same, but the thinner metal of the firebox is more suitable for wood chunks than large logs. What you sacrifice in capability and features, you make up in savings. Prices start around two hundred dollars and seem to be dropping as the competition increases.

One of the best established manufacturers, the New Braunfels Smoker Company (800-232-3398), produces a variety of popular pits under different brand names, including Hondo, Cattleman's, and Black Diamond. The Hondo is particularly versatile, capable of burning small logs as well as wood chunks, and it is fitted with an opening on the lid for an optional industrial thermometer.

Other companies are jumping into this booming market. Brinkmann (800-527-0717) entered the market in the early 1990s, and other major manufacturers such as Char-Broil (800-241-8981) are considering it as we go to press. Within the next decade sales could rival those of charcoal grills.

Wood-Burning Ovens

Another good option for barbecuing is an outdoor oven. These ovens generally produce less smoky flavor than a log or chunk pit, but they are easy and economical to use. An Oregon company, Traeger Industries (800-TRAEGER), makes a line of grills that cook with wood pellets. You set the oven for the lowest of three temperatures and load a supply of pellets. Then a patented auger mechanism feeds the pellets into a small, efficient firebox under the cooking grate. Prices start at less than five hundred dollars.

Cookshack ovens are similar in cost and convenience. Primarily a manufacturer of commercial barbecue equipment, Cookshack (800-423-0698) makes a model suitable for home use that operates just like the bigger restaurant ones. Powered by electricity, it burns wood chunks in a tightly sealed oven that you turn on and don't touch again until you're done. You can even install the smoker inside, venting it through a standard kitchen ventilation system.

If you want to cook indoors, though, you should also consider one of the "stove-top smokers" introduced in recent years. The Cameron model made by C.M. International (719-390-0505) can't handle a full range of barbecue like the Cookshack can, but it's one-tenth the price and requires no installation or outside venting. Designed to fit over a back and front burner on a range, the metal container with a sliding lid holds several fish fillets or pieces of chicken. Your stove provides the heat, which ignites wood dust (packaged with the cooker) to generate smoke. The canny little contraption produces a mild but distinctive smoke flavor, ideal for some dishes.

Charcoal Grills and Ovens

Many people barbecue with a combination of charcoal and wood chunks or chips. You don't get the same level of smoky flavor as you do from logs, but that can be an advantage at times. With practice you can do a reasonable job on traditional barbecue meats, particularly pork, and even an inexperienced barbecuer can make superior chicken, fish, and vegetable dishes.

The conventional charcoal grill on your patio is all you need for many of our recipes, though you have to use it in a much different way for barbecuing than for grilling. Since grills are designed for high-heat cooking, the biggest challenge is keeping the temperature low enough for long enough to get the right result. A thermometer is essential, at least until you've mastered the trick.

Some kind of vented cover, even an aluminum-foil tent, is necessary for smoking, along with an ample supply of wood chips and chunks presoaked in water. The rest is straightforward, if not simple. On the most common grills, you cook with indirect heat by placing the food over a pan of water on the opposite side of the grill from the hot charcoal and wood. Close the vents on the grill most of the way, to hold down the intensity of the fire, and try not to lift the lid except to add more heated coals or pieces of wood.

The drawing illustrates how to barbecue using a popular style of charcoal grill. Start by soaking your wood—at least 30 minutes for chips and 3 hours for chunks—and lighting 20 to 25 charcoal briquettes or 10 to 12 handfuls of lump charcoal. When the fuel is ready, place a metal pan, half full of water, on the lower grate. The hot charcoal goes alongside, directly over one of the three bottom vents. Put the wet wood on the coals, and set the food on the upper grate above the water pan and under the top vent of the closed lid. Place the probe of a candy thermometer through the top vent, with the

15

round temperature gauge wedged on the outside and the tip near the food. Some people center the pan and the food on the two grates, with the coals and wood on both sides of the bottom grid, but we prefer the other approach because it allows us to position the thermometer better.

Regulate the heat mainly with the opposite bottom and top vents, opening them a notch to increase the temperature and closing them to decrease it. Leave the other bottom vents closed. With food that requires an extended cooking time, add a small amount of preheated coals—about a quarter of the initial quantity—as soon as the temperature drops below 180° F, usually every hour or two. Use tongs to place the coals through the gap between the top grill handle and the kettle rim. Replenish the wood at the same time or even more often, whenever the smoke dies down.

Barbecuing is simpler in an oven-style grill with an adjustable firebox, a built-in thermometer, and a side door for loading fuel. You can regulate the temperature by raising or lowering the firebox, and you can add charcoal and wood without opening the lid and releasing heat. Several companies make versions, but the Hasty-Bake Charcoal Oven (800-4AN-OVEN) is the original, first built in 1948. It's still a favorite among barbecuers, used by two award-winners at the big 1993 Memphis in May cook-off. The main drawback may be the price, which is high for a charcoal grill, sometimes in the same range as a wood-burning pit.

Water Smokers

Unlike charcoal grills, gas and electric grills don't work well with real barbecue. You can add wood chips to the lava rocks or other heat element in many models, but they aren't designed for slow cooking at low temperatures. If you want a similar level of ease and convenience, it's best to invest $50 to $150 in a water smoker. Usually powered by electricity or charcoal, water smokers don't always excel with traditional barbecue meat, but they do work great on food that benefits from light smoking and added moisture.

The advantages of an electric water smoker can be compelling. You plug it into an outdoor socket or an extension cord running inside, add presoaked pieces of wood, and you don't need to tamper with anything again for a couple of hours or longer. It maintains a steady low cooking temperature without any need for adjustments. If you're cooking a large cut of meat, you'll have to replenish the wood and water once or twice, but otherwise the smoker almost begs you to leave it alone.

That's the rub for many barbecuers. You don't feel like you are contributing much to the cooking. Instead of sitting around with friends tending the fire, you are inside paying bills or watching TV. Some of the credit for success has to go to the local utility company, not exactly a bragging secret.

Charcoal water smokers provide a little more direct involvement in the cooking process, though they are also simple to operate. You start the fire with a large amount of charcoal—usually a minimum of 5 pounds—and seldom have to add more. You buy the low attention level with high fuel costs, which over the long haul make the charcoal smokers more expensive than the electric ones, despite their lower initial price. The charcoal models also fluctuate more in cooking temperature, firing up at the top end of real barbecue range, or maybe higher, and then dropping steadily over time to more appropriate levels, or even lower.

All water smokers look much the same and operate on similar principles. Shaped like something a dinosaur dropped on the patio, they have a domed lid (often fitted with an imprecise thermometer), one or two grates for food, a pan for holding water or other liquids, and the heat source on the bottom. The water helps keep the temperature low and prevents the undesirable smoke produced by fat falling in the fire. It also adds considerable moistness to food, much more than you get from a water reservoir in a log pit. When you want a crisp, crunchy finish in a dish, you may need to cook without the water pan, or at least remove the pan during the last stages of cooking.

Ceramic smokers made originally in China and Japan look a bit like water smokers and also retain moisture because of the insulating properties of their walls. More common in the States a generation ago than today, they seem to be disappearing just as the market for water smokers has boomed. Even Weber (800-999-3237) and Char-Broil (800-241-8981) make water smokers now, though Meco (800-346-3256) and particularly Brinkmann (800-527-0717) offer a more extensive line, as well as greater experience in the field.

Homemade Smokers

Barbecuing was America's original and most popular form of outdoor cooking until grilling surged into the forefront after the Second World War. Equipment was a major reason for the shift. By the 1950s factories were turning out basic, cheap grills faster than Formica, but those who wanted a barbecue smoker for home use had to make it for themselves. That's still a good option for some people, even with the solid commercial products available today. A lot of barbecue cook-off champions work on homemade equipment, sometimes expensively fabricated pits in special shapes ranging from armadillos to whiskey bottles.

Most do-it-yourselfers start with 55-gallon metal drums—well-scrubbed ones that never contained anything toxic. They are moderately easy to convert into a smoker and, most important, they project an authentic homespun feel, letting everyone know you're no drugstore dude.

A single drum cut in half horizontally, the most common design, is better for grilling than for smoking, but it can manage either. You split the barrel lengthwise, adding hinges on the back and a handle in front for a lid. Any kind of heavy metal grid can serve as a grate for holding the food. The most difficult part is attaching legs, usually accomplished by welding or bolting angle irons to the drum.

To avoid that job, you can use the barrel vertically, which elevates the working area to a comfortable height and also improves the smoke circulation needed for real barbecue. Among several options for rigging it, you can cut one end from the drum, place the opening over a brick fire pit, and hang meat from hooks secured to the vented top.

A double-barrel configuration is even better for barbecuing, though the construction is more complex. The bottom drum serves as an offset firebox, allowing you to keep the flame at an optimum distance from the food. Some experts recommend using parts from wood stoves for such elements as the firebox door, cast-iron supports, flues, and chimneys with dampers. Wood stove dealers and large hardware stores should have sources.

An experienced welder can build any of these barrel smokers from the illustration, but a few tips may help you to get it right. Remove any existing paint as well as you can and refinish all surfaces with a high-temperature paint. Install a good thermometer near the cooking area, so you can check the temperature easily. Make sure you have a well-controlled flow of air from the firebox, across the food, and out through a chimney or vent at the opposite end of the smoker. A baffle may help insure proper smoke circulation. If you want to burn logs instead of charcoal, as you should, line the bottom of the barrel with sand and firebrick to keep the wood from burning through and to reinforce the heat-retention properties of the thin metal.

A brick pit is another option for anyone with a lifetime address and basic masonry skills. A simple brick rectangle with a metal grate and lid will work, though it's better to add an attached outside firebox at one end of the pit and a chimney at the other, both fitted with mechanisms for regulating air circulation. Even someone who isn't handy at all can make a temporary version of a similar pit. Just stack concrete blocks about four feet high in a cleared, level area—perhaps a driveway—borrow a grate from your grill or oven, and use heavy-duty aluminum foil as a lid.

What you can barbecue well depends on what you build. A double-barrel pit or a sophisticated brick pit has the same kind of broad range as a store-bought log-burner, though they are trickier to master. Other homemade options are more limited in capabilities, but any that can handle a true wood fire have more potential than a manufactured charcoal smoker.

Whether you build or buy, your equipment is your key to barbecue success. You may be inclined after awhile to give more credit to your skills and secrets, but you won't be bragging about much if you ever forget that the fire comes before the food.

Fuels and
☆ Tools ☆

If someone ever discovers a way to fix real barbecue by pushing a button, life will be as dull as a dance at a bankers' convention. Cooks add the soul to barbecue, and they do it through their fuels and tools.

Wood

Cigars produce smoke and so does burning fat, but you don't want to cook with either one. The smoke flavor in real barbecue should come mainly from wood. If you aren't using it in one form or another, you aren't barbecuing.

Only hardwoods work. Soft, resinous woods, such as pine, cedar, and spruce, contain too much sap, which makes their smoke harsh and foul-tasting. Avoid plywood, construction scraps, or anything you cannot positively identify as an appropriate, untreated hardwood.

The most common barbecue woods are listed in the flavoring chart on page 28. Many pitmasters swear by a certain wood, particularly hickory or oak, but the differences are less substantial than the similarities. Usually people prefer what grows in their neck of the woods, and that always seems to suit the food they fix.

If you have a log-burning pit, the optimum kind, your choice of woods will be limited to your region anyway, unless you're willing to pay some heavy freight charges. To find out what's available, check the yellow pages for firewood dealers. You can also call local restaurants that smoke food and ask about their wood sources, but unless they are authentic Bar-B-Q joints, they may not cook with logs.

Most backyard barbecuers get their smoke flavor from wood chips or chunks, both sold in small bags in stores that carry outdoor cooking supplies. Chips should be soaked in water or another liquid—perhaps beer, wine, or juice—for a minimum of 30 minutes, preferably longer, so they will smoke instead of flame. When they are well saturated, you place them on top of a charcoal fire right before the food goes on the grate. One handful produces a mild smoke flavor in anything that cooks for less than an hour. For a deeper smoke taste, add more chips, and replenish them periodically over an extended cooking time, whenever the vented smoke starts dying out, perhaps as often as every thirty minutes.

Wood chunks work better than chips for most barbecuing and are a little more versatile. You can cook with them straight from the bag, burning them down to embers. Or presoak them and put them on a charcoal fire for a few hours. The dry chunks produce a lot of smoky flavor, but they tend to burn unevenly, making it difficult to maintain a steady temperature unless you have an offset firebox and a good thermometer. Several soaked chunks used in combination with charcoal result in the same flavor as a handful of chips, but they last longer, an asset in slow and low cooking.

Charcoal

Many people who cook with charcoal pick up any old bag that's handy or cheap. This can be a mistake. Charcoal varies as much as Madonna's moods and has almost the same chance of being a real stinker.

The problem is in the contents. Standard charcoal briquettes are made by turning sawdust to carbon in a combustion process that excludes oxygen. This burns away the wood flavor, but even worse things may happen after that point. To bind the carbonized wood into briquettes and promote ignition, many manufacturers add other substances, sometimes including petroleum products, coal, and sodium nitrate. When lit, these briquettes are bound to pollute the air, and they may do a little jig on your taste buds as well.

The advantage of the standard briquettes is that they provide an even, constant heat for a considerable period of time. With practice you can control their rate of burning to maintain the low, steady temperatures needed for real barbecue, and you can avoid the need to add more coals to the fire on a frequent basis. By themselves the briquettes won't provide any wood smoke flavor, but you can get that with the addition of wood chips or chunks.

Recently, some manufacturers have started putting in the wood for you, making briquettes studded with noncarbonized pieces of hardwood. It's a convenient way to get the kind of smoke you want, but you may still have the undesirable additives, and you lose control over the amount of wood you're burning in the charcoal fire.

We prefer to add chips or chunks ourselves, and we prefer to use briquettes bound together with vegetable starches only. Likely to be labeled "all-natural" briquettes, they offer the strengths of their conventional cousins without the drawbacks, and they burn for as long or longer than any kind of charcoal on the market. The only difficulty is finding them. If you can't locate a version in a local store, a good source is Nature's Own, a company that makes a range of superior charcoal and wood products. Their products are available by mail-order from Peoples Smoke 'n Grill (800-729-5800).

Lump hardwood charcoal, sometimes called chunk charwood, is another good option when used in combination with wood chips or chunks. It is carbonized, like all charcoal, but it's left in irregular shapes instead of being compressed into briquettes, eliminating the need for fillers and binders. It burns cleanly, ignites easily, and produces a steady, long-lasting fire.

The main problem with lump hardwood charcoal is that it burns hotter than briquettes, so you have to be more careful about controlling the temperature. The solution is to reduce the amount of charcoal used in cooking and to keep the lumps spread slightly apart from each other.

That's merely an extension of what you do with any charcoal fire in barbecuing. Except in a water smoker, you use fewer coals than you would for grilling the same food and you keep them loosely spaced rather than stacked together. The number of coals needed varies with the kind of equipment, but a good starting point for experimentation is twenty to fifty briquettes or ten to twenty-five handfuls of hardwood lumps, depending on the size of the firebox and its distance from the food. If you need to add more charcoal after an hour or two, preheat it in a metal container and use tongs to place the pieces in the fire.

Fire Starters

Starting a log fire in a barbecue pit is similar to doing the same thing in a fireplace or wood stove. You stack a few logs carefully to allow room for air to circulate around them, and ignite the wood with kindling. Just don't use resinous kindling, such as fatwood, in a pit. We put a few chunks of hardwood under the logs and get them burning with Weber Flamegos, white cubes made of natural, nonpetroleum materials that seem to us more effective, safer, and environmentally sensitive than lighter fluids.

To begin a charcoal fire, we recommend using the metal chimneys designed for the purpose and sold in almost any store that carries outdoor cooking supplies. You just light crumpled newspaper in the bottom of the sheet metal cylinder, and that ignites the charcoal you pile in the top portion. If you need to heat additional coals later, the chimneys are ready-made for the purpose. Best of all, they're inexpensive and hassle-free. Electric fire starters are equally easy to use, but the odd blend of technologies seems to us a little like drinking bourbon with root beer.

Charcoal is ready for grilling purposes as soon as it's covered completely with a thin layer of gray ash. For barbecuing, you can let it burn down a few minutes longer, until it's thickly coated with ash and no red glow is visible. You should be able to hold your hand about five inches above the coals for a minimum of five seconds.

Barbecue Tools

Heat-resistant gloves. The best way to remove food from a smoker, or to shift it around, is with your hands, securely wrapped in heat-resistant gloves. Never puncture your vittles with a fork. Tongs work with small items, but if you point a pair of the overgrown tweezers at a ten-pound brisket, the poor pincers are going to wilt in your paws. Kitchen or welder's mitts offer good protection for your hands, but we prefer neoprene gloves designed for firemen. They can handle anything and they clean quickly. Besides, the big, black, shiny mitts have a certain pitmaster sex appeal. We ordered ours from Pitt's & Spitt's (800-521-2947), which also sells the next two items and a full range of other barbecue supplies.

Mopping brushes. Mopping or basting is a big part of barbecuing, as we explain in the next chapter. Cotton string dish mops work best, but pastry brushes or even nylon paintbrushes do an adequate job. Clean them thoroughly at the end of the day, even dunking cotton mop heads in boiling water.

Kitchen syringe. Some foods, especially poultry, benefit from the injection of spices and liquid into the meat to add flavor and moistness. This is done with an inexpensive kitchen syringe, an oversized needle resembling something a veterinarian might use to inoculate a cow. To use, push the plunger down to expel any air and then dip the needle into your injection liquid. Draw the plunger back slowly until the syringe fills fully and then inject the liquid deep into the food in several spots. Be sure to clean the syringe after each use with hot, soapy water.

Instant-read meat thermometer. In addition to a cooking thermometer, most barbecuers will want a thermometer that can give an instant reading of the internal temperature of meat. You don't need to check traditional barbecue meats for doneness because they are cooked so long, but you'll want that capability with many other foods. Some of the handiest models are designed to clip in your pocket.

Fireplace poker or shovel. For a pit in particular, and some other smokers as well, you need a metal poker or hand-held shovel to move around coals, logs, and ashes. You can find them at any store that carries fireplace or wood stove supplies.

Wire brush. It's important to keep your cooking grate clean, so food doesn't stick or taste like what you cooked the last time. Instead of soap or other scouring agents, use a heavy-duty wire brush, available at hardware stores. Some are designed specifically for cleaning grills, but general-purpose versions also work. Scrub the grate when it's hot, preferably right after cooking or, if you forget, the next time you fire up the smoker.

Sturdy work table. An outdoor cook shouldn't be running to the kitchen to work. You want your supplies, sauces, and refreshments handy, and you need an area for prepping, cutting, and serving the day's feast. A card table will work, but the more you barbecue, the more you'll want something larger and heavier.

Tidbit utensils. If you're planning to cook bite-size morsels or fish in your smoker, it's worth investing in a portable grate with a small mesh that prevents food from falling through. Griffo Grill and Oscarware make models widely distributed around the country. A set of metal skewers is also useful.

Drip pan. To barbecue on a covered charcoal grill, you need a drip pan to place beneath the food alongside the coals. If you use a regular kitchen pan, instead of a disposable aluminum one, wrap it in foil or spray it with a nonstick cooking spray to make cleaning easier. Fill the pan halfway with water or another liquid.

Smokeproof dishes. Use pans and dishes that won't discolor easily from smoke, such as cast-iron pots or something that can be cleaned with relative ease, such as a Pyrex dish. Disposable foil pans are a good option, too. Heavy-duty foil can be fashioned into trays for lightweight food or used for wrapping various items. Other baking dishes and heat-proof utensils can be used with barbecuing, but they may require a lot of scrubbing to remove the dark smoke color, particularly if you're smoking in a wood-burning pit.

Cooking accessories. An apron may feel funny at first, but you learn quickly why people have them. The same is true of pot holders, paper towels, a cutting board, plastic trash bags, aluminum foil, and other normal kitchen fixtures.

Gimme cap. Professional chefs wear toques. Barbecue cooks wear caps, usually the "gimme" kind people give away or sell cheaply to promote a business, team, or event. They just look right, and they're certainly handy when you've forgotten the pot holders, paper towels, or fly swatter.

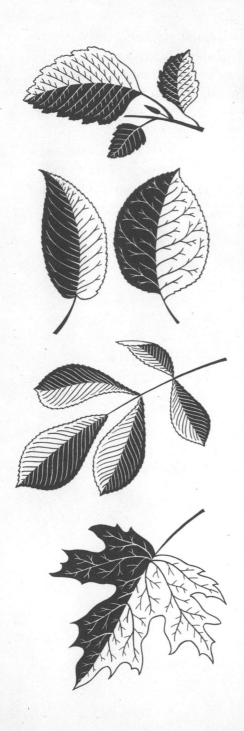

Wood Flavoring Chart

Alder: The traditional wood for smoking salmon in the Pacific Northwest, alder also works well with other fish. It has a light, delicate flavor.

Apple and Cherry: Both woods produce a slightly sweet, fruity smoke that's mild enough for chicken or turkey, but capable of flavoring a ham.

Hickory: Hickory is the king of the woods in the Southern barbecue belt, as basic to the region's cooking as cornbread. The strong, hearty taste is perfect for pork shoulder and ribs, but it also enhances any red meat or poultry.

Maple: Mildly smoky and sweet, maple mates well with poultry, ham, and vegetables.

Mesquite: The mystique wood of the past decade, mesquite is also America's most misunderstood wood. It's great for grilling because it burns very hot, but below average for barbecuing for the same reason. Also, the smoke taste turns from tangy to bitter over an extended cooking time. Few serious pitmasters use mesquite, despite a lot of stories about its prevalence in the Southwest.

Oak: If hickory is the king of barbecue woods, oak is the queen. Assertive but always pleasant, it's the most versatile of hardwoods, blending well with a wide range of flavors. What it does to beef brisket is probably against the law in some states.

Pecan: The choice of many professional chefs, pecan burns cool and offers a subtle richness of character. Some people call it a mellow version of hickory.

Part Two

★ ★ ★

Smoking Slow and Low

Spicing Up ☆ Your Life ☆

The first step in barbecuing, most of the time, is the application of a dry rub, paste, or marinade to the food you're fixing. Then, after you start cooking, you often "mop" the food with a liquid containing some of the same ingredients. These are vital processes in barbecuing, best approached with playful exuberance, even if you're a little squeamish about working with raw meat.

Flavor is the main function of the various potions, and their role is frequently more important to the taste of barbecue than anything you add to food at the end. Sometimes a dry rub, paste, marinade, or mop becomes the basis of a finishing or table sauce—the subject of a separate chapter—but even then, they have worked much of their wizardry before the cooking is completed. In barbecuing, you don't get a real treat without some serious foreplay.

Dry Rubs

☆

Dry rubs are combinations of dried spices massaged into food before cooking. Originally developed long ago for preservation, rubs in barbecuing help seal in flavor, add another dimension to the taste, and form a savory crust. While the technique is old, it wasn't widely used in American cooking outside of barbecue circles until recently, when New Orleans chef Paul Prudhomme created blackened redfish and other dishes using his line of seasoning blends.

The appropriate ingredients in dry rubs vary with the kind of food you're cooking, but some items are more common than others. Salt and sugar probably appear more often than anything else, in both commercial and homemade rubs, though they are also the most controversial ingredients. Some pitmasters say that salt draws the moisture out of meat, and everyone agrees that white or brown sugar burns on the surface of food. We follow the course of moderation, using salt and sugar when they round out the taste of a rub, but keeping the quantity in careful balance with other ingredients. From a flavor standpoint, if nothing else, they are normally better in a supporting rather than starring role.

Garlic powder, onion powder, and lemon-pepper seasonings are a close second in popularity, particularly in homemade rubs. They all work better in a dry spice mix than they do in most kitchen preparations, but by themselves their potential for adding punch is pretty limited. We usually supplement them, or even supplant them, with pepper and dried chiles, plus some combination of secondary seasonings, such as dry mustard, cumin, sage, thyme, allspice, cinnamon, nutmeg, and ginger.

When applying a rub, add it thoroughly and evenly. Generally you don't skimp on the amount, though some dishes benefit from a light touch. If you're cooking chicken or other poultry, spread the seasoning both over and under the skin, being careful to avoid tearing the skin. If you're rubbing vegetables, cover them first with a thin layer of oil. Always wash your hands well with soap and hot water before moving on to other tasks.

After coating the food, let it absorb the spices in the refrigerator, wrapped in plastic. We favor zipper-lock bags or industrial-size food-safe plastic bags, depending on the size of the item. Oven-roasting bags, the type used for Thanksgiving turkeys, work, too. As we indicate in our recipes in later chapters, fish fillets and shrimp need to sit for thirty to forty-five minutes before cooking, big cuts of meat like an overnight sleep, and other kinds of food require some amount of time in between.

The following collection of master rubs illustrates typical spice blends for different dishes. We repeat all the instructions when we use one of these in a particular recipe—so you don't have to turn back here—but it may help in understanding rubs to see a sample set of them in one place. Also, if you want to make up a batch of your own custom rubs at the beginning of the barbecue season, as we do each year, you'll find this a useful starting point. Figure that two cups of rub will yield enough to flavor a couple of briskets or a half-dozen slabs of ribs.

Wild Willy's Number One-derful Rub

This is our main all-purpose rub, good on ribs, brisket, chicken, and more.

3/4 TABLESPOON CILANTRO FLAKES

¾ cup paprika
¼ cup ground black pepper
¼ cup salt
¼ cup sugar *(BROWN)* DRY
1 TABLESPOON MUSTARD

2 tablespoons chili powder
2 tablespoons garlic powder
2 tablespoons onion powder
1 teaspoons cayenne
2 TEASPOONS NEW MEXICO CHILI PEPPER

Makes about 2 cups

Mix the spices thoroughly in a bowl. Store covered in a cool, dark pantry.

BBQ tips Derived from a mild chile, paprika is a common dry rub ingredient. Most store-bought varieties have as much flavor as redwood sawdust, but with a little effort you can find good Hungarian products.

Southern Succor Rub

We use this on many cuts of pork, including shoulder.

½ cup ground black pepper
½ cup paprika
½ cup turbinado sugar

¼ cup salt
4 teaspoons dry mustard
2 teaspoons cayenne

Makes about 2 cups

Mix the spices thoroughly in a bowl. Store covered in a cool, dark pantry.

Originally developed to make Texas chili con carne, but now used in many other ways as well, chili powders combine dried red chiles (usually anchos) with other spices, such as cumin and garlic. One of the oldest and best brands is Gebhardt's, created in salute to the San Antonio "Chili Queens" of a century ago and now distributed nationally.

BBQ tips Jim Quessenberry, one of the planet's premier pitmasters, gave us the idea of using turbinado sugar in rubs. A coarsely granulated raw sugar, turbinado has a light molasses flavor and doesn't break down under barbecuing temperatures to the same extent as other sugars. You can find turbinado sugar at natural food stores.

Jim uses turbinado in his commercial dry rub, Arkansas Trav'ler Spice Beautiful, which may be the best on the market anywhere. To order it and other superb barbecue products by mail, write 206 East Merriman, Wynne, Arkansas 72396 or call 501-588-4442.

Poultry Perfect Rub

Chicken and other poultry can take a variety of rubs well, depending on the flavor you want, but this is often our top choice.

¾ cup paprika	2 tablespoons onion powder
¼ cup ground black pepper	2 tablespoons dry mustard
¼ cup celery salt	2 teaspoons cayenne
¼ cup sugar	Zest of 3 to 4 lemons, dried and minced

Makes about 2 cups

Mix the spices thoroughly in a bowl. Store covered in a cool, dark pantry.

BBQ tips Lemon zest can be air-dried overnight. If you're in a hurry to get your poultry in the pit, dry the zest in a 225° F oven or smoker for 8 to 10 minutes.

Cajun Ragin' Rub

This blend dances on your taste buds. Pair it with pork ribs or shoulder, or try it with a meaty fish, such as snapper or redfish.

¼ cup celery salt	2 tablespoons garlic powder
¼ cup ground black pepper	1 tablespoon cayenne
¼ cup white pepper	1 tablespoon dried thyme
¼ cup brown sugar	2 teaspoons dried sage

Makes about 1¼ cups

Mix the spices thoroughly in a bowl. Store covered in a cool, dark pantry.

BBQ tips Some ready-made seasoning blends make great dry rubs, either on their own or in combination with other spices. Cajun and Creole seasonings, Asian five-spice powder, even crab boil, can each make a worthy dry rub or at least the foundation for one.

Sweet Sensation

These spices match the sweetness and succulence of tender cuts of pork, such as tenderloin or rib roast.

¼ cup ground allspice	2 teaspoons ground nutmeg
¼ cup brown sugar	2 teaspoons ground cinnamon
¼ cup onion powder	2 teaspoons dried thyme
2 tablespoons salt	

Makes about 1 cup

Mix the spices thoroughly in a bowl. Store covered in a cool, dark pantry.

BBQ tips When you have leftover rub, seal it in plastic zipper-lock bags or in jars. Keep the spice blend in a cool pantry or refrigerator until your next round of barbecuing, or try it with other preparations, such as broiling or sautéing.

Southwest Heat

Hard to beat when you want some heat.

½ cup ground dried New Mexican red chile

½ cup ground dried ancho chile

3 tablespoons salt

3 tablespoons ground cumin

1 tablespoon dried oregano, preferably Mexican

Makes about 1½ cups

Mix the spices thoroughly in a bowl. Store covered in a cool, dark pantry.

BBQ tips Chiles in a rub should leave an afterglow in the throat, not a raging conflagration. Dried ground chiles, such as ancho or New Mexican red, offer earthy savor and sweetness with a moderate level of firepower. Powders made from jalapeños and chipotles (smoked jalapeños) turn up the thermostat a little higher, and cayenne or habanero chiles can shoot the mercury right out the top.

Jamaican Jerk Rub

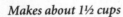

6 tablespoons onion powder
6 tablespoons dried onion
   flakes
2 tablespoons ground allspice
2 tablespoons fresh-ground
   black pepper
2 tablespoons cayenne

2 tablespoons sugar
4½ teaspoons dried thyme
4½ teaspoons ground cinnamon
1½ teaspoons ground nutmeg
¼ teaspoon dried ground
   Habanero chile (optional)

Makes about 1½ cups

Mix the spices thoroughly in a bowl. Store covered in a cool, dark pantry.

Pastes

A paste is a wet version of a dry rub, a combination of seasonings bound together in a thick emulsion by liquid or fat. Occasionally called "slathers," they add both flavor and moisture to food. Typical core ingredients range from stock to lemon juice, from oil to fresh herbs. Puréed garlic, onions, anchovies, horseradish, mustard, or even peanut butter might bind the mixture.

Dry rubs are great on traditional barbecue meats, which don't need extra moisture, but pastes work better on some lean meats. They usually impart a milder taste than rubs, making them suitable for delicate fish or seafood preparations. Pastes are also a good way to add herb flavors, allowing you to coat a chicken with basil or a lamb chop with mint.

A paste needs to be thick enough to adhere to the food but thin enough to smear easily. As with dry rubs, you massage it into every surface and then put the food in the refrigerator in a plastic bag to soak for an appropriate period. Pastes with fresh herbs lose their potency after a few days, but others keep for several weeks when refrigerated.

The paste preparations that follow show some of the possibilities. If none of these sound exactly right for your favorite food, they may at least inspire your own creations.

Primo Paste

This is a basic, general-purpose paste, good for a range of lean foods, particularly turkey.

1 *whole bulb* garlic, peeled
6 tablespoons coarse-ground black pepper
6 tablespoons kosher salt

¼ teaspoon cayenne or ground chipotle chile
6 tablespoons garlic-flavored oil

Makes about 1 cup

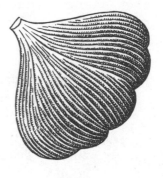

In a mortar and pestle or with a food processor, combine the paste ingredients, mashing the garlic with the pepper, salt, and cayenne or chipotle. Add the oil to form a thick paste. Refrigerate the paste, covered, for up to 2 weeks.

BBQ tips Oil-based pastes work especially well on fish and lean meats, such as venison, cabrito, and chicken. Experiment with oils of varied flavors, infused with garlic, basil, or other herbs. Unrefined or lightly refined oils, such as corn or peanut, add their own pleasing taste.

Some paste recipes promise more than others. We came across one, based on mustard, that claimed equal effectiveness as a flavoring agent and as a medicinal plaster for combating bronchial infections.

Name-Your-Herb Paste

Mix and match your favorite flavors in this paste. We like mint with trout and lamb, basil on chicken and tuna, parsley for beef, cilantro with shrimp and salmon, and sage on cabrito, duck, and pork.

1½ cups fresh herbs (mint, basil, Italian flat-leaf parsley, cilantro, or sage)
10 to 14 garlic cloves

1 teaspoon salt
1 cup oil, preferably olive or another type of flavorful oil that complements your recipe

Makes about 1½ cups

In a food processor, combine the herbs, garlic, and salt. Process until the herbs are finely chopped. Add the oil in a slow stream, mixing thoroughly. The paste should be refrigerated and used within a day or two.

Kentucky Pride

This smoky sweet paste can enhance better cuts of pork and beef.

1 medium onion, preferably a sweet variety, chunked
¼ cup bourbon
2 tablespoons brown sugar

2 tablespoons ground black pepper
1 tablespoon oil, preferably canola or corn

Makes about 1¼ cups

Combine the paste ingredients in a food processor or blender and process until the onion is finely chopped and a thick purée forms. Refrigerate the paste, covered, for up to 2 weeks.

☆**Variation:** Substitute beer or tequila for the bourbon and match the paste with chicken or game birds.

Thunder Paste

A more exotic blend that's superb on chicken and shrimp.

1 small onion, chunked
⅓ cup orange juice
2 tablespoons peanut oil
2 teaspoons ground anise seeds
1 teaspoon turmeric

1 teaspoon curry powder
1 teaspoon salt
½ teaspoon ground allspice
½ teaspoon ground cinnamon

Combine the paste ingredients in a food processor or blender and process until the onion is finely chopped and a thick purée forms. Refrigerate the paste, covered, for up to 2 weeks.

Marinades

Normally a combination of acid, oil, and spices, marinades are liquid flavoring agents used to bathe food before cooking. Like pastes, they aren't as common in barbecuing as dry rubs, but they are gaining favor. Some marinades tame an undesirable taste, as a buttermilk soak does for wild game, but most often they are intended to complement and enrich the food's natural flavor.

The acid might be vinegar, lemon or other fruit juice, milk, yogurt, or wine. The fat in a marinade is normally a vegetable oil, since butter and bacon drippings coagulate when chilled. The proportions depend a lot on the type of food you're cooking, with the amount of oil increasing substantially with fish and lean cuts of meat. Spices and herbs are used in assertive quantities because their pungency is diminished by the soaking process.

Some people think marinades tenderize meat, but that's not quite accurate. Actually the liquid softens tissue, a subtle but important distinction. Food marinated for too long becomes mushy and flabby. Extra time doesn't help the flavoring process either, because marinades don't penetrate much beyond the surface of the food and don't need to go any deeper.

Prepare marinades right before they are needed and don't reuse them with other raw foods. If you plan to use a marinade for mopping or basting, or as part of a sauce, first boil the mixture vigorously to kill any harmful bacteria.

Marinate food in a glass, stainless steel, or plastic container; aluminum can react with the acid. Choose a shallow dish just larger than the food, a zipper-lock freezer bag, or, for big cuts of meat, an industrial-size food-safe plastic bag or an oven-roasting bag. Bag-wrapped food is easier to stash in the fridge and requires only about half the amount of liquid to cover the food.

Turn food you are marinating once or twice during the process to make sure you're saturating all surfaces. Figure that 2 cups of marinade will flavor about 2 pounds of meat.

James Beard's Basic Barbecue Marinade

The master of American cooking, James Beard, used a marinade similar to this on many outdoor dishes.

½ cup soy sauce	1 teaspoon fresh-ground black pepper
½ cup dry sherry	
½ cup strong brewed tea	½ teaspoon ground anise seeds
2 tablespoons honey	½ teaspoon ground cloves
2 tablespoons peanut oil	1 garlic clove, minced

Makes about 2 cups

Combine the ingredients in a food processor. The marinade can be refrigerated for several days.

James Bond's Basic Barbecue Marinade

If you like vodka martinis as much as James Bond does, you'll relish this marinade on seafood and chicken.

1½ cups vodka	3 tablespoons minced onion
½ cup dry vermouth	Juice of 1 large lemon
3 tablespoons oil, preferably canola or corn	

Makes about 2½ cups

Combine the ingredients. Mr. Bond would implore you to shake it rather than stir it. The marinade is best the day it's made.

James Beard helped inspire the suburban resurgence of outdoor cooking after the Second World War. His *Cook It Outdoors*, published in 1941, and the 1960 *Treasury of Outdoor Cooking* are still grilling classics.

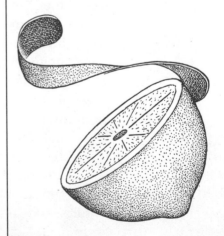

Red Wine Marinade

A stout, classic combo for beef and venison.

2 cups dry red wine
½ cup red wine vinegar
¼ cup oil, preferably olive or another type of flavorful oil that complements your recipe

10 to 12 fresh sage leaves or 2 teaspoons dried sage
2 garlic cloves, minced

Makes about 2¾ cups

Combine the ingredients in a food processor or blender. The marinade is best the day it's made.

BBQ tips Don't waste money on expensive wines for marinades, but do use something that's good enough to drink—you will be eating it in your food, after all.

Former Houston Oilers star Earl Campbell marinates his beef brisket in an unusual mixture of brown sugar—as much as two pounds' worth—black pepper, garlic, meat tenderizer, and Lawry's sauce.

Jalapeño-Lime Marinade

This feisty mixture adds a kick to shrimp and chicken.

⅓ cup pickled jalapeño slices
¼ cup pickling liquid from jar or can of pickled jalapeños
Juice of 2 limes
4 tablespoons corn oil, preferably unrefined

3 tablespoons minced fresh cilantro
4 green onions, sliced
3 garlic cloves, minced

Makes about 1½ cups

Purée the marinade ingredients in a food processor or blender. The marinade is best the day it's made.

Red-Eye Marinade

An eye-opener any time of day—try it with pork or beef.

2 cups strong brewed coffee
1 medium onion, chunked
½ cup cider vinegar

¼ cup dark unsulphured
   molasses

Makes about 3 cups

Blend the ingredients in a blender. The marinade is best the day it's made.

BBQ tips Since marinades flavor only the surface of food, the larger the surface area relative to weight, the more of the marinade taste you will get. A flank steak, for example, drinks up the juice like a jilted cowboy out on the town.

Cheryl's Cider Soak

Here's a fruity favorite of ours for pork, duck, and game birds. We skip the oil when we use the soak for ribs or other fatty cuts of pork.

1½ cups apple cider
¾ cup cider vinegar
½ medium onion, minced
3 tablespoons oil, preferably canola or corn (optional)

1½ tablespoons Worcestershire sauce
1 teaspoon ground cinnamon
1 teaspoon dried thyme

Makes about 2¾ cups

Combine the ingredients in a food processor or blender. The marinade can be refrigerated for several days.

BBQ tips Cheryl's Cider Soak is a good example of a marinade that can do double-duty as a mop. For basting food, simply heat the ingredients in a saucepan and apply the warm liquid to the vittles while they're cooking. If you marinated meat in the mixture first, bring the marinade to a vigorous boil before using it as a mop.

Mops

☆

Mops, or bastes, play an important role in traditional barbecuing. These liquids that you apply to meat during the cooking process are an old and honored way of keeping food moist and adding an extra layer of flavor. Their usefulness today, however, varies considerably, depending on the kind of cooking equipment you have. We include mops in most of our barbecue recipes, but we make them optional because the design of some smokers precludes or discourages basting. See the chart on page 55 for guidance on whether "To Mop or Not."

A mop can be something as simple as beer or meat stock, or a combination of ingredients as complex as an IRS form. Butter or oil are primary elements when cooking fish, chicken, and other food that dries out easily. It's also common to use vinegar or lemon juice, some Worcestershire, and a healthy dose of the same seasonings you used in your rub, paste, or marinade. In some cases, the marinade itself simply becomes the mop after a vigorous boiling.

You usually baste the food with a cotton string tool that resembles a miniature floor mop, often available at restaurant supply stores or businesses specializing in outdoor cooking supplies. Keep the liquid warm during the cooking process to kill any bacteria the tool might pick up from the surface of the food and to avoid lowering the temperature of the food. When you're working with a pit, the baste can simmer in a heavy pan on top of the firebox or you may need to keep it on the stove inside. Replenish the liquid as needed. The long cooking concentrates the flavor and creates an increasingly robust brew that is sometimes boiled and served as a table sauce with the meat.

Foods with little or no fat may require regular mopping, as our recipes indicate, but don't overdo it. Every time you lift the lid of your smoker, you lower the temperature inside and increase the cooking time. That's desirable only if the fire gets too hot, when it helps to release heat and cool the meat with a little moisture.

We suggest many different bastes in our recipes later in the book, but the ones that follow are representative of the range. They demonstrate the core principles and ingredients, and may give you ideas for developing special mops of your own.

Southern Sop

This is one version, among hundreds, of the traditional pork baste used throughout the South.

2 cups cider vinegar	1 tablespoon Worcestershire sauce
1 cup water	
3 tablespoons ground black pepper	1 tablespoon paprika
2 tablespoons salt	1 tablespoon cayenne

Makes about 3½ cups

Combine the ingredients in a saucepan. Heat the mop and use it warm.

Basic Beer Mop

Anything from Texas brisket to Boston butt will happily lap up this brew.

12 ounces beer	1 tablespoon Worcestershire sauce
½ cup cider vinegar	
½ cup water	1 tablespoon Wild Willy's Number One-derful Rub (page 36) or other dry rub or seasoning that complements the flavor of your dish
¼ cup oil, preferably canola or corn	
½ medium onion, chopped	
2 garlic cloves, minced	

Makes about 3 cups

Combine the ingredients in a saucepan. Heat the mop and use it warm.

On Labor Day weekend Colonial Williamsburg stages an authentic version of an eighteenth-century barbecue. The pitmasters cook a whole hog the original way, basting with saltwater and butter.

Lemon Mop

A delicious baste for chicken, fish, and seafood.

1½ cups chicken stock
½ cup fresh lemon juice
½ medium onion, chopped
½ cup butter
1 tablespoon Worcestershire sauce

1 tablespoon prepared yellow mustard
2 teaspoons Poultry Perfect Rub (page 37)

Makes about 3 cups

Combine the ingredients in a saucepan. Heat the mop and use it warm.

Lightning Mop

C. Clark "Smoky" Hale is an "Ol' Baster" extraordinaire. In his folksy *Great American Barbecue Instruction Book* (Abacus Publishing), Smoky argues that the basting sauce or mop is the secret of great barbecue, capable of making "a pine knot tender and delicious."

We developed this for our Hot Times Jalapeño Turkey Breast, but it's also good with other poultry and shrimp dishes.

3 cups chicken or turkey stock
⅓ cup oil, preferably canola or corn

¼ cup minced pickled jalapeños
¼ cup jalapeño jelly

Makes about 4 cups

Combine the ingredients in a saucepan. Heat the mop and use it warm.

Pop Mop

Unless you brag too much, no one is likely to guess the source of the interesting sweet flavor in your food. The mop is especially good on onions.

3 cups Dr Pepper, Coca-Cola,   2 tablespoons oil, preferably
   or R.C. Cola   canola or corn

Makes about 3 cups

Combine the ingredients in a saucepan. Heat the mop and use it warm.

To Mop or Not

The equipment you use for barbecuing determines whether and how often you baste food while it cooks. We list mops as "optional" in most of our barbecue recipes, but you should use them if they are appropriate to your style of smoker. In a few cases, we suggest basting food before or after cooking, rather than during the process, and in those unusual situations, the mop works well with any kind of equipment.

Wood-burning pits: Mops were made for pits. If you burn logs or wood chunks in a manufactured or homemade pit of traditional design, basting your food will improve its quality. Mop as often as the recipes indicate.

Wood ovens: Never apply a mop during cooking in an oven that operates on electrical power. It's not only dangerous, but, in some cases at least, also unnecessary. In ovens that seal as tightly as the Cookshack, for example, food retains its internal moisture and doesn't require any basting. Follow the manufacturer's directions with other brands of wood ovens.

Charcoal grills and ovens: You should baste food in a charcoal grill, but not as often as you do in a wood-burning pit because grills lose far more of their heat any time you lift the lid. In a conventional kettle grill, such as a Weber, we mop only when we have the top off to add charcoal or pieces of wood. In an oven-style grill, such as the Hasty-Bake, we mop with about half the frequency we would in a wood-burning pit.

Water smokers: Basting isn't really necessary in a water smoker because the cooking process itself adds moisture to food. We like to mop occasionally for the flavor value, but we limit the frequency for the same reason we do in a charcoal grill—heat loss. We baste every 1 to 2 hours, or when we have the lid off for another purpose.

Pork You Can
☆ Pull Apart ☆

When you're talking barbecue in the South, you're talking pork. To express a preference for barbecued beef or smoked fish is akin to announcing that you're the grandchild of General William Tecumseh Sherman. You can even stir up a helluva of an argument over the *part* of the pig you like. In some areas of the Carolinas you go whole hog or nothing, barbecuing the entire animal and eating it all in a variety of forms. Just a county away, folks won't touch anything except the shoulder; down the road, the ribs are the only cut that matters.

If you get beyond the feud about parts, you're still confronted with passionate differences about saucing and serving the pork. Some pitmasters base their sauce on ketchup, others won't let a tomato through the door. Some think spice is nice, others are set on sweet, and still others won't abide anything on their meat. The pork may be pulled, chopped, or minced. If you order a dinner plate, the accompaniments could be anything from hush puppies to burgoo. If you opt for a sandwich, you can usually count on a white bun or bread, but you never know whether the coleslaw will be inside or on the side.

In truth, barbecued pork is good any of these ways and many others. Our favorite version is always what's in front of us at the moment, and right now that's a whole heap of deliciously different recipes.

The Renowned Mr. Brown

In old Southern slang, "Mr. Brown" is the dark, smoky outside part of barbecued pork, usually the shoulder. This is the traditional cooking style, perfected by generations of pitmasters to give Mr. Brown his deserved renown.

SOUTHERN SUCCOR RUB

¼ cup ground black pepper	2 tablespoons salt
¼ cup paprika	2 teaspoons dry mustard
¼ cup turbinado sugar	1 teaspoon cayenne

6-pound to 8-pound Boston butt

SOUTHERN SOP (OPTIONAL)

Remaining Southern Succor Rub	2 tablespoons salt
2 cups cider vinegar	1 tablespoon Worcestershire
1 cup water	sauce
3 tablespoons ground black	1 tablespoon paprika
pepper	1 tablespoon cayenne

Golden Mustard Barbecue Sauce (page 293), Carolina Red (page 292), or Vaunted Vinegar Sauce (page 292) (optional)

Serves 8 to 10

The night before you plan to barbecue, combine the rub ingredients in a small bowl. Massage the pork well with about half of the rub. Transfer the pork to a plastic bag, and refrigerate it overnight.

Before you begin to barbecue, remove the pork from the refrigerator. Pat down the butt with another coating of rub. Let the pork sit at room temperature for about 45 minutes.

Prepare the smoker for barbecuing, bringing the temperature to 200° F to 220° F.

If you plan to baste the pork (see chapter 3, "To Mop or Not"), stir any remaining rub together with the mop ingredients in a saucepan and warm the mixture over low heat.

Leonard Heuberger conceived the most famous barbecue sign in the country, a fixture for many years at Leonard's in Memphis. A neon pig in top hat and tails, swinging a cane, carries the caption, "Mr. Brown Goes To Town."

Transfer the pork to the smoker and cook it for about 1½ hours per pound, or until the internal temperature reaches 170° F to 180° F. Mop the pork about once an hour in a wood-burning pit, or as appropriate for your style of smoker.

Remove the pork from the smoker and let it sit for about 15 minutes, until cool enough to handle. Pull off chunks of the meat, and either shred or chop them as you wish. Make sure each serving has some of the darker, chewier Mr. Brown along with the lighter interior meat. If you wish, serve the pork with Golden Mustard Barbecue Sauce, Carolina Red, or Vaunted Vinegar Sauce.

BBQ tips Butchers normally cut pork shoulder into two big pieces of meat, the Boston butt and the picnic, both likely to weigh 6 to 8 pounds on the average hog. If you want to cook the whole shoulder, an overnight job, you may have to make a special order in advance. Most backyard barbecuers and restaurants these days are satisfied with just the butt, the portion that has the least bone.

Red-Eye Butt

Anything as tasty as a barbecued shoulder warrants a little experimentation. Here we add some extra tang, using an old American pork enhancer—coffee—and we speed up the cooking time by starting with just half of a Boston butt, a common supermarket cut.

RED-EYE MARINADE AND MOP

2 cups strong coffee	½ cup dark unsulphured
2 cups cider vinegar	molasses
1 medium onion, chunked	

½ pork butt, 3½ to 4 pounds
Bar-BQ Ranch Sauce (page 295) (optional)

Serves 4 to 6

The night before you plan to barbecue, combine the marinade ingredients in a blender. Pour the marinade over the pork in a plastic bag. Refrigerate the meat overnight.

Before you begin to barbecue, drain the pork, reserving all of the marinade and adding 1 cup of water to it if you plan to baste the meat. If your smoker isn't appropriate for basting, save only 1 cup of marinade with the onion solids. Let the pork sit at room temperature for 30 to 40 minutes.

Prepare the smoker for barbecuing, bringing the temperature to 200° F to 220° F.

Bring the reserved marinade to a boil over high heat. Reduce the heat to a simmer and cook for several minutes. Keep the liquid warm over low heat.

Transfer the pork to the smoker and cook it for 4 hours. Baste the meat with the warmed marinade at 45-minute intervals in a wood-burning pit, or as appropriate for your style of smoker. After 4 hours, wrap the pork in heavy-duty foil, pouring about ½ to 1 cup of the warmed marinade and the onion solids over the meat.

In the past decade, the number of barbecue cook-offs and festivals around the country grew from a few dozen to about four hundred. They are scattered from Florida to Alaska, from California to Massachusetts, and the prizes range from a ribbon up to $30,000 at the American Royal competition in Kansas City in October.

Discard any remaining marinade. Seal the edges of the foil well. Return the pork to the smoker for about 2 more hours, cooking it to the fall-apart stage, with an internal temperature near 190° F.

Allow the pork to sit at room temperature for 10 to 15 minutes before pulling the pork apart in shreds. Offer Bar-BQ Ranch Sauce on the side, if you wish.

BBQ tips Pork works better than any other meat for barbecuing on a charcoal grill. The Red-Eye Butt is particularly well suited, and so is The Renowned Mr. Brown, using half of a butt instead of the full cut.

BBQ tips You have more control over your cooking temperature in a log-burning pit than in other kinds of smokers, but the mechanisms of control are not always well explained in the owner's manual. First in importance is the size and intensity of the fire. In an efficient, well-constructed pit you seldom need more than three logs burning at once, or more than a small flame going. The air intake control is a close second in significance. You open it to increase the draft—which stirs the flame and raises the heat—or close it to dampen the blaze and reduce the temperature. The outtake adjustment on the smoke stack is most useful in reining back a fire that's gotten too hot. Unless that happens, leave it fully open to keep the smoke circulating freely. If it's shut down for an extended period, food will get sooty.

Perfect Picnic

The bony portion of a pork shoulder, the picnic, is as delectable as the butt end, but slightly different in flavor, closer in flavor to ham.

PERFECT PICNIC RUB

5 tablespoons ground black pepper	2 tablespoons salt
¼ cup turbinado sugar	1 tablespoon dry mustard
3 tablespoons paprika	2 teaspoons onion powder
	1 teaspoon cayenne

6-pound to 8-pound pork picnic

PICNIC MOP (OPTIONAL)

Remaining Perfect Picnic Rub	2 tablespoons salt
3 cups cider vinegar	1 tablespoon dry mustard
1 cup water	4 garlic cloves, minced
1 medium onion, minced	1 teaspoon cayenne
¼ cup ground black pepper	

Golden Mustard Barbecue Sauce (page 293), Vaunted Vinegar Sauce (page 292), or Creole Classic Barbecue Sauce (page 299) (optional)

Serves 8 to 10

The night before you plan to barbecue, combine the rub ingredients in a small bowl. Massage the pork well with about half of the rub. Transfer the pork to a plastic bag and refrigerate it overnight.

Before you begin to barbecue, take the pork from the refrigerator. Pat down the pork with another coating of rub. Let the pork sit at room temperature for about 45 minutes.

Prepare the smoker for barbecuing, bringing the temperature to 200° F to 220° F.

If you plan to baste the pork (see chapter 3, "To Mop or Not"), stir any remaining rub together with the mop

Except for the major events, barbecue contests tend to come and go because they are usually run by volunteers. The best way to keep up is to subscribe to barbecue newsletters. The Kansas City Barbeque Society (11514 Hickman Mills Drive, Kansas City, Missouri 64134) and the Pacific Northwest Barbecue Association (4244 134th Avenue SE, Bellevue, Washington 98006) include their regular publications in the membership dues ($20 and $10 respectively). Among the independents, the *National Barbecue News* (P.O. Box 981, Douglas, Georgia 31533, $18) provides good coverage of cookoffs, and you get plenty of that and more in the *Goat Gap Gazette* (5110 Bayard Lane No. 2, Houston, Texas 77006, $18) and *The Pits* (7714 Hillard, Dallas, Texas 75217, $18).

Tips from the Pit
(P.O. Box 31, Carlisle, Massachusetts 01741, $12) offers thorough coverage of barbecue news and events in New England and the Northeast, along with essays, articles, and reviews of interest to barbecuers anywhere.

ingredients in a saucepan and warm the mixture over low heat.

Transfer the pork to the smoker and cook it for about 1½ hours per pound, or until the internal temperature reaches 170° F to 180° F. Mop the meat every 50 to 60 minutes in a wood-burning pit, or as appropriate for your style of smoker.

Remove the pork from the smoker and let it sit for about 15 minutes, until cool enough to handle. Pull off chunks of the meat, then either shred or chop them as you like. If you wish, serve the pork with Golden Mustard Barbecue Sauce, Vaunted Vinegar Sauce, or Creole Classic Barbecue Sauce.

☆**Serving Suggestion:** A smoked picnic makes for a memorable small-scale "pig-picking." Add Creamy Coleslaw, Candied Sweet Potatoes, Carolina Jerusalem Artichoke Pickles, and maybe a pot of Brunswick Stew. For a prodigious finish, offer Prodigal Pecan Pie for dessert.

BBQ tips The time needed to bring a smoker to the proper temperature for barbecuing varies from less than 5 minutes to as much as 1 hour, depending on the style of smoker, your fire-building techniques, the moisture content of the wood or charcoal, and the weather. Our recipe instructions assume an average warm-up time of 30 to 45 minutes. If your smoker requires more or less time, you may need to adjust the sequence of recipe steps accordingly.

Going Whole Hog

If you have a large barbecue pit, a few assistants, and an urge for the ultimate challenge, you should tackle a whole hog. This was the original barbecue meat of the South, and it's still the first choice of many prominent pitmasters. Among all the experts, no one does a better job than Jim Quessenberry, founder and leader of the Arkansas Trav'lers barbecue team. We had the honor of cooking with the Trav'lers one year at the Memphis in May World Championship Barbecue Contest, where Jim taught us his techniques.

As Quessenberry says, "The most important factor in whole hog is in fact the hog, himself." Bribe your butcher for the best animal in the area. Jim gets his hogs from a Mennonite farmer in Tennessee who custom raises them on corn for a firm white meat that's as mild as turkey. The butcher should gut the hog, skin it, and trim the outside fat to a ¼-inch thickness.

One full-grown hog, 120 to 150 pounds, skinned and trimmed
10 to 15 cups Arkansas Trav'ler Spice Beautiful (see BBQ Tip, page 37) or Southern Succor Rub (page 36)

QUESSENBERRY'S QUINTESSENTIAL HOG MOP

3 quarts cider vinegar   ¾ cup salt
1½ quarts water

Golden Mustard Barbecue Sauce (page 293), Carolina Red (page 292), or Vaunted Vinegar Sauce (page 292) (optional)

Serves 25 to 40 (or half of Arkansas)

Fire up the pit, preferably with a combination of hickory and oak, and bring it to a temperature of 250° F.

Rub the hog thoroughly with the dry spices and lift it onto the pit, belly side down. If the pit has an offset firebox, position the head facing away from the fire

Jim Quessenberry's Arkansas Trav'lers are one of the most respected teams on the barbecue contest circuit. Based in Wynne, Arkansas, the group has competed at the Memphis in May cook-off every year since it began and has twice won the Irish Cup International Barbecue Contest. Quessenberry and his crew are true world champions.

and cover the hams loosely with aluminum foil. Every hour or so, sprinkle on more dry spices or mop the meat with the vinegar mixture, alternating between the two applications.

Maintain a steady cooking temperature of 200° F to 250° F for 18 to 20 hours, or until the internal temperature of the meat is 165° F to 170° F.

While the fire dies, allow the hog to sit in the pit for several hours before carving. Serve accompanied by Golden Mustard Barbecue Sauce, Carolina Red, or Vaunted Vinegar Sauce, if you wish.

Miss White's Delights

Most of the time Southerners serve pork shoulder in a sandwich, a simple concept that's been perfected to a folk art. This traditional sandwich, Carolinas-style, blends a bit of The Renowned Mr. Brown with a pile of stringy "pulled" pieces of "Miss White," the luscious inside meat.

The slaw and sauce can be made a day ahead of serving, if desired.

CAROLINA SANDWICH SLAW

2	cups chopped cabbage	2 teaspoons sugar
2	tablespoons minced onion	¼ teaspoon salt
2	tablespoons white vinegar	Generous grinding of black
1½	tablespoons mayonnaise	pepper

VAUNTED VINEGAR SAUCE

1	cup white vinegar	½ teaspoon cayenne or hot red
1	tablespoon sugar	pepper flakes
1	teaspoon salt	
½	teaspoon fresh-ground black pepper	

The North Carolina Pork Producers Association improves on Mr. Webster in its definition of barbecue: "1. the premiere ethnic food of North Carolina. 2. pig pickin'. 3. catalyst for great debate. 4. a method of cooking. 5. pig as a culinary art. 6. a cultural rite. 7. all of the above."

About 3 cups pulled or chopped smoked pork shoulder, such as
    meat from The Renowned Mr. Brown (page 58), Red-Eye Butt
    (page 60), Perfect Picnic (page 62), or Going Whole Hog (page
    64), warmed
6 to 8 spongy white bread buns

Serves 6 to 8

To prepare the slaw, mix all the ingredients together in a bowl. Refrigerate, covered, for at least
30 minutes.

To prepare the sauce, combine all the ingredients in a
bowl and stir until the sugar dissolves. Refrigerate the
sauce, too, if you are not planning to use it within the
next hour. It can be served cold or reheated.

Place the pork on a serving platter along with the
buns. Let each person make his or her own sandwich,
piling portions of the coleslaw, pork, and sauce on the
bun, then squishing the bun together so that the meat
juices and sauce mingle. Devour immediately.

☆**Serving Suggestion:** Offer Peppery 'Pups, our
Carolinas-style hush puppies, on the side and maybe
Moon Pies for dessert.

BBQ tips Don't try to slice a barbecued butt with a
knife to make sandwiches or anything else. If it's cooked
right, the meat is easy to pick or pull apart when it's still
warm, and that's the time-honored way to serve it. Allow
the pork to cool a little, but not for too long, and use
gloves or a fork. The only role for a knife is to chop or
mince the pieces of meat after they are pulled off, and
that's an optional step.

"There may be religious, political, athletic, or sexual images that stir deeper emotions—*may be*—but nothing in the realm of Southern food is regarded with more passionate enthusiasm by the faithful than a perfectly cooked and seasoned pork shoulder or slab of ribs." John Egerton, *Southern Food* (Knopf)

Memphis Mustard Sandwich

This is a tasty variation on the standard pork sandwich, based on a version served in Memphis at Payne's, a former gas station converted mainly in its menu of fuels.

The slaw and sauce can be made a day ahead of serving, if desired.

MEMPHIS MUSTARD SLAW

2 cups chopped cabbage	1½ tablespoons white vinegar
½ cup minced onion	¾ teaspoon sugar
2½ tablespoons prepared yellow mustard	¼ teaspoon salt

MEMPHIS MAGIC BARBECUE SAUCE

3 tablespoons butter	1 teaspoon sugar
¼ cup minced onion	¼ teaspoon fresh-ground black pepper
1 cup tomato sauce	⅛ teaspoon cayenne or hot red pepper flakes
1 cup white vinegar	
3 tablespoons Worcestershire sauce	Dash of Tabasco or other hot red pepper sauce
1 teaspoon salt	

About 3 cups pulled or chopped smoked pork shoulder, such as meat from The Renowned Mr. Brown (page 58), Red-Eye Butt (page 60), Perfect Picnic (page 62), or Going Whole Hog (page 64), warmed
6 to 8 spongy white bread buns

Serves 6 to 8

To make the slaw, mix all the ingredients in a bowl. Refrigerate, covered, for at least 30 minutes.

To make the sauce, melt the butter in a heavy saucepan over medium heat. Add the onion and sauté until softened. Mix in the remaining ingredients and simmer until the sauce has thickened and reduced, about 25 minutes. Refrigerate the sauce, too. It can be served cold or reheated.

To serve, place the pork on a serving platter along with the buns. Let each person make his or her own sandwich, piling portions of the slaw, pork, and sauce on the bun, then squishing the bun together so that the meat juices and sauce mingle. Chow down.

☆**Variation:** In some scattered spots, particularly in Kentucky, people like their barbecue sandwiches on cornbread. If you want to try the idea, pile the pork on Cracklin' Cornbread.

BBQ tips Resist any upscale urge you may have to improve on the soft, spongy white buns traditionally used for barbecue sandwiches, unless you want to try cornbread. A "whole-grain sesame seed sourdough baguette" won't soak up enough juice to do the sandwich justice.

Most Memphis barbecue restaurants serve their ribs wet, but Charlie Vergos' Rendezvous downtown has probably sold more dry ribs than any place in the country. Layered with spices, the ribs come out of the kitchen as crunchy as corn chips, a perfect accompaniment to the barrels of beer served nightly in the raucous rathskeller.

Lone Star Spareribs

In Kansas City, Memphis, and other rib capitals, most barbecuers cook in a "wet" style, applying a sauce near the end of the cooking and again before serving. In Texas, where people love to be contrary, the ribs are often left "dry," as they are here.

BARBECUED RIB RUB

⅓ cup ground black pepper
¼ cup paprika
2 tablespoons sugar
1 tablespoon salt

1 tablespoon chili powder
1½ teaspoons garlic powder
1½ teaspoons onion powder

3 full slabs of pork spareribs, "St. Louis cut" (trimmed of the chine bone and brisket flap), preferably 3 pounds each or less

BASIC BEER MOP (OPTIONAL)

12 ounces beer
½ cup cider vinegar
½ cup water
¼ cup oil, preferably canola or corn
½ medium onion, chopped

2 garlic cloves, minced
1 tablespoon Worcestershire sauce
1 tablespoon Barbecued Rib Rub

Serves 6

The night before you plan to barbecue, combine the rub ingredients in a small bowl. Apply the rub evenly to the ribs, reserving about half of the spice mixture. Place the slabs in a plastic bag and refrigerate them overnight.

Before you begin to barbecue, take the ribs from the refrigerator. Pat them down with the remaining rub, reserving 1 tablespoon of it if you plan to use the mop. Let the ribs sit at room temperature for 30 to 40 minutes. Prepare the smoker for barbecuing, bringing the temperature to 200° F to 220° F.

If you are going to baste the ribs (see chapter 3, "To Mop or Not"), mix together the beer, vinegar, water, oil, onion, garlic, Worcestershire sauce, and rub in a large saucepan. Warm the mop liquid over low heat.

Transfer the meat to the smoker. Cook the ribs for 5 to 6 hours, turning and basting them with the mop about once an hour in a wood-burning pit, or as appropriate in your style of smoker.

When ready, the meat should be well-done and falling off the bones. Allow the slabs to sit for 10 minutes before slicing them into individual ribs.

BBQ tips We suggest different cooking times for our various rib recipes, but you may want to adjust the times for your taste. Spareribs are usually done in 3½ to 4 hours, when you can crack them apart with a gloved hand. At that point the meat is firm, chewy, and juicy. If you prefer the ribs crunchier, leaner, and falling apart, as we do with "dry" styles, cook them longer, about 5 hours for a 3-pound slab or up to 6 hours for a larger slab.

Kansas City Sloppy Ribs

Kansas City folks love to make a mess with ribs, layering them with so much sweet, hot sauce that you're licking your fingers as often as you're licking your chops.

KC RIB RUB

1 cup brown sugar	1½ tablespoons chili powder
½ cup paprika	1½ tablespoons garlic powder
2½ tablespoons ground black pepper	1½ tablespoons onion powder
	1 to 2 teaspoons cayenne
2½ tablespoons salt	

3 full slabs of pork spareribs, "St. Louis cut" (trimmed of the chine bone and brisket flap), preferably 3 pounds each or less

Struttin' Sauce (page 290), Boydesque Brew (page 291), or other sweet, tomato-based barbecue sauce

Serves 6

The night before you plan to barbecue, combine the rub ingredients in a bowl. Apply about one-third of the rub evenly to the ribs, reserving the rest of the spice mixture. Place the slabs in a plastic bag and refrigerate them overnight.

Before you begin to barbecue, take the ribs from the refrigerator. Sprinkle the ribs lightly but thoroughly with rub, reserving the rest of the mixture. Let the ribs sit at room temperature for 30 to 40 minutes.

Prepare the smoker for barbecuing, bringing the temperature to 200° F to 220° F.

Transfer the meat to the smoker. Cook the ribs for about 4 hours, turning and sprinkling them with more dry rub about halfway through the time. In the last 45 minutes of cooking, slather the ribs once or twice with Struttin' Sauce, Boydesque Brew, or other sweet tomato-based barbecue sauce.

When ready, the meat will bend easily between the ribs, and the sauce will be gooey and sticky. Allow the slabs to sit for 10 minutes before slicing them into individual ribs. Serve with more sauce on top or on the side and plenty of napkins.

☆**Serving Suggestion:** For a stick-to-your-ribs rib feast, add Tangy Buttermilk Potato Salad, Kansas City Baked Beans, garlic bread, and Wild Huckleberry Pie with Coconut Crumble. Don't forget the napkins.

BBQ tips   Rib cuts can get confusing. Pork spareribs come from the belly of the hog, next to the bacon, and are great for barbecuing because of their combination of meat, fat, and pork flavor. Butchers used to discard the tough cut until they discovered it could be tenderized through slow smoking. Loin ribs, baby back ribs (the loin ribs of a small pig), and country ribs are all "better," more expensive cuts. They taste good barbecued, too, but they don't depend as much on the process for their flavor.

BBQ tips   Barbecue sauces and other glazes added to meat in the last hour of cooking are often important to the flavor of a dish, particularly ribs, but you need to adjust their use to your style of smoker. Like mops, they work best in a wood-burning pit, where they should be applied the maximum number of times suggested in a recipe. With a charcoal grill, water smoker, or other kind of equipment that loses a lot of heat when the lid is raised, we normally use glazes only once during the cooking. With some electric-powered smokers, such as a Cookshack, you should wait to apply the sauce when you remove the food from the oven.

Martin Luther King, Jr., loved barbecue, particularly the pork ribs and sandwiches at Aleck's Barbecue Heaven in downtown Atlanta. Opened by Ernest Alexander in 1942, and now run by his daughter Pam, Aleck's was an important hangout for the early leaders of the civil rights movement.

Bourbon-Glazed Ribs

This Kentucky-inspired recipe is our personal favorite for "wet" spareribs. They're finished at the end with a mellow glaze that also serves as a table sauce.

BARBECUED RIB RUB

⅓ cup ground black pepper	1 tablespoon chili powder
¼ cup paprika	1½ teaspoons garlic powder
2 tablespoons sugar	1½ teaspoons onion powder
1 tablespoon salt	

3 full slabs of pork spareribs, "St. Louis cut" (trimmed of the chine bone and brisket flap), preferably 3 pounds each or less

BOURBON MOP (OPTIONAL)

¾ cup bourbon	½ cup water
¾ cup cider vinegar	

BOUR-BQ SAUCE

¼ cup butter	½ cup pure maple syrup
¼ cup oil, preferably canola or corn	⅓ cup dark unsulphured molasses
2 medium onions, minced	2 tablespoons Worcestershire sauce
¾ cup bourbon	
⅔ cup ketchup	½ teaspoon fresh-ground black pepper
½ cup cider vinegar	
½ cup fresh orange juice	½ teaspoon salt

Serves 6

The night before you plan to barbecue, combine the rub ingredients in a bowl. Apply the rub evenly to the ribs, reserving about half of the spice mixture. Place the slabs in a plastic bag and refrigerate them overnight.

Before you begin to barbecue, take the ribs from the refrigerator. Pat them down with the remaining rub. Let the ribs sit at room temperature for 30 to 40 minutes.

Prepare the smoker for barbecuing, bringing the temperature to 200° F to 220° F.

If you plan to baste the meat (see chapter 3, "To Mop or Not"), mix together the bourbon, vinegar, and water. Warm the mop liquid over low heat.

Transfer the meat to the smoker. Cook the ribs for about 4 hours, turning and mopping them after 1½ and 3 hours in a wood-burning pit, or as appropriate in your style of smoker.

While the slabs are smoking, prepare the Bour-BQ Sauce so that it is ready to apply to the ribs approximately 45 minutes before the meat is done. In a large saucepan, melt the butter with the oil over medium heat. Add the onions and sauté for about 5 minutes, or until they begin to turn golden. Add the remaining sauce ingredients, reduce the heat to low, and cook until the mixture thickens, approximately 40 minutes, stirring it frequently.

Brush the ribs with sauce once or twice in the last 45 minutes of cooking. Return the remaining sauce to the stove and simmer for 15 to 20 minutes, or until reduced by one-third.

When the slabs are ready, the meat will bend easily between the ribs, and the sauce will be gooey and sticky. Allow the slabs to sit for 10 minutes before slicing them into individual ribs. Serve with the reduced sauce on the side.

☆**Serving Suggestion:** We like the ribs best with a simple salad like Killed Salad, which means there's still room for Run for the Roses Pie afterward.

BBQ tips The preferred size of spareribs for barbecuing is "3 and down," meaning 3 pounds or smaller, a variable that depends on the weight of the pig when butchered. Don't fret if all you can find are larger slabs, but do smoke them a little longer.

The small burg of Murphysboro, Illinois, has acquired a big reputation in barbecue circles in recent years. In addition to the champion Apple City BBQuers, three other teams from the area made it to the famed Memphis in May cook-off in 1993.

Apple City Baby Back Ribs

This recipe is inspired by the award-winning ribs made by the Apple City BBQuers from Murphysboro, Illinois, the most successful barbecue contest team in the country in recent years.

CHERYL'S CIDER SOAK

1½ cups apple cider or juice	1 tablespoon oil, preferably
¾ cup cider vinegar	canola or corn
½ medium onion, minced	1 teaspoon ground cinnamon
1½ tablespoons Worcestershire sauce	1 teaspoon dried thyme

2 slabs of baby back ribs, preferably 1¼ to 1½ pounds each

APPLE RIB RUB

¼ cup brown sugar	1 teaspoon dry mustard
4 teaspoons onion powder	1 teaspoon salt
1 teaspoon ground cinnamon	½ teaspoon dried thyme

APPLE RIB MOP (OPTIONAL)

1½ cups apple cider or juice	4 teaspoons Worcestershire
½ cup cider vinegar	sauce

Apple City Apple Sauce (page 303) preferably, or Boydesque Brew (page 291)

Serves 3 to 4

The night before you plan to barbecue, combine the soak ingredients in a large lidded jar. Place the slabs of ribs in a plastic bag or shallow dish and pour the marinade over the ribs. Refrigerate them overnight.

Prepare the smoker for barbecuing, bringing the temperature to 200° F to 220° F.

Remove the ribs from the refrigerator and drain them, discarding the marinade. In a bowl, mix together the dry rub ingredients and pat the ribs with about half the mixture. Let the ribs sit at room temperature for 25 to 30 minutes.

If you plan to baste the meat (see chapter 3, "To Mop or Not"), mix together the cider, vinegar, and Worcestershire sauce in a saucepan. Warm the mop liquid over low heat.

Transfer the meat to the smoker. Cook the ribs for approximately 3 hours, turning and basting them with the mop every hour in a wood-burning pit, or as appropriate in your style of smoker. About 45 minutes before the ribs are done, brush them with Apple City Apple Sauce or Boydesque Brew, and repeat the step shortly before you remove the meat from the smoker.

When the slabs are ready, the meat will bend easily between the ribs, and the sauce will be gooey and sticky and caramelized in spots. Allow the slabs to sit for 5 to 10 minutes before slicing them into individual ribs. Serve with more sauce on the side.

BBQ tips The Apple City BBQuers cook their ribs over apple wood, which is common in their neighborhood. The sweet wood works well with many pork dishes, though we usually like to mix it with hickory.

New Yorkers are always looking for weekend getaways, as you might expect. We would opt for spending a night in a motel in Stratford or Stamford, Connecticut, and pigging out at Stick to Your Ribs, an authentic Yankee barbecue joint. Historic country inns are certainly in good taste, but their flavor doesn't rival real 'Q.'

West Coast Baby Backs

FIVE-SPICE RUB

⅓ cup five-spice powder, store-bought or homemade

⅓ cup brown sugar

2 slabs of baby back ribs, preferably 1¼ to 1½ pounds each

¼ cup soy sauce

West Coast Wonder barbecue sauce (page 300) or Plum Good Slopping Sauce (page 305) (optional)

Serves 3 to 4

At least 2 hours before you plan to barbecue, and preferably the evening before, mix together the rub ingredients in a small bowl. Rub the ribs with the soy sauce followed by a liberal coating of the spice mixture. Reserve the remaining rub. Place the ribs in a plastic bag and refrigerate them overnight, or for at least 2 hours.

Prepare the smoker for barbecuing, bringing the temperature to 200° F to 220° F.

Remove the ribs from the refrigerator. Pat them down with the remaining rub. Let the ribs sit at room temperature for 25 to 30 minutes.

Transfer the meat to the smoker. Cook the ribs for approximately 3 hours, turning and sprinkling them with the remaining dry rub about halfway through the cooking time.

When done, the ribs will have a thin coating of crispy spices on the surface and will pull apart easily. Allow the slabs to sit for 5 to 10 minutes before slicing them into individual ribs. Serve warm, with West Coast Wonder barbecue sauce or Plum Good Slopping Sauce, if you wish.

☆**Serving Suggestion:** Add some sliced water chestnuts and minced red bell pepper to cooked white rice, and serve it along with steamed broccoli spears drizzled with a little soy sauce. Finish with creamy 'Nana Pudding.

BBQ tips Perfectionists strip the membrane from the bone side of ribs, but this step isn't really necessary, particularly if you cook the meat longer than it needs to be done.

BBQ tips You can usually find five-spice powder in the Chinese section of your supermarket or certainly in Asian markets. To make a fresher version, grind up equal amounts of cinnamon sticks, star anise, cloves, fennel seeds, and Szechwan peppercorns. The mixture will keep for several months in an airtight jar in a cool pantry.

Cajun Country Ribs

Country-style ribs come from the blade ends of pork loin. Meaty and full of flavor, they pair well with hearty Louisiana spices.

CAJUN RAGIN' RUB

2 tablespoons celery salt	1 tablespoon garlic powder
2 tablespoons ground black pepper	1½ teaspoons cayenne
	1½ teaspoons dried thyme
2 tablespoons white pepper	1 teaspoon dried sage
2 tablespoons brown sugar	

Four to six 10-ounce to 14-ounce country-style rib sections

QUICK SOUTHERN SOP (OPTIONAL)

Remaining Cajun Ragin' Rub	1 tablespoon Worcestershire sauce
1½ cups cider vinegar	
¾ cup water	

Creole Classic Barbecue Sauce (page 299), Memphis Magic (page 294), or other spicy tomato-based barbecue sauce

Everywhere you turn in northern Alabama you find a Gibson's Bar-B-Q joint. They all go back, one way or another, to Big Bob Gibson, who started barbecuing hogs for the public in 1925 in an open underground pit. At first Big Bob barbecued only on Saturdays, and his farm doubled as the restaurant, with tables arranged under the shade of the trees.

Serves 4

The night before you plan to barbecue, combine the rub ingredients in a small bowl. Apply the rub evenly to the ribs, reserving about half of the spice mixture. Place the ribs in a plastic bag and refrigerate them overnight.

Prepare the smoker for barbecuing, bringing the temperature to 200° F to 220° F.

Remove the ribs from the refrigerator. Pat them down with a liberal sprinkling of the remaining rub, reserving at least 1 tablespoon if you plan to use the mop. Let the ribs stand at room temperature for 25 to 30 minutes.

If you are going to baste the meat (see chapter 3, "To Mop or Not"), mix together the vinegar, water, Worcestershire sauce, and remaining rub in a saucepan. Warm the mop liquid over low heat.

Transfer the meat to the smoker. Cook the ribs for 2½ to 3 hours, basting them with the mop at 45-minute intervals in a wood-burning pit, or as appropriate in your style of smoker.

When ready, the meat will be well-done and quite tender, with a coating of crispy spices on the surface. Serve hot.

☆**Serving Suggestion:** Mix cultures tastefully, serving the ribs with Kraut Salad, Sweet Potato Biscuits, and Santa Fe Capirotada for the finale.

Ginger-Glazed Ham

In Virginia, Kentucky, and other nearby states, traditional country hams—rare today—are cured in a bed of dry salt for some 5 weeks, smoked in an old-fashioned smokehouse for up to 2 months, and hung to age for almost a year. Barbecuing a ham is much simpler, and the result is just as tasty.

SOUTHERN SUCCOR RUB

2 tablespoons ground black pepper	1 tablespoon salt
	1 teaspoon dry mustard
2 tablespoons paprika	½ teaspoon cayenne
2 tablespoons turbinado sugar	

12-pound to 14-pound cooked ready-to-eat ham

PINEAPPLE MOP (OPTIONAL)

1½ cups chicken stock	2 teaspoons dry mustard
1½ cups pineapple juice	1 teaspoon ground cloves
3 tablespoons oil, preferably canola or corn	

GINGER GLAZE

⅔ cup ginger preserves or jelly	¼ teaspoon dry mustard
2 to 3 tablespoons pineapple juice	Pinch of ground cloves

Serves 10 to 12

The night before you plan to barbecue, combine the rub ingredients in a small bowl. Apply the rub evenly to the ham. Place the ham in a plastic bag and refrigerate it overnight.

Before you begin to barbecue, take the ham from the refrigerator and let it sit at room temperature for 45 to 60 minutes.

Prepare the smoker for barbecuing, bringing the temperature to 200° F to 220° F.

G.W. "Toots" Caston founded Fresh Air Bar-B-Que, deep in the Georgia woods, near Jackson, back in 1929. His family added concrete floors and pine paneling in the 1950s, but not much else has changed. Fresh Air is still a shack, and the fall-apart hams are still pit smoked for a full day.

If you like smokehouse-style country hams, you'll love the Loveless Motel and Cafe, just outside Nashville, Tennessee. The small roadhouse eatery specializes in hams and jams, and the kitchen does a magnificent job with both. You can even order by phone; just call 615-646-0067.

If you plan to baste the meat (see chapter 3, "To Mop or Not"), mix together the mop ingredients in a saucepan. Warm the mop liquid over low heat.

Transfer the ham to the smoker. Cook for 5½ to 6 hours, basting the meat with the mop about once an hour in a wood-burning pit, or as appropriate in your style of smoker. Brush the ham with the glaze twice during the last hour of cooking.

Let the ham sit for 15 minutes before carving. Save some of the leftovers for Monday Night Ham Loaf.

☆**Serving Suggestion:** Ham has always made a Sunday dinner special. Prepare a crock of Supper Spread and serve it with crackers as a taste teaser. Accompany the ham with Country Collard Greens, Mamie's Macaroni and Cheese, Corn and Watermelon Pickle-lilli, and Buttermilk Biscuits with peach butter or jam. Sweet Potato Pudding slides down easily for dessert.

When the first permanent British colonists landed at Jamestown, Virginia, in May, 1607, their limited cargo included domesticated pigs. The pork in your pit today may have as good an ancestry as any Colonial Dame.

Sweet and Fruity Tenderloin

SWEET SENSATION RUB

1 tablespoon ground allspice	½ teaspoon ground nutmeg
1 tablespoon brown sugar	½ teaspoon ground cinnamon
1 tablespoon onion powder	½ teaspoon dried thyme
1½ teaspoons salt	

Two 12-ounce to 14-ounce pork tenderloins
Oil, preferably canola or corn

TENDERLOIN MOP (OPTIONAL)

Remaining Sweet Sensation Rub	1 tablespoon cider vinegar
1½ cups chicken stock	1 tablespoon honey
2 tablespoons oil, preferably canola or corn	

Jalapeach Barbecue Sauce (page 302) or Jamaican Barbecue Sauce (page 300)

Serves 4

The night before you plan to barbecue, combine the rub ingredients in a small bowl. Massage the tenderloins with a thin film of the oil followed by a couple of tablespoons of the rub. Wrap them in plastic and refrigerate overnight.

Prepare your smoker for barbecuing, bringing the temperature to 200° F to 220° F.

Remove the tenderloins from the refrigerator and let them sit at room temperature for 30 minutes.

If you plan to baste the meat (see chapter 3, "To Mop or Not"), stir together the remaining rub with the other mop ingredients in a small saucepan and warm the mixture over low heat.

Warm a heavy skillet over high heat. Quickly sear the tenderloins on all sides. Transfer the tenderloins to the smoker. Cook for 2 to 2¼ hours, turning the meat and basting it with the mop about once every 30 minutes in a wood-burning pit, or as appropriate in your style of smoker. Brush the tenderloins lightly with Jalapeach Barbecue Sauce or Jamaican Barbecue Sauce during the last 30 minutes of cooking.

The tenderloins are ready when the internal temperature reaches 160° F. Let the meat sit for 10 minutes before carving. Serve with additional sauce on the side.

☆**Serving Suggestion:** Provide a decorative bowl of Curry Pecans and a pitcher of Maui Mai Tais for openers. With the pork, serve roasted potatoes and carrots, Blue Corn Muffins, and later a Liar's Lime Pie.

Pork Loin Mexicana

In this succulent preparation, tropical fruits combine with spice for a south-of-the-border flavor reminiscent of Veracruz.

SWEET SENSATION RUB

1 tablespoon ground allspice	½ teaspoon ground nutmeg
1 tablespoon brown sugar	½ teaspoon ground cinnamon
1 tablespoon onion powder	½ teaspoon dried thyme
1½ teaspoons salt	

3½-pound to 4-pound boneless center-cut pork loin, with a pocket sliced lengthwise through the center

FRUIT SALSA

1 cup fresh orange juice	1 teaspoon ground dried red chile, preferably ancho or New Mexican, or chili powder
2 small ripe tomatoes, preferably Romas or Italian plum	
1 small ripe banana, chopped	2 garlic cloves, minced
½ medium onion, minced	Dash of cider vinegar
1 fresh jalapeño, minced	
2 teaspoons extra-virgin olive oil	

FILLING

6 to 8 ounces uncooked Cha-Cha Chorizo (page 96) or other chorizo or spicy sausage	1 egg
	½ medium onion, minced
	3 green onions, sliced

MEXICANA MOP

Juice of 2 oranges	1 tablespoon extra-virgin olive oil
½ cup cider vinegar	
½ cup water	2 garlic cloves, minced

Serves 4

The night before you plan to barbecue, combine the rub ingredients in a small bowl. Massage the pork with the rub inside and out. Wrap the meat in a small plastic bag, and refrigerate overnight.

Before you begin to barbecue, prepare the salsa by combining all the ingredients in a small bowl. Refrigerate it until needed.

Prepare the smoker for barbecuing, bringing the temperature to 200° F to 220° F.

Remove the pork from the refrigerator and let it sit at room temperature for 30 minutes.

In a small bowl, mix together the filling ingredients. Stuff the loin with the chorizo mixture and tie it with kitchen twine in several places.

Mix together the mop ingredients in a small saucepan and keep the liquid warm over low heat.

Warm a heavy skillet over high heat. Add the loin and sear it quickly on all sides. Transfer the pork to the smoker. Cook for 2½ to 2¾ hours, basting the loin at 30-minute to 40-minute intervals in a wood-burning pit, or as appropriate for your style of smoker.

After the initial cooking period, remove the pork from the smoker and wrap it in heavy-duty foil, pouring about 2 tablespoons of the mop and ¼ cup of the salsa over the meat. Discard any remaining mop. Seal the edges of the foil well. Return the pork to the smoker for another 1 to 1¼ hours, cooking to an internal temperature of 160° F.

Allow the pork to sit at room temperature for about 10 minutes before slicing. Serve slices topped with spoonfuls of the salsa. Offer the remaining salsa on the side.

BBQ tips If you run short of mop in any recipe, extend it with additional splashes of the main liquid or even a little water. While we call for specific proportions, always feel free to take liberties—that's part of the fun of barbecuing.

The Great Pork BarbeQlossal each June brings the bacon back home. Iowa, the pork capital of the country, hasn't had a strong barbecue tradition, but the BarbeQlossal at Des Moines' State Fairgrounds aims to change that. If you lose out at the cook-off, you can hop over to the simultaneous World Pork Expo and enjoy events such as the pig races and the Pig-Casso art competition.

Purely Pork Chops

SOUTHERN SUCCOR RUB

1 tablespoon ground black pepper
1 tablespoon paprika
1 tablespoon turbinado sugar
1½ teaspoons salt
½ teaspoon dry mustard
¼ teaspoon cayenne

6 bone-in center-cut pork chops, ½-inch to ¾-inch thick

CHOP MOP (OPTIONAL)

½ cup cider or white vinegar

Old-Fashioned High-Cholesterol Great-Tasting Southern Sauce (page 293), Apple City Apple Sauce (page 303), or other barbecue sauce (optional)

Serves 6

At least 2 hours, and preferably 4 hours, before you plan to barbecue, combine the rub ingredients in a small bowl. Massage the chops with several tablespoons of the rub. Place the chops in a plastic bag and refrigerate for 1½ to 3½ hours.

Prepare the smoker for barbecuing, bringing the temperature to 200° F to 220° F.

Remove the chops from the refrigerator and let them sit at room temperature for 30 minutes.

If you plan to baste the chops (see chapter 3, "To Mop or Not"), warm the vinegar in a small saucepan over low heat.

Warm a heavy skillet over high heat. Quickly sear the chops on both sides and transfer them to the smoker. Cook the meat for 55 to 65 minutes, turning and basting it with the mop once or twice in a wood-burning pit, or as appropriate in your style of smoker.

The chops are ready when the internal temperature reaches 160° F. Serve hot, with Old-Fashioned High-Cholesterol Great-Tasting Southern Sauce, Apple City

Apple Sauce, or other barbecue sauce on the side, if you wish.

☆**Variation:** For Pop Chops, marinate and/or mop the chops with Pop Mop, using Dr Pepper, Coca-Cola, or R.C. Cola.

Stuffed Chops

These tender chops are stuffed with a moist cornbread dressing.

KENTUCKY PRIDE PASTE

½ medium onion, preferably a sweet variety, chunked

2 tablespoons bourbon

1 tablespoon brown sugar

1 tablespoon ground black pepper

1½ teaspoons oil, preferably canola or corn

6 bone-in double-thick center-cut pork chops, about 1½ inches thick, cut with a pocket for stuffing

STUFFING

4 tablespoons butter

½ medium green bell pepper, chopped fine

⅓ medium onion, chopped fine

1 celery rib, chopped fine

1 cup dry cornbread crumbs

1 dozen pitted prunes, chopped

2 tablespoons chopped fresh parsley

1 tablespoon minced fresh sage or ½ tablespoon dried sage

¼ teaspoon dry mustard

Salt to taste

1 to 3 tablespoons water or chicken stock

DRUNK CHOP MOP (OPTIONAL)

1 cup cider or white vinegar

2 tablespoons bourbon

2 tablespoons water

Serves 6

At least 2 hours, and preferably 4 hours, before you plan to barbecue, combine the paste ingredients in a food processor or blender. Massage the chops inside and out with the paste. Place the chops in a plastic bag and refrigerate for 1½ to 3½ hours.

Prepare the smoker for barbecuing, bringing the temperature to 200° F to 220° F.

Remove the chops from the refrigerator and let them sit at room temperature for 20 to 30 minutes.

To make the stuffing, melt the butter in a small skillet. Add the bell pepper, onion, and celery, sautéing until soft. Spoon the mixture into a bowl and stir in the remaining ingredients, adding only enough water or stock to bind the stuffing loosely. Stuff the chops with equal portions of the mixture.

If you plan to baste the chops (see chapter 3, "To Mop or Not"), warm the vinegar, bourbon, and water in a small saucepan over low heat. Keep the mop warm over low heat.

Warm a heavy skillet over high heat. Quickly sear the chops on both sides and transfer them to the smoker. Cook for 1¾ to 2 hours, turning and basting the meat with the mop about every 30 minutes in a wood-burning pit, or as appropriate in your style of smoker.

The chops are ready when the internal temperature reaches 160° F. Serve hot.

☆**Serving Suggestion:** For a casual supper, pair the chops with Sweet Sally's Sweet Potato Salad. Poach apple slices in apple juice and cinnamon and top with crystallized ginger for dessert.

East L.A. Pork Tacos

Shoulder chops start out a little tougher and fattier than their center-cut cousins, but many pork fans prefer their richer flavor and cheaper cost. Cooked this style, they'll be plenty tender and taste great, too. Many well-stocked super-markets carry achiote, as do Mexican, Latin American, and East Indian markets.

BORRACHO MARINADE AND OPTIONAL MOP

2   cups orange juice
⅔ cup tequila
Juice of 2 limes
Juice of 1 lemon
½ medium onion, minced
1   tablespoon olive oil
3   garlic cloves, minced
2   teaspoons dried oregano,
    preferably Mexican

1   teaspoon achiote (annatto)
    paste
1   teaspoon ground cumin
Several dashes of Melinda's
    Original Habanero Hot
    Sauce or other fiery habanero
    hot sauce

6 shoulder pork chops, 12 to 14 ounces each

Warm corn tortillas
Chopped onion and cilantro, and lime and orange wedges, for
    garnish
Sauce Olé (page 296) or additional habanero hot sauce

Serves 4 to 6

The night before you plan to barbecue, combine the marinade ingredients in a blender or food processor. Pour the marinade over the pork in a plastic bag. Refrigerate the chops overnight.

Prepare the smoker for barbecuing, bringing the temperature to 200° F to 220° F.

Drain the pork, reserving all of the marinade if you plan to baste the meat during cooking. Let the chops sit at room temperature for 30 minutes.

To make the optional mop (see chapter 3, "To Mop or Not"), bring the marinade to a boil over high heat and boil for several minutes. Keep warm over low heat.

Stan Gambrell, the city administrator of Vienna, Georgia, recalls a barbecue cooking team that entered the town's first Big Pig Jig in 1982. He says they "insisted on burying their pig in the ground Hawaiian style, and kept insisting that the hole be dug wider. And wider. And WIDER. We dug the way they said they wanted it, but when judging time came and they tried to dig up their pig, they never could find it."

Transfer the chops to the smoker. Cook for 2½ to 2¾ hours, basting at 45-minute intervals in a wood-burning pit, or as appropriate for your style of smoker.

When done, the pork will pull easily away from the fat and bone. Allow the chops to sit at room temperature for 10 to 15 minutes and pull the pork into shreds. Arrange the pork on a platter with the warm tortillas and garnishes. Serve with Sauce Olé or additional habanero hot sauce.

BBQ tips Most authorities today agree that pork is done enough to eat when the internal temperature reaches 160° F or even a little less. Most barbecuers cook the meat to a temperature of at least 170° F, when it begins to fall apart, and some go as high as 190° F.

Creole Crown Roast

A crown pork roast, elegantly presented and carved at the table, symbolizes a special occasion. Call your butcher ahead for the roast, formed by tying the rib section of the loin into a circle.

CREOLE RUB

2 tablespoons celery salt	1½ teaspoons dried thyme
1 tablespoon paprika	½ teaspoon cayenne
1 tablespoon ground black pepper	1 tablespoon brown sugar
	1½ teaspoons garlic powder
1 tablespoon white pepper	

5-pound crown pork roast (10 to 12 chops)
1 to 2 tablespoons Worcestershire sauce

CREOLE MOP (OPTIONAL)

Remaining Creole Rub	¼ cup Worcestershire sauce
2 cups chicken or beef stock	¼ cup butter
2 cups water	

Serves 8 to 10

The night before you plan to barbecue, combine the rub ingredients in a small bowl. Massage the roast well with the Worcestershire sauce and then with about half of the rub. Transfer the roast to a plastic bag and refrigerate it overnight.

Before you begin to barbecue, remove the roast from the refrigerator. Pat down the roast lightly with another coating of rub. Let the roast sit at room temperature for 40 to 45 minutes.

Prepare the smoker for barbecuing, bringing the temperature to 200° F to 220° F.

If you plan to baste the roast (see chapter 3, "To Mop or Not"), stir any remaining rub together with the other mop ingredients in a saucepan and warm the mixture over low heat.

Transfer the roast to the smoker and cook for 4¾ to 5 hours, or until the internal temperature reaches 160° F. Mop the pork every 40 to 45 minutes in a wood-burning pit, or as appropriate for your style of smoker.

Remove the pork from the smoker and let it sit at room temperature for 10 to 15 minutes. Carve the roast, slicing downward between each bone to cut into individual chops.

☆**Serving Suggestion:** Serve the crown roast as the centerpiece for a Mardi Gras meal. Sip Firewater first, then sit down to a first course of Shrimp Rémoulade. Present the roast with twice-baked potatoes, Maque Choux Peppers, and sautéed chayote squash. Offer pralines and coffee laced with bourbon for dessert.

BBQ tips When mops include butter or oil, much of the fat drips away from the food it's protecting, leaving behind moist meat and a hint of flavor.

Ca-Rib-bean Roast

CA-RIB-BEAN RUB

1 tablespoon brown sugar	½ teaspoon dried thyme
2 teaspoons ground allspice	1 teaspoon salt
2 teaspoons onion powder	½ teaspoon ground nutmeg

2½-pound to 2¾-pound pork rib roast
1 tablespoon rum, preferably dark

CA-RIB-BEAN MOP (OPTIONAL)

1 cup chicken or beef stock	¼ cup rum, preferably dark
1 cup water	2 tablespoons oil, preferably
½ cup cider vinegar	canola or corn

MANGO SAUCE

1 mango, chopped	2 tablespoons cream of coconut
½ medium onion, chopped	1 teaspoon Ca-Rib-bean Rub
2 tablespoons mango chutney	Splash or two of Pickapeppa
½ cup chicken stock	sauce (optional)
2 to 3 tablespoons rum,	Salt to taste
preferably dark	1½ teaspoons butter

Serves 4 to 5

The night before you plan to barbecue, combine the rub ingredients in a small bowl. Massage the pork well with the rum and then with about half of the rub. Transfer the pork to a plastic bag and refrigerate it overnight.

Prepare the smoker for barbecuing, bringing the temperature to 200° F to 220° F.

Remove the pork from the refrigerator. Pat down the pork lightly with another coating of rub. Let the meat sit at room temperature for 30 to 40 minutes.

If you plan to baste the pork (see chapter 3, "To Mop or Not"), stir any remaining rub together with the other mop ingredients in a saucepan and warm the mixture over low heat.

Transfer the pork to the smoker, fattier side up, and cook for 4¾ to 5 hours, or until the internal temperature reaches 160° F. Mop the meat every 40 to 45 minutes in a wood-burning pit, or as appropriate for your style of smoker.

While the roast cooks, prepare the sauce. In a food processor or blender, purée together the mango, onion, and chutney, pouring in a bit of the stock if necessary. Spoon the mixture into a heavy saucepan and add the remaining stock, rum, cream of coconut, and dry rub. Warm the mixture over medium heat and simmer for about 20 minutes. Taste and add as much Pickapeppa and salt as necessary to balance the savory and sweet flavors. The sauce can be kept warm or refrigerated until the roast is ready and then reheated. Add the butter to the warm sauce just before serving.

Remove the pork from the smoker and let it sit at room temperature for 10 to 15 minutes. Carve the roast and serve, accompanied by the warm sauce.

The same German butchers who created modern Texas barbecue also made great link sausage, which they smoked with the brisket in the pit at the back of the meat market. It's still as popular as beef in central Texas joints.

Hill Country Links

If you own or can borrow a meat grinder, you can stuff your own sausage links for barbecuing.

4 pounds pork butt, with fat	1 tablespoon salt
2 pounds beef chuck or round steak, with fat	1 tablespoon coarse-ground black pepper
1 large onion, minced	1 to 2 tablespoons chile caribe or other crushed dried red chile of moderate heat
6 garlic cloves, minced	
2 tablespoons minced fresh sage or 1 tablespoon dried sage	½ to 1 teaspoon cayenne

4 yards hog sausage casings

Oil, preferably canola or corn

Makes about twenty-four 4-ounce sausages, serving 12 or more

At least one evening before you plan to barbecue the sausages, grind the pork and beef together, using the coarse-grind blade of a meat grinder. Add the rest of the ingredients, except the casings and oil. If you wish, grind the mixture again. Refrigerate, covered, overnight.

Prepare the casings, soaking them in several changes of water over several hours.

With the stuffing attachment of a meat grinder, stuff the cold sausage mixture into the casings, making 1-inch-thick links about 5 inches long. With your fingers, twist the casing and tie off the individual sausages with kitchen twine. Cut between the links. If you end up with any air bubbles, prick the casing in those spots with a needle. The sausage is ready to barbecue, but it can be refrigerated for several days or frozen for at least a month.

Prepare the smoker for barbecuing, bringing the temperature to 200° F to 220° F. Rub the sausages lightly with the oil.

Transfer the links to the smoker and cook for 2 to 2¼ hours, until the skin of the sausage looks ready to pop. Always err on the side of caution with the timing and cut one of the sausages open to check for doneness before eating any of them. Serve hot.

BBQ tips Sausage casings are the intestines of various farm animals. You want casings from a pig in this instance. Inexpensive and hard to damage, the casings generally come packed in brine. These days most casing comes "preflushed," eliminating the need to clean the casing interiors with running water. You'll want to soak them, though, to eliminate the brine. When stuffing the sausages, it's easiest to work with the casings in sections no longer than a yard long, and to have the meat well-chilled.

If you plan to make a lot of sausage, some sausage companies or meat markets sell casings in bulk. You can usually get casings for 100 pounds of sausage and change back from a twenty dollar bill. The brined casings keep, refrigerated, for up to a year.

Barbecue cook-offs go hog wild with names. It's Swine Days in Natchez, Mississippi, a Pig Pickin' Party in Columbia, South Carolina, an Ozark Hawg contest in Batesville, Arkansas, and a Hogtoberfest in Roanoke Rapids, North Carolina.

Store-Bought Hot Brats

If you don't want to grind and stuff your own sausage, you can start with a store-bought variety and still add an abundance of smoky, barbecue taste. Around the barbecue cook-off circuit, nationally distributed Johnsonville bratwurst from Sheboygan, Wisconsin, is a popular choice. Personally, we prefer brats with more spice—nutmeg, coriander, ginger, or caraway—though they are a little harder to find.

1 dozen 4-ounce to 6-ounce
  uncooked bratwursts
Oil, preferably canola or corn

1 to 2 teaspoons Wild Willy's
  Number One-derful Dry Rub
  (page 36) or other savory
  seasoning blend (optional)

Golden Mustard Barbecue Sauce
  (page 293) or other mustardy
  barbecue sauce (optional)

Serves 6

Prepare the smoker for barbecuing, bringing the temperature to 200° F to 220° F.

Rub the brats lightly with oil and sprinkle them with rub if you wish. Let the brats sit at room temperature for 20 minutes.

Transfer the brats to the smoker and cook for 1½ to 2 hours, depending on size, or until the skin of the sausage looks ready to pop. Serve hot, perhaps with Golden Mustard Barbecue Sauce.

BBQ tips You can barbecue any kind of store-bought sausage. In addition to bratwurst, our biggest hits have included a robust Molinari Italian sausage and several varieties of Bruce Aidells' links, both from the San Francisco Bay area, but with some national distribution. If you use precooked sausage, get something that was smoked originally, because it will need only about 30 minutes in your smoker—not long enough to absorb much smoke flavor.

☆**Serving Suggestion:** Don't wait for October for an Oktoberfest menu. Barbecue several varieties of sausage, and buy loaves of hearty breads like pumpernickel and rye, several kinds of mustard, some garlicky dill pickles, and loads of German beer. Make up a hefty bowl of Hot German Potato Salad and Black Walnut Cake to round out the celebration.

Cha-Cha Chorizo

A popular sausage throughout the Southwest, spicy chorizo is delicious smoked.

1¾ pounds pork butt, with fat, ground by your butcher or with a meat grinder at home	1 jalapeño, minced
	1½ teaspoons dried oregano, preferably Mexican
3 tablespoons chili powder, preferably Gebhardt's	1½ teaspoons ground cumin
	1 teaspoon salt
½ cup minced onion	½ teaspoon cayenne or ground chile de árbol
½ cup cider vinegar	
Juice of 1 orange	½ teaspoon *canela* (Mexican cinnamon) or cinnamon
6 garlic cloves, minced	

CHA-CHA MOP (OPTIONAL)

Juice of 1 orange	1½ teaspoons olive oil
¼ cup cider vinegar	

Serves 4 to 6

At least an evening before you plan to smoke the sausages, start the preparations. In a large bowl, mix together the sausage ingredients. Refrigerate, covered, overnight or for a couple of days.

Prepare the smoker for barbecuing, bringing the temperature to 200° F to 220° F.

Allen & Son Bar-B-Que remains a bastion of the old "Down East" barbecue style that's been popular in eastern North Carolina since the locals talked with British accents. In several branches around Chapel Hill, the restaurant cooks whole hogs in an open pit over wood coals and serves the meat with a thin vinegary sauce full of pepper and spice.

Form the sausage mixture into 8 patties, about 3 ounces each. Let the patties sit at room temperature for about 15 minutes.

If you plan to baste the sausage patties (see chapter 3, "To Mop or Not"), mix together the mop ingredients in a small saucepan and warm over low heat.

Transfer the patties to the smoker. Cook for about 1 hour, mopping once or twice in a wood-burning pit, or as appropriate in your style of smoker. The patties should be ready when they are richly browned and cooked through. Always err on the side of caution with the timing, though, and cut one of the patties open to check for doneness before eating any of them. Serve hot.

☆**Serving Suggestion:** Chorizo is a great breakfast sausage. It puts real zing in a simple dish like scrambled eggs.

B.C. Canadian Bacon

We got this idea from friends in British Columbia, Canada, where they call this cut of pork "back bacon."

1 pound Canadian bacon
Oil, preferably canola or corn
1 teaspoon Wild Willy's Number
   One-derful Rub (page 36),
   Southern Succor Rub (page
   36), Cajun Ragin' Rub
   (page 38), or other savory
   seasoning blend

PINEAPPLE MOP (OPTIONAL)

½ cup chicken stock
½ cup pineapple juice
1 tablespoon oil, preferably
   canola or corn

¾ teaspoon dry mustard
¼ teaspoon ground cloves

Serves 2 to 4

Prepare the smoker for barbecuing, bringing the temperature to 200° F to 220° F.

Rub the Canadian bacon lightly with oil and sprinkle it with rub. Let the meat sit at room temperature for 30 minutes.

If you plan to baste the meat (see chapter 3, "To Mop or Not"), stir together the mop ingredients in a small saucepan and warm the mixture over low heat.

Transfer the Canadian bacon to the smoker and cook for 1 to 1¼ hours, turning and mopping twice in a wood-burning pit, or as appropriate in your style of smoker.

Let the meat sit at room temperature for 5 to 10 minutes before slicing and serving.

☆**Serving Suggestion:** Smoked Canadian bacon is a natural for eggs Benedict. To add some extra punch, we like to substitute chile con queso or another spicy cheese sauce for the Hollandaise.

Triple Play Tube Steak

Barbecuing elevates bologna to a new taste sphere, and all it requires is a quick score, slather, and smoke.

2-pound stick of bologna Memphis Magic (page 294), Bar-BQ Ranch Sauce (page 295), or other not-too-sweet, tomato-based barbecue sauce	1 tablespoon cider or white vinegar

Serves 6 to 8

Score the bologna ¼-inch deep with wide criss-cross cuts. Thin ⅓ cup of the barbecue sauce with the vinegar. Cover the bologna thoroughly with the thinned sauce. Let the bologna sit at room temperature for 20 to 30 minutes.

Prepare the smoker for barbecuing, bringing the temperature to 200° F to 220° F.

Transfer the bologna to the smoker and cook for about 2 hours. The sauce will have caramelized on the bologna's surface. Serve sliced, hot or cold, with additional barbecue sauce.

☆**Serving Suggestion:** Make sandwiches out of the bologna, topped with barbecue sauce, Green Tomato Chowchow, and some chopped onions. If you liked baloney sandwiches as a kid, you'll relish this one.

Monday Night Ham Loaf

1 pound Ginger-Glazed Ham (page 80) or other well-smoked fully-cooked ham
¾ pound ground pork
1 medium onion, chopped
1 tablespoon oil, preferably canola or corn
1 cup cornbread crumbs or other bread crumbs
2 eggs

1 cup milk
2 tablespoons prepared yellow mustard
2 tablespoons Worcestershire sauce
1½ tablespoons cider vinegar
¼ teaspoon ground cloves
Pinch of ground ginger
Salt to taste

MONDAY NIGHT GLAZE

2 tablespoons ginger preserves or jelly
1 tablespoon pineapple or apple juice

1 teaspoon prepared yellow mustard

Serves 6 to 8

Preheat the oven to 350° F. Process the ham in a food processor until minced fine, or grind the ham in a meat grinder. Transfer the ham to a bowl, add the remaining ingredients, and combine well.

Spoon the moist ham mixture into a loaf pan and smooth its surface. Bake the loaf for 45 minutes. While the loaf bakes, combine the glaze ingredients in a small bowl. Brush the loaf with the glaze. Continue baking for another 15 to 20 minutes, for a total cooking time of 60 to 65 minutes.

Remove the meat from the oven and let it sit for at least 10 minutes before cutting. Serve hot or cold. Leftovers keep for 3 to 4 days.

☆**Serving Suggestion:** Ham loaf makes good mini-sandwiches on split Sweet Potato Biscuits or tiny wedges of Cracklin' Cornbread. Serve the sandwiches with ginger preserves or jelly, mango or peach chutney, or tangy mustard.

Supper Spread

This is an all-American version of rillettes, the rich, savory potted French dish. Our recipe is modeled on one from Southern food authority Nathalie Dupree.

¼ cup butter	2 teaspoons minced fresh sage
1 cup finely chopped smoked	or 1 teaspoon dried sage
pork butt or picnic	Tabasco or other hot pepper
½ cup water	sauce to taste
2 garlic cloves, minced	Salt and coarse-ground black
1 teaspoon Worcestershire	pepper to taste
sauce	

Serves 2 as a main course or 4 to 6 as an appetizer

In a small heavy saucepan, melt the butter over low heat. Add the pork, water, garlic, and Worcestershire sauce. Barely simmer the mixture over very low heat for 15 to 20 minutes, or until the liquid evaporates but the pork still looks moist. The pork should be quite tender. Remove the pan from the heat and mix in the sage, Tabasco, and salt and pepper to taste. Spoon the mixture into a small crock, cover, and refrigerate at least until chilled, but preferably overnight.

Let the spread sit at room temperature for about 10 minutes before serving. Serve the spread with a crusty country-style white bread.

☆**Serving Suggestion:** To complete an early winter supper, add South-of-the-Border Garlic Soup, a couple of varieties of pickles, and Southern Caesar Salad. Offer fresh pears to round out the meal.

Barbecue Spaghetti

This may never make it in Italy, but it's sure big in Memphis.

1½ to 2 cups Memphis Magic (page 294) or other tomato-based barbecue sauce

1½ cups pulled or shredded smoked pork butt or picnic

1 pound cooked spaghetti

Chopped onion, for garnish (optional)

Serves 4

Warm the barbecue sauce in a saucepan. Add the pork and heat through. Mix the sauce with the spaghetti and serve on a platter. Garnish with the onion, if you wish.

Pork is ancient fare the world over. According to food historian Waverley Root, pigs are second only to dogs as the oldest domesticated animals on earth.

☆ Bodacious Beef ☆

Some Southern pitmasters think Texans started barbecuing beef simply because they couldn't tell a steer from a pig. Texans, in turn, reckon that anyone who prefers hogs to cattle doesn't know the difference between a trough and a table.

The pork and beef barbecue traditions are entirely different animals in all respects, including origins. British colonists brought pigs to the East Coast and adopted Native American cooking methods to create their style of barbecue. Long before these settlers moved west, Mexican ranchers and *vaqueros*, the earliest cowboys, introduced the Southwest to their specialty, *barbacoa de cabeza*. It's whole head barbecue, preferably made with a big bull's head that is smoked overnight in an underground pit.

Barbacoa de cabeza remained a chuck-wagon treat throughout the epic era of the cowboy, but the dish never had a chance in Dallas. German butchers in central Texas intervened around the turn of the century to change the nature of beef barbecue. For them, sweetbreads, brains, and other parts of the head were too much of a delicacy to put in a pit. They took up barbecuing as a way to get rid of their worst cuts of beef, like brisket, sometimes a throw-away piece in the days before fast-food hamburgers. The thrifty butchers found that long, slow smoking tenderized even the toughest meat, turning a waste product into a hunk of Heaven—not to mention a profitable sideline.

From small Texas towns like Lockhart, Taylor, and Elgin, beef barbecue spread throughout the Southwest and Midwest. It met the pork barbecue tradition in Kansas City, one of the capitals of the 'Q,' and the two learned to live together in mutual respect on that neutral turf. Elsewhere, partisans may continue to clash on the merits of the meats, but anyone who tries both with an open mind will end up on the Kansas City side of the street. Even if pork ribs tickle you pink, you'll discover that the burnt ends of a brisket can't be beat.

Braggin'-Rights Brisket

The medieval alchemists, who sought to turn base metals into gold, should have tried barbecuing a brisket on a wood-burning pit. The transformation of the meat is on the same magnitude of magic and much more successful. If you're cooking on a charcoal or electric smoker, skip to the recipe for Dallas Dandy Brisket.

WILD WILLY'S NUMBER ONE-DERFUL RUB

¾ cup paprika
¼ cup ground black pepper
¼ cup salt
¼ cup sugar

2 tablespoons chili powder
2 tablespoons garlic powder
2 tablespoons onion powder
2 teaspoons cayenne

8-pound to 12-pound packer-trimmed beef brisket

BASIC BEER MOP

12 ounces beer
½ cup cider vinegar
½ cup water
¼ cup oil, preferably canola or corn
½ medium onion, chopped

2 garlic cloves, minced
1 tablespoon Worcestershire sauce
1 tablespoon Wild Willy's Number One-derful Rub

Struttin' Sauce (page 290), Bar-BQ Ranch Sauce (page 295), or other tomato-based barbecue sauce (optional)

Serves 12 to 18

The night before you plan to barbecue, combine the rub ingredients in a small bowl. Apply the rub evenly to the brisket, massaging it into every little pore, reserving at least 1 tablespoon of the rub. Place the brisket in a plastic bag and refrigerate it overnight.

Before you begin to barbecue, remove the brisket from the refrigerator. Let the brisket sit at room temperature for 45 minutes.

Prepare the smoker for barbecuing, bringing the temperature to 200° F to 220° F.

In a saucepan, mix together the mop ingredients and warm over low heat.

Transfer the brisket to the coolest part of the smoker, fat side up, so the juices will help baste the meat. Cook the brisket until well-done, 1 to 1¼ hours per pound. Every hour or so, baste the blackening hunk with the mop.

When the meat is cooked, remove it from the smoker and let it sit at room temperature for 20 minutes. Then cut the fatty top section away from the leaner bottom portion. An easily identifiable layer of fat separates the two areas. Trim the excess fat from both pieces and slice them thinly against the grain. Watch what you're doing because the grain changes direction. If you wish, serve Struttin' Sauce, Bar-BQ Ranch Sauce, or other tomato-based barbecue sauce on the side.

☆**Serving Suggestion:** For a rousing ranch barbecue, start with Can't Wait Queso and Chicken from Hell, served with an iced tub of beer and a gargantuan pitcher of Sunny Sweet Tea. Accompany the brisket with Creamy Coleslaw, Cowpoke Pintos, San Antonio Cactus and Corn Salad, and Cracklin' Cornbread. To finish, what else but Texas Peach Cobbler?

BBQ tips The best barbecued brisket is heavily smoked and significantly shrunk during the cooking process. The only way to succeed completely is with a wood-burning pit or similar homemade smoker. If you have the right equipment, be sure to start with a packer-trimmed brisket, the whole cut with a thick layer of fat on one side. You may need to contact your butcher a few days ahead to get what you want.

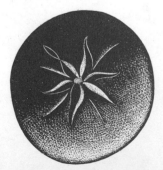

Hayward Spears, another guy from Hope, Arkansas, may make the best burnt ends in Kansas City. His suburban restaurant, Hayward's, isn't too slack on other kinds of meat either, cooking more than nine tons of barbecue a week.

Burnt Ends

A Kansas City specialty, the burnt ends of a barbecued brisket are fit for a royal feast. Any pit-smoked brisket has plenty of blackened surface to cut into ends, but we prefer to use the fatty top portion, sliced off in one piece and cooked again. If you don't want to take the time for this on the same day you barbecue initially, freeze the meat and put it back on the pit when you fire up again.

1 fully barbecued fatty top section Braggin'-Rights Brisket (page 105)

Struttin' Sauce (page 290), Bar-BQ Ranch Sauce (page 295), or other tomato-based barbecue sauce (optional)

Serves 4 to 6

Prepare the smoker for barbecuing, bringing the temperature to 200° F to 220° F.

Transfer the brisket section to the smoker and cook it for 3 to 4 hours, depending on its size. Let the brisket sit at room temperature for 10 minutes and then slice or shred it. After you break through the coal-like crust, the meat will pull apart into succulent shreds with chewy, deep-flavored ends. Savor at once, with Struttin' Sauce, Bar-BQ Ranch Sauce, or other tomato-based barbecue sauce on the side, if you wish.

BBQ tips You should seldom trim the fat from meat before you barbecue it. The fat is a natural basting agent that helps to keep the meat moist and flavorful, particularly when it's on the top side of the cut while it's cooking. Much of the fat melts away in your smoker—just check the water pan or reservoir—and the rest can be trimmed before serving.

Dallas Dandy Brisket

Even if you have a wood-burning pit, you may not want to fire it for a full day every time you want some brisket. This is the best alternative style we've found and it works great in a water smoker or charcoal grill. You won't get a full measure of the old-time barbecued brisket flavor, but you'll still have plenty to boast about.

DALLAS DANDY RUB

2 tablespoons hickory-flavored salt

2 tablespoons brown sugar

2 tablespoons paprika

2 tablespoons chili powder

2 tablespoons ground black pepper

DALLAS DANDY MARINADE

2 tablespoons Dallas Dandy Rub

12 ounces beer

1 medium onion, chopped

½ cup cider or white vinegar

¼ cup oil, preferably canola or corn

2 canned chipotle chiles plus 2 tablespoons adobo sauce

2 tablespoons pure liquid smoke

4-pound fully trimmed brisket section (sometimes called the flat cut)

Struttin' Sauce (page 290), Bar-BQ Ranch Sauce (page 295), or other tomato-based barbecue sauce (optional)

Serves 6 to 8

The night before you plan to barbecue, stir together the dry rub ingredients in a small bowl. Combine 2 tablespoons of the rub with the other marinade ingredients in a blender and purée. Place the brisket in a plastic bag and pour the marinade over it. Refrigerate the brisket overnight.

Before you begin to barbecue, take the brisket from the refrigerator. Drain and discard the marinade. Pat the brisket down with all but 2 tablespoons of the remain-

Dallas chef Stephan Pyles, author of *The New Texas Cuisine*, says that barbecue is a way of life in his home state. He calls it "a ritual that's bred in the bone."

ing rub, coating the slab well. Let the brisket sit at room temperature for about 45 minutes.

Prepare the smoker for barbecuing, bringing the temperature to 200° F to 220° F.

Transfer the brisket to the smoker and cook for 3 hours. Place the meat on a sheet of heavy-duty foil, sprinkle it with the rest of the rub, and close the foil tightly. Cook for an additional 1½ to 2 hours, until well-done and tender.

Let the brisket sit at room temperature for 15 minutes. Trim any excess fat and slice the brisket thinly against the grain, changing direction as the grain changes. If you wish, serve Struttin' Sauce, Bar-BQ Ranch Sauce, or other tomato-based barbecue sauce on the side.

☆**Serving Suggestion:** For a summer supper, round out the meal with Burstin' with Black-Eyed Peas Salad and Boarding House Macaroni Salad. No dessert beats The Best Cure for a Southern Summer.

BBQ tips Chipotle chiles, which are smoked jalapeños, contribute their smoldering heat and smokiness to many great barbecue dishes. They can be found dried, but we often prefer the canned variety for its flavorful adobo sauce, a heady concoction of vinegar, tomato, onions, spices, and smoke. *Muy sabrosa.*

Bona Fide Fajitas

In addition to barbacoa de cabeza, *Mexican ranchers and* vaqueros *in the Southwest gave the world* fajitas, *another slow-starter. The diaphragm muscle of cattle,* fajitas *or skirt steak, didn't win acceptance even in Texas until the last couple of decades. After the dish became trendy across the country, restaurants began misusing the Spanish term to refer to almost any kind of grilled meat rolled in a flour tortilla. The only true* fajitas *are made with beef skirt, and the best ones are still slow-smoked outdoors over a wood fire. If you want to be literal, this is a* taco de fajitas, *but most people know it simply by the name of the meat itself.*

FAJITAS MARINADE AND OPTIONAL MOP

12 ounces beer
¾ cup oil, preferably canola or corn
½ medium onion, chopped
Juice of 2 limes
4 garlic cloves, minced
1 bay leaf
2 tablespoons Worcestershire sauce
1 tablespoon chili powder
1 teaspoon fresh-ground black pepper
1 teaspoon crushed chiltepins or chiles pequíns or Tabasco sauce
1 teaspoon ground cumin

2-pound to 3-pound whole beef skirt, trimmed of fat and membrane

PICO DE GALLO

4 small red-ripe tomatoes, preferably Romas or Italian plum, diced
½ bell pepper, preferably red, chopped
¼ cup chopped fresh cilantro
¼ cup chopped red onion
2 to 3 fresh serranos or 3 to 4 fresh jalapeños, minced
Juice of ½ lime
½ teaspoon salt or more to taste
2 to 4 tablespoons tomato juice (optional)

Warm flour tortillas
Lime wedges and cilantro sprigs, for garnish
Sour cream

Serves 6 to 8

On the old California *ranchos*, beef head's barbecue was a special feast for the full family. In her delightful 1988 *California Rancho Cooking* (Olive Press), Jacqueline Higuera McMahan recounts how the men dug a pit and tended the fire overnight, women made tortillas and salsas, and the children stuffed mint, oregano, and rosemary into the bull's ears and mouth. When they dug up the head after hours of covered smoking, the chief cook got the eyes and the cheek meat, and the boys grabbed "the huge set of teeth so they could run off to frighten any squeamish young ladies on the sidelines."

The night before you plan to barbecue, combine the marinade ingredients in a blender and purée. Place the skirt steak in a plastic bag or shallow dish and pour the marinade over it. Refrigerate the skirt steak overnight, turning occasionally if needed to saturate the surface with the marinade.

Prepare the smoker for barbecuing, bringing the temperature to 200° F to 220° F.

Remove the skirt from the refrigerator and drain it, reserving the marinade if you plan to baste the meat. Let the skirt sit at room temperature for 30 minutes.

Make the pico de gallo by combining all the ingredients except the tomato juice in a bowl. If you prefer a more liquid consistency, add some or all of the tomato juice. Refrigerate until serving time.

If you are going to baste the meat (see chapter 3, "To Mop or Not"), boil the marinade in a saucepan over high heat for several minutes and then keep the mop warm over low heat.

Transfer the skirt to the smoker. Cook for approximately 1 hour, mopping every 20 minutes in a wood-burning pit, or as appropriate for your style of smoker.

If your smoker has a separate grill area for cooking directly over the fire, or if you have another grill handy, move the meat there and sear it for 1 to 2 minutes per side. This step adds a pleasant crispy exterior texture, but isn't necessary for flavor. Alternatively, smoke the meat for about 15 minutes longer.

Let the skirt sit for 10 minutes and then slice thinly at a diagonal angle against the grain. Pile the meat and warm tortillas on a platter garnished with lime wedges and cilantro, and serve the pico de gallo and sour cream on the side.

A red-orange, pea-shaped chile pod that grows wild in parts of the Southwest, chiltepins add serious zing to barbecue marinades. Their pointed-pod cousins, chiles pequíns, pack similar firepower. If your market has neither, Tabasco or a similar hot sauce makes a good substitute.

Drunk and Dirty Tenderloin

This one owes its inspiration to our old Kentucky home— the one in Bourbon County. It was there, in the same year that the country adopted the Constitution, that a Baptist preacher named Elijah Craig invented the wonderful American whiskey that flavors this tenderloin. We developed the recipe originally, like a couple of others in the chapter, for our Texas Home Cooking *(Harvard Common Press, 1993).*

Starnes Bar-B-Q in Paducah thrives on Kentucky contrariness. Though mutton is the barbecue of choice in the western part of the state, pork and beef are the stars at Starnes. Even more ornery, the two-booth joint serves its delicious meat on *toasted* bread, an idea that takes just a bite to like.

DRUNK AND DIRTY MARINADE

1 cup soy sauce	2 tablespoons brown sugar
½ cup bourbon	½ teaspoon ground ginger
¼ cup Worcestershire sauce	4 garlic cloves, minced
2-pound beef tenderloin	¼ cup oil, preferably canola or
2 tablespoons coarse-ground	corn
black pepper	¼ cup water
1 teaspoon white pepper	

Serves 6

At least 4 hours, and up to 12 hours, before you plan to barbecue, combine the marinade ingredients in a lidded jar. Place the tenderloin in a plastic bag or shallow dish and pour the marinade over the meat. Turn the meat occasionally if needed to saturate the surface with the marinade.

Prepare the smoker for barbecuing, bringing the temperature to 200° F to 220° F.

Remove the tenderloin from the refrigerator and drain the marinade, reserving it. Cover the tenderloin thoroughly with the black pepper first, then the white pepper. Let the tenderloin sit for 30 minutes.

Pour half the marinade into a saucepan and refrigerate it until the tenderloin is cooked. If you plan to baste the meat (see chapter 3, "To Mop or Not"), pour the other half of the marinade into another saucepan and stir in the oil and water. Bring this mop mixture to a boil over high heat and boil for several minutes. Keep the mop warm over low heat.

In a heavy skillet, sear the meat quickly on all sides over high heat. Transfer the tenderloin to the smoker and cook for 1½ to 2 hours, mopping every 20 minutes in a wood-burning pit, or as appropriate for your style of smoker. The meat is ready when the internal temperature reaches 140° F to 145° F. Be careful not to overcook since tenderloin is best rare to medium-rare.

Bring the reserved portion of marinade to a boil, and boil for several minutes, until the marinade is reduced by one-fourth. Slice the tenderloin and serve topped by spoonfuls of the sauce.

☆**Serving Suggestion:** When you need an impressive but homey menu, start with Smoked Olives and Drop-Dead Trout Spread with crackers or bread. Alongside the tenderloin, offer garlicky scalloped potatoes and spinach sautéed with baby tomatoes. Run for the Roses Pie completes a memorable meal.

BBQ tips The layer of pink, or smoke ring, you find just under the surface of most slow-smoked meat is not an indication of undercooking. When the pink runs from the outside in, as it does in barbecue, it results from the smoking process. When the pink runs from the center out, like in a rare steak, the meat is cooked less thoroughly than possible.

Carpetbag Steak

CREOLE RUB

1 tablespoon celery salt
1½ teaspoons paprika
1½ teaspoons ground black
   pepper
1½ teaspoons white pepper

1½ teaspoons brown sugar
¾ teaspoon garlic powder
¾ teaspoon dried thyme
¾ teaspoon cayenne

Two 12-ounce to 14-ounce New York sirloin strip steaks, cut with
   a pocket for stuffing
⅓ to ½ cup shucked oysters, with their liquor

CARPETBAG MOP (OPTIONAL)

Reserved oyster liquor
½ cup beef stock or clam juice
½ cup water
2 tablespoons cider vinegar

1 tablespoon extra-virgin olive
   oil
1 teaspoon Creole Rub

Serves 2 to 4

About 1 to 2 hours before you plan to barbecue, combine the dry rub ingredients together in a small bowl. Rub the steaks well with the mixture inside and out, saving at least 1 teaspoon of the rub for the stuffing and 1 teaspoon for the mop. Wrap the steaks in plastic and refrigerate them.

Prepare the smoker for barbecuing, bringing the temperature to 200° F to 220° F.

About 20 minutes before barbecuing, remove the steaks from the refrigerator and let them sit at room temperature. Drain the oysters gently. Reserve their liquor if you plan to baste the steaks. Toss the oysters with 1 teaspoon of the rub and stuff half the oysters into each steak.

If you are using the mop (see chapter 3, "To Mop or Not"), combine the oyster liquor with the remaining mop ingredients in a small saucepan. Bring the mixture to a boil and then keep it warm over low heat.

In a heavy skillet, sear the meat quickly on both sides over high heat. Transfer the steaks to the smoker and cook for 45 to 60 minutes, depending upon your desired doneness. Mop twice in a wood-burning pit, or as appropriate for your style of smoker. We prefer the steaks when the internal temperature reaches 145° F to 150° F, or medium-rare.

Let the steaks sit for 5 minutes and serve. Cut the steaks in half for more delicate appetites.

☆**Serving Suggestion:** Add baked beets, white rice, good bread with garlic-dill butter, and Candy Bar Cheesecake.

Scented Sirloin

This may not be the scent you want if you're feeling frisky, but the heap of garlic in this sirloin sure keeps the meat moist.

BASIC BLACK RUB

1½ tablespoons ground black pepper

1½ teaspoons kosher salt

2-pound to 2½-pound boneless top sirloin steak about 2 inches thick, cut with a pocket for stuffing, or two 1-pound to 1½-pound steaks of similar shape, each about 1 inch thick

FILLING

1 medium *whole bulb* garlic, roasted (baked for about an hour at 350° F)
1 tablespoon butter

⅛ teaspoon anchovy paste
½ cup sliced green onions
2 tablespoons red wine

SCENTED MOP (OPTIONAL)

½ cup red wine
½ cup red wine vinegar
½ cup water

2 tablespoons butter
2 garlic cloves, minced

Dallas chef Dean Fearing, from the Mansion on Turtle Creek, once said that in Texas, "Barbecue is God." Thinking about his comment a minute, he added, "or maybe it's just God's work."

Serves 6

About 1 to 2 hours before you plan to barbecue, combine the dry rub ingredients together in a small bowl. Rub the steak well with the mixture inside and out. Wrap the steak in plastic and refrigerate it.

Prepare the smoker for barbecuing, bringing the temperature to 200° F to 220° F.

About 20 minutes before barbecuing, remove the meat from the refrigerator and let it sit at room temperature.

To make the filling, break the garlic bulb apart and squeeze each soft clove from its skin.

In a small skillet, heat the butter with the anchovy paste. Add the garlic, mashing it with a fork to form a rough purée. Stir in the green onions and wine, and cook a minute or two, until the onions are limp. Remove the pan from the heat and let the filling cool briefly. Spoon the filling into the pocket of the sirloin or, if you are using two individual steaks, layer the filling on one steak and top it with the other. It is not necessary (or desirable) to secure the pair with toothpicks as long as you handle the sirloin "sandwich" with care.

If you plan to baste the meat (see chapter 3, "To Mop or Not"), stir together the mop ingredients in a small saucepan and warm over low heat.

In a heavy skillet, sear the sirloin quickly on both sides over high heat. Transfer the meat to the smoker and cook for about 1¾ hours, depending upon your desired doneness. Mop every 30 minutes in a wood-burning pit, or as appropriate for your style of smoker. We prefer the meat when the internal temperature reaches 145° F to 150° F, or medium-rare. Let the meat sit for 5 minutes and serve.

☆**Serving Suggestion:** Dinner could begin with Brined Bluepoints. Accompany the steak with a mixed vegetable salad, perhaps marinated green beans and carrots, and Blue Corn Muffins. Try a fruity dessert, such as spears of fresh pineapple topped with a little rum and brown sugar.

Bar-B-Q joints in Evansville, Indiana, like to simmer pieces of meat in a robust broth to make "soaks" or beef and pork "sauce." Usually served on rye bread with onions, the Sloppy Joe mixture saturates the sandwich with the distilled essence of the 'Q.'

Soy-Soaked Steak

Flank steaks make excellent barbecue, particularly when marinated.

SOY-SOAKED MARINADE AND GLAZE

¾ cup soy sauce, preferably a low-sodium variety
⅓ cup Pickapeppa sauce
⅓ cup Worcestershire sauce
¼ cup red wine
¼ cup red wine vinegar

3 tablespoons brown sugar or more to taste
1½ tablespoons oil, preferably sesame
2 garlic cloves, minced

2 flank steaks (about 2½ pounds total)

Serves 6 to 8

The night before you plan to barbecue, combine the marinade ingredients in a lidded jar. Place the flank steaks in a plastic bag or shallow dish and pour the marinade over them. Refrigerate the steaks overnight.

Prepare the smoker for barbecuing, bringing the temperature to 200° F to 220° F.

Remove the steaks from the refrigerator. Drain them and reserve the marinade. Let the steaks sit at room temperature for 25 minutes.

In a heavy saucepan, bring the marinade to a boil and boil it for 5 to 10 minutes, until reduced by one-third. Keep the mixture warm for glazing the meat.

Brush the glaze over the steaks and transfer them to the smoker. Brush the steaks with the glaze again after about 25 minutes. Cook for a total of 45 to 55 minutes, until the meat is rare to medium-rare.

Let the steaks rest for 5 or 10 minutes before slicing thinly across the grain. Serve the slices with additional glaze on the top or on the side.

BBQ tips Allowing food to come to room temperature before barbecuing promotes quick and even cooking, and with meat, fowl, and fish, it reduces the chance that a cold center will harbor bacteria. It's unsafe, however, to leave most food at room temperature for any longer than 1 hour. Always adjust the order of the recipe steps to prevent leaving your meat out for too long.

PJ's Spicy Soul Steak

We got the idea for this stuffed round steak from Wayne Whitworth, manufacturer of Pitt's & Spitt's pits. We named it for his delightful wife, PJ, who's as spicy and spirited as the steak.

1-pound top round steak
2 teaspoons Wild Willy's Number One-derful Rub (page 36), Cajun Ragin' Rub (page 38), or other savory seasoning blend

FILLING

3 tablespoons oil, preferably peanut
½ pound bulk chorizo or other spicy sausage
2 tablespoons minced onion
2 garlic cloves, minced
1½ cups cooked greens (collards, kale, and spinach are especially good)

1 cup dry bread crumbs
½ cup Parmesan cheese
2 tablespoons dry mustard
Salt and fresh-ground black pepper to taste
1 egg, lightly beaten

SPICY SOUL MOP (OPTIONAL)

1 cup beer
½ cup water
2 tablespoons cider or white vinegar

1 tablespoon oil, preferably peanut

PJ and Wayne got married in style—real barbecue style. They were hitched between two pits at the barbecue cook-off that opens the Houston Livestock Show and Rodeo, and they celebrated the blessed event afterwards by serving 'Q' to a thousand witnesses. The wedding cake was tiered layers of jalapeño cornbread topped with a Velveeta cheese frosting.

Serves 4

About 1 hour before you plan to barbecue, cut the steak into quarters and pound each quarter into a ¼-inch-thick rectangle. Combine the dry rub ingredients together in a small bowl and sprinkle the steaks with the spice mixture. Let the steaks sit at room temperature while you finish the preparations.

Prepare the smoker for barbecuing, bringing the temperature to 200° F to 220° F.

Warm the oil in a heavy skillet over medium heat. Add the chorizo, onion, and garlic, and sauté briefly until the chorizo is cooked through. Mix in the remaining filling ingredients. Spoon equal portions of the filling over each piece of steak. Roll up each piece of steak from one of its long sides, jelly-roll style. Make the rolls snug but leave some room for the filling to expand. Secure the rolls with toothpicks.

If you plan to baste the meat (see chapter 3, "To Mop or Not"), stir together the mop ingredients in a small saucepan and warm the mixture over low heat.

Transfer the rolls to the smoker and cook for 35 to 45 minutes. Mop once before closing the smoker and again after 25 minutes in a wood-burning pit, or as appropriate for your style of smoker. Serve immediately.

BBQ tips Oak is the best all-around wood for barbecuing beef. For additional flavor, we like to add some cherry wood or a little mesquite near the end of the cooking.

Cinderella Short Ribs

The fatty beef short rib, a cheap cut often made into stew meat, is always one of the ugliest things in a grocery store. A little slow-smoking does wonders for the appearance and sure makes it taste pretty.

WILD WILLY'S NUMBER ONE-DERFUL RUB

¾ cup paprika	2 tablespoons chili powder
¼ cup ground black pepper	2 tablespoons garlic powder
¼ cup salt	2 tablespoons onion powder
¼ cup sugar	2 teaspoons cayenne

5 to 6 pounds bone-in beef short ribs, cut between the ribs

BASIC BEER MOP (OPTIONAL)

12 ounces beer	2 garlic cloves, minced
½ cup cider vinegar	1 tablespoon Worcestershire sauce
½ cup water	
¼ cup oil, preferably canola or corn	1 tablespoon Wild Willy's Number One-derful Rub
½ medium onion, chopped	

CINDERELLA GLAZE AND SAUCE

1½ cups ketchup	2 garlic cloves, minced
1 cup beer	2 teaspoons ground cumin
¾ cup cider vinegar	1½ teaspoons ground anise
¼ cup minced fresh cilantro	1½ teaspoons salt
3 tablespoons brown sugar	1 teaspoon Tabasco or other hot pepper sauce
2 tablespoons Worcestershire sauce	

Serves 6

The night before you plan to barbecue, combine the rub ingredients in a bowl. Apply about half of the rub evenly to the ribs, reserving the rest of the spice mixture. Place the slabs in a plastic bag and refrigerate them overnight.

Goldie's Trail Bar-B-Que is something of a Western outpost in Vicksburg, Mississippi, a bastion of beef brisket in the Southern pork belt. Gola "Goldie" Marshall learned his barbecuing in Arkansas, where he opened a combination restaurant and liquor store in the 1950s. After the county voted to go dry, he moved down the Old Muddy to the present location, bringing his style of 'Q' along.

Prepare the smoker for barbecuing, bringing the temperature to 200° F to 220° F.

Remove the ribs from the refrigerator. Sprinkle the ribs lightly but thoroughly with more rub. Let the ribs sit at room temperature for 30 minutes.

If you plan to baste the meat (see chapter 3, "To Mop or Not"), combine the mop ingredients in a small saucepan and warm over low heat.

Transfer the meat to the smoker, fatty side up. Cook for 4 to 5 hours, depending on the size of the ribs, until well done. Mop the meat once an hour until the last hour in a wood-burning pit, or as appropriate for your type of smoker.

While the ribs are barbecuing, prepare the glaze. Mix the ingredients in a saucepan and bring the liquid to a simmer. Reduce the heat to low and cook the mixture for 30 minutes, stirring frequently. Brush the ribs with the glaze once or twice during the last hour of cooking. Return the remaining sauce to the stove and simmer for an additional 15 minutes to thicken it.

Remove the ribs from the smoker and let them sit at room temperature for 10 minutes. Trim the fat from the meat. Serve with the reduced Cinderella Sauce on the side.

BBQ tips Any tomato-based sauce, including a barbecue sauce, will burn on the surface of food if applied as a glaze before the last hour of cooking. In rare instances, that's desirable, but not as a general rule.

Standing Tall Prime Rib

Try to get a true prime rib for this recipe, one that meets USDA standards for the highest grade beef. The cut that most supermarkets sell as a prime rib is actually just a USDA choice rib roast, a good piece of meat but not superior.

STANDING TALL MARINADE AND OPTIONAL MOP

1⅓ cups red wine
1⅓ cups red wine vinegar
⅓ cup olive oil

4 teaspoons dried rosemary
4 garlic cloves, minced
2 teaspoons dried thyme

3-pound prime standing rib roast

BASIC BLACK RUB

1½ tablespoons coarse-ground
   black pepper

½ tablespoon kosher salt

Sprigs of fresh rosemary, for garnish (optional)

Serves 4

The night before you plan to barbecue, combine the marinade ingredients in a lidded jar. Place the roast in a plastic bag, pour the marinade over it, and refrigerate it overnight.

Prepare the smoker for barbecuing, bringing the temperature to 200° F to 220° F.

Remove the roast from the refrigerator and drain it, reserving the marinade if you plan to mop the meat. Combine the dry rub ingredients in a small bowl and rub the roast with the mixture. Let the roast sit at room temperature for about 30 minutes.

If you are using the mop (see chapter 3, "To Mop or Not"), bring the marinade to a boil in a saucepan and boil for several minutes. Keep the mop warm over low heat. Transfer the roast to the smoker, fatty side up. Cook for about 2½ hours, mopping every 30 minutes in a wood-burning pit, or as appropriate for your style of

Talk about dedication. Carolyn Wells, of the Kansas City Barbeque Society and Pig Out Publications, puts in about 1200 to 1300 hours a year of volunteer work on behalf of barbecue organizations and events. She's a great competition pitmaster, but can't find the time to enter cook-offs these days.

smoker. Cook the meat rare, to an internal temperature of about 140° F for the best flavor.

Remove the roast from the smoker and let it sit at room temperature for 10 minutes before carving. Serve immediately.

☆**Serving Suggestion:** Use this as the centerpiece for a special meal, such as Christmas Eve or New Year's Eve dinner. Creamy Catfish Spread and 007 Shrimp make good nibbles. Parmesan-topped baked potatoes, steamed broccoli with orange butter, Squash Relish, and Butter-milk Biscuits with fruit preserves round out the main course. For dessert, poach pears or other winter fruit in sugar syrup with a touch of vermouth.

Just south of Kansas City, Snead's looks the part of a barbecue bastion, a plain, rural roadhouse cafe with an aging sign no taller than the trees. Try one of the magnificent log sand-wiches, a long bun stuffed with a robust mixture of barbecued beef, pork, and ham. It'll turn a city slicker into a lumberjack.

Pit Pot Roast

WILD WILLY'S NUMBER ONE-DERFUL RUB

¾ cup paprika	2 tablespoons chili powder
¼ cup ground black pepper	2 tablespoons garlic powder
¼ cup salt	2 tablespoons onion powder
¼ cup sugar	2 teaspoons cayenne

3-pound boneless shoulder chuck roast
3 to 4 garlic cloves, slivered
1 to 2 pickled jalapeños, slivered

PIT POT MOP (OPTIONAL)

16 ounces beer	2 tablespoons pickling liquid
½ cup cider vinegar	from jar or can of pickled
1 medium onion, chopped	jalapeños
2 tablespoons oil, preferably canola or corn	

10-ounce can Ro-Tel tomatoes with green chiles or an equal quantity of canned whole tomatoes and juice
¼ cup beef stock or beer (if you're not using the mop)

Serves 6 to 8

The night before you plan to barbecue, combine the dry rub ingredients in a small bowl. Insert the garlic and jalapeño slivers into openings in the meat's surface. Massage the meat well with the dry rub, place it in a plastic bag, and refrigerate it overnight.

Before you begin to barbecue, remove the roast from the refrigerator and let it sit at room temperature for 45 minutes.

Prepare the smoker for barbecuing, bringing the temperature to 200° F to 220° F.

If you plan to mop the meat (see chapter 3, "To Mop or Not"), stir together the mop ingredients in a small saucepan and warm over low heat.

Transfer the roast to the smoker and cook for 4 hours, mopping every 45 minutes in a wood-burning pit, or as appropriate for your style of smoker. Place the roast on a large sheet of heavy-duty aluminum foil and pour the tomatoes over the meat. Add ¼ cup mop, beef stock, or beer. Seal the foil tightly and continue cooking the roast for 3 more hours, until the meat is falling-apart tender.

Remove the roast from the smoker and let it sit at room temperature for 10 minutes before serving.

BBQ tips Aluminum foil is a wonder wrap in barbecuing, useful in many ways. When you cover food with it during the cooking process, as with the Pit Pot Roast, the foil creates a little steam oven that keeps meat moist. In other situations it can prevent delicate items from getting too smoky.

The Taylor, Texas, International Barbecue Cook-off started in the late 1970s in response to the legislature declaring chili the official state dish. Every August the local organizers prove to the politicos that 'Q' is still the queen of Lone Star cooking.

Southwest Stew on a Stick

An old favorite, beef stew, tastes as good in kebob form as in a bowl. You'll want to use a tender cut of beef, though, for the relatively short cooking period.

STEW RUB

2 teaspoons chili powder	¾ teaspoon ground cumin seed
1½ teaspoons salt or more to taste	½ teaspoon ground cayenne
1 teaspoon dry mustard	½ teaspoon fresh-ground black pepper

2 pounds sirloin, cut in 1-inch cubes
1½ cups pearl onions, peeled and parboiled
6 carrots, cut into thick chunks and parboiled

STEW GLAZE

¾ cup beer	2 tablespoons dark, unsulphured molasses
¾ cup beef stock	
2 tablespoons tomato paste	½ teaspoon chili powder

Serves 6

About 2 to 4 hours before you plan to barbecue, combine the dry rub ingredients in a small bowl. Toss the meat cubes with the rub, spoon them into a large plastic bag, and refrigerate.

Prepare the smoker for barbecuing, bringing the temperature to 200° F to 220° F.

Remove the meat from the refrigerator and skewer pieces of meat alternately with the onions and carrots. Cover the kebobs loosely with plastic and let them sit at room temperature while you prepare the glaze.

In a saucepan, combine the glaze ingredients and simmer over medium heat for 20 minutes or until reduced by about a third. Keep the glaze warm.

Brush the skewers with the glaze and transfer them to the smoker. Cook for 30 to 45 minutes, until your desired doneness, brushing the kebobs with glaze about 5 minutes before they are done. Serve hot, brushed again with the glaze, if you wish.

High Plains Jerky

Jerky was the meat of the West when drying food was one of the main means of preservation. This is a simulated barbecue version, developed for flavor rather than longevity.

1 pound top round steak

JERKY MARINADE

½ cup Worcestershire sauce
½ cup soy sauce
¼ cup brown sugar
4 garlic cloves, minced
2 teaspoons fresh-ground black pepper

2 teaspoons ground dried red chile, preferably New Mexican or ancho
1 teaspoon onion powder

Serves 6 to 8 as a snack

About 2 hours before you plan to barbecue, place the meat in the freezer to make slicing it easier. After 30 to 40 minutes, remove the meat from the freezer and slice it as thin as you can with a good sharp knife. Trim the meat of all fat.

Combine the marinade ingredients in a lidded jar. Place the meat in a plastic bag or shallow dish and pour the marinade over it. Marinate for about 1 hour.

Prepare the smoker for barbecuing, bringing the temperature to 200° F to 220° F.

Remove the meat from the refrigerator, drain it, and let it sit at room temperature for 10 to 15 minutes.

Transfer the meat to a sheet of heavy-duty foil, separating the pieces. Place the meat in the coolest part of your smoker and cook until the meat begins to blacken, about 45 minutes. Wrap the foil loosely over the meat and continue barbecuing for another 1 to 1¼ hours, until well-dried.

Remove the jerky from the smoker and let it cool to room temperature before serving. Refrigerate any leftovers.

BBQ tips When you order logs for a barbecue pit, ask for the smallest ones the supplier has. The ideal size is 12 to 14 inches, but anything up to 16 inches will work fine in most fireboxes.

Barbecue restaurants in California range from fancy to funky. In Beverly Hills, pricey ribs come with a selection from the salad bar. You're better off in Oakland, where you may get a side of collard greens. Our favorite spot—partially for the name—is Dr. Hogly-Wogly's Tyler, Texas Bar-B-Que in Los Angeles. The brisket is terrific, but if you want endive, you better bring your own.

The Humble Hot Dog

Los Angeles Dodgers fans once raised a big stink and forced the ballpark to start grilling its Dodger Dogs again instead of steaming them. That's a step in the right direction, but the difference in taste is nothing compared to a smokin' dog.

All-beef hot dogs, probably lots of them, of a good brand, such as Boar's Head

Squishy white bread hot dog buns	Pickle relish
Mustard	Barbecue sauce, maybe Golden Mustard Sauce (page 293) or
Chopped onions	Struttin' Sauce (page 290)

Serves as many as you wish

Prepare the smoker for barbecuing, bringing the temperature to 200° F to 220° F.

Transfer the hot dogs to the smoker and cook for about 1 hour, or until the skins look ready to burst. Remove them from the smoker and serve immediately with all the trimmings.

Humdinger Hamburgers

This is the way to one-up uppity neighbors who brag about their grilled hamburgers. Smoking makes ground meat taste like tenderloin.

WILD WILLY'S NUMBER ONE-DERFUL RUB

3 tablespoons paprika	1½ teaspoons chili powder
1 tablespoon ground black pepper	1½ teaspoons garlic powder
1 tablespoon salt	1½ teaspoons onion powder
1 tablespoon sugar	½ teaspoon cayenne

2 pounds cheapest grade ground beef
½ medium onion, chopped
3 chopped roasted green chiles, preferably New Mexican, Anaheim, or poblano, fresh or frozen (optional)

BASIC BEER MOP (OPTIONAL)

6 ounces beer	1 garlic clove, minced
¼ cup cider vinegar	1½ teaspoons Worcestershire sauce
¼ cup water	
2 tablespoons oil, preferably canola or corn	1½ teaspoons Wild Willy's Number One-derful Rub
¼ medium onion, chopped	

Sourdough bread, sliced
Mustard, mayonnaise, dill pickles, tomatoes, lettuce, and Bar-BQ Ranch Sauce (page 295) (optional)

Serves 4

About 1 to 2 hours before you plan to barbecue, combine the rub ingredients in a small bowl.

In another bowl, mix together the hamburger, onion, and chiles with your hands. Form the mixture into 4 thick patties and apply the dry rub thoroughly to all surfaces, reserving at least 1½ teaspoons of the spice mixture. Cover the patties with plastic and refrigerate them.

Prepare the smoker for barbecuing, bringing the temperature to 200° F to 220° F.

The biggest barbecue cook-off in Texas launches the Houston Livestock Show and Rodeo each February, a little ol' event that relies on ten thousand volunteers and attracts a million and a half spectators.

Remove the patties from the refrigerator and let them sit at room temperature for 15 minutes.

If you plan to baste the meat (see chapter 3, "To Mop or Not"), stir the mop ingredients together in a small saucepan and warm over low heat.

Transfer the patties to the smoker and cook for about 1 hour, mopping every 20 minutes in a wood-burning pit, or as appropriate for your style of smoker.

Serve the burgers between slices of sourdough bread. Try a bite before you reach for any of the optional toppings, all good but less than essential with the richly flavored meat.

☆**Serving Suggestion:** Make the Humdinger Hamburger and The Humble Hot Dog the stars of a fall picnic. Add some Devil-May-Care Eggs, California Crunch salad, Peanut Butter Cake, and a light, fruity red wine.

BBQ tips For the best ground beef for barbecuing, ask your butcher to twice grind a piece of chuck, top or bottom round, or rump, with enough fat to make up about 20 percent of the whole.

Ain't Momma's Meat Loaf

As with a hamburger, smoking can raise meat loaf from the mundane to the sublime. We like this version, but if you— or your momma—have a favorite recipe, it can be modified for barbecuing by making the meat mixture extra moist and by adding plenty of Worcestershire sauce, vinegar, or other sharp flavor to cut the richness of the smoke.

MEAT LOAF

1 tablespoon oil, preferably canola or corn	1¼ pounds ground beef
½ cup minced onion	¾ pound ground pork
½ green or red bell pepper, chopped fine	1½ cups dry bread crumbs
3 garlic cloves, minced	3 tablespoons sour cream
1 teaspoon fresh-ground black pepper	2 tablespoons Worcestershire sauce
1 teaspoon salt	1 egg
½ teaspoon ground cumin	¼ cup stock, preferably beef
	1 teaspoon Tabasco or other hot pepper sauce to taste

BASIC BEER MOP (OPTIONAL)

12 ounces beer	1 tablespoon Worcestershire sauce
½ cup cider vinegar	
½ cup water	1 tablespoon Wild Willy's Number One-derful Rub (page 36), Cajun Ragin' Rub (page 38), or other savory seasoning blend
¼ cup oil, preferably canola or corn	
½ medium onion, chopped	
2 garlic cloves, minced	

Bar-BQ Ranch Sauce (page 295), Creole Classic Barbecue Sauce (page 299), or other spicy tomato-based barbecue sauce

Serves 6

Prepare the smoker for barbecuing, bringing the temperature to 200° F to 220° F.

In a heavy skillet, warm the oil over medium heat. Add the onion, bell pepper, garlic, pepper, salt, and cumin, and sauté until the vegetables are softened. Spoon the vegetable mixture into a large bowl.

Add the remaining meat loaf ingredients and mix well with your hands. Mound the meat into a smoke-proof loaf pan.

If you plan to baste the meat (see chapter 3, "To Mop or Not"), stir the mop ingredients together in a small saucepan and warm the mixture over low heat.

Transfer the loaf to the smoker. Cook for 45 minutes, or until the meat has shrunk away from the sides of the pan. Gently ease the meat loaf out of the pan and place directly onto the grate of the smoker. Continue cooking the meat for an additional 1½ hours, dabbing it every 30 minutes with the mop in a wood-burning pit, or as appropriate for your style of smoker. When 30 minutes of cooking time remain, apply the barbecue sauce to the top of the meat loaf.

After removing the loaf from the smoker, allow it to sit at room temperature for 10 minutes before slicing and serve warm or refrigerate for later use in sandwiches.

☆**Serving Suggestion:** No meat loaf is ever complete at our house without Mamie's Macaroni and Cheese on the side and, usually, Country Collard Greens as well. Dessert's not essential, but we'd never turn down 'Nana Pudding.

BBQ tips If you want to create a real mess for your spouse to clean up, try starting a meat loaf in a smoker outside a pan. It isn't pretty. You don't even really need to remove the meat from the pan, but the step allows the meat to soak up extra smoke flavor.

Brisket Hash

When you barbecue a brisket, you're likely to have left-overs unless you've invited a small town to dinner. This and the following recipe will clear out the fridge fast.

2 tablespoons oil, preferably
  corn or canola
1 tablespoon butter
2½ cups diced potatoes,
  preferably unpeeled
1½ cups diced onions
1 cup diced red bell pepper
1 to 2 pickled jalapeños, minced
4 cups shredded smoked
  brisket, such as Braggin'-
  Rights Brisket (page 105),
  Burnt Ends (page 107), or
  Dallas Dandy Brisket (page 108)

¾ cup beef stock
1½ tablespoons prepared yellow
  mustard
1 tablespoon ketchup
1 teaspoon coarse-ground
  black pepper
Salt to taste

Serves 4 to 6

In a heavy skillet, warm the oil and butter together over medium heat. Add the potatoes, onions, bell pepper, and jalapeños, and sauté for 10 minutes until the potatoes have begun to soften. Mix in the remaining ingredients. Simmer, covered, for 10 minutes, stirring the mixture up from the bottom once after 6 or 7 minutes and patting it back down. Uncover the skillet and continue cooking for another minute or two, until the liquid is absorbed and the mixture just begins to get crusty on the bottom. Serve hot.

☆**Serving Suggestion:** For a hearty breakfast, serve the hash with Buttermilk Biscuits with berry preserves and fresh fruit.

BBQ tips Traditional barbecue meats are cooked well done. However rare you may like some naturally tender meat, you'll enjoy beef brisket, pork shoulder, ribs, and similar cuts the most when they are thoroughly cooked. It's almost impossible to get them too done, which gives you a fair range of flexibility for timing how long to leave them in your smoker.

Salpicón

The pride of El Paso, Texas, and the adjoining town of Juarez, Mexico, a salpicón *typically combines a mélange of colorful vegetables with baked or boiled brisket in a lively vinaigrette. Ours pairs the mixture instead with smoked meat. The hearty salad can serve as a main dish or, when accompanied by tortilla chips for dipping, as an appetizer. It makes a fast-food taco salad look as appetizing as cold gravy.*

SALPICÓN DRESSING

7-ounce can chipotle chiles in
   adobo sauce
1 cup extra-virgin olive oil
⅔ cup fresh lime juice

¼ cup cider vinegar
2 garlic cloves, minced
Salt and coarse-ground black
   pepper to taste

SALPICÓN SALAD

3½ pounds shredded smoked
   beef brisket, such as Braggin'-
   Rights Brisket (page 105),
   Burnt Ends (page 107), or
   Dallas Dandy Brisket (page
   108)
4 small red-ripe tomatoes,
   preferably Romas or Italian
   plum, diced

2 ripe avocados, preferably
   Hass, diced
1 large red bell pepper, diced
1 medium red onion, diced
6 ounces Monterey jack cheese,
   grated
⅔ cup chopped fresh cilantro
6 medium radishes, grated
1 head romaine, shredded

Serves 12 to 14

Barbacoa de cabeza, or beef head barbecue, is still a festive tradition in southwest Texas. Mexican-American families cook the whole head in a mesquite-fired pit on a Saturday and serve the various parts on Sunday morning, eating the meat and organs on tortillas with salsa. Refried beans and eggs are customary side dishes.

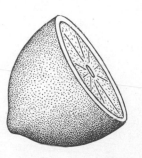

Combine all the dressing ingredients in a blender or food processor and process until well combined.

In a large bowl, combine the brisket with half to three-quarters of the salad dressing. Refrigerate for at least 2 hours, or up to overnight.

Remove the meat from the refrigerator and let it sit at room temperature for about 30 minutes. Add the remaining ingredients to the brisket and toss well. Drizzle on more dressing as you wish, keeping in mind it will increase the salad's heat level. Serve immediately.

☆**Serving Suggestion:** Salpicón stars as the centerpiece of a fiesta meal. Accompany it with Blue Corn Muffins, Santa Fe Capirotada, and Turquoise Margaritas.

BBQ tips Some of our recipes call for fresh green chiles, such as New Mexican or Anaheim, which must be roasted first to blister the tough skin. You can roast them individually over a gas stove burner, the same way you toast marshmallows over a fire. Spear the chiles on a fork, place them near the flame, and heat them until the skins have blistered and darkened uniformly. If you're roasting several chiles, you might want to do it in an oven. Place a layer of pods on a baking sheet and broil them until all are dark, turning the chiles frequently. After roasting, place the hot chiles in a plastic bag to steam and cool. Peel the roasted pods if you want to use them immediately, or freeze them, which makes the peeling easier. Canned chiles make a poor substitute for a homemade version, whether fresh or frozen.

Lean and Mean ☆ Meats ☆

The people of Owensboro, Kentucky, and Brady, Texas, don't believe that either pork or beef is all that special as barbecue meat. Neither do the growing number of game farmers in the country, or some folks who favor fancy food.

In Owensboro, barbecue means mutton. In other places, pitmasters usually prefer their sheep young and tender, perhaps in the form of a succulent leg of lamb. Upscale restaurant chefs from Hawaii to Houston cherish the local venison. Down around Brady, where they raise a lot of goats, you don't want to kid anyone about what goes on the grate. Barbecue, like love, is a many-splendored thing.

Almost Owensboro Mutton

We cheat a bit with this recipe, since mutton is seldom available commercially in most of the country. The closest substitute we've found is a shoulder roast from a full-grown "yearling" lamb, which comes out much like Owensboro's best when barbecued in this straightforward style. The flavor is distinctive but mild—definitely worth a try. You may need to order this cut from your butcher in advance.

MUTTON AND LAMB RUB

½ cup ground black pepper   1½ tablespoons garlic powder
2½ tablespoons brown sugar   ½ teaspoon ground allspice
2   tablespoons salt

7-pound to 8-pound lamb shoulder roast, preferably from a
    "yearling" lamb
¼   cup Worcestershire sauce

MUTTON AND LAMB MOP (OPTIONAL)

Remaining Mutton and Lamb   ¾ cup white vinegar
    Rub   ¾ cup water
1½ cups beer or beef stock   ¼ cup Worcestershire sauce

Black Sauce (page 297) or Moonlite and Moonshine sauce (page
    297) (optional)

Serves 6

The evening before you plan to barbecue, combine the rub ingredients in a small bowl. Coat the meat with the Worcestershire sauce and then massage it with two-thirds of the rub. Transfer the meat to a plastic bag and refrigerate it overnight.

Prepare the smoker for barbecuing, bringing the temperature to 200° F to 220°F.

Remove the meat from the refrigerator and let it sit at room temperature for about 30 minutes.

The 14th Annual International Bar-B-Q Festival in 1992 attracted sixty thousand hungry people to downtown Owensboro. From thirty-four states and six foreign countries, the spectators consumed twenty tons of barbecued mutton and fifteen hundred gallons of burgoo in one three-hour feed.

If you plan to baste the meat (see chapter 3, "To Mop or Not"), mix together the remaining rub with the other mop ingredients in a saucepan and warm over low heat. Transfer the meat to the smoker, fatty side up. Cook for approximately 1½ hours per pound, basting the lamb with the mop about once an hour in a wood-burning pit, or as appropriate in your style of smoker. When ready, the meat should be well done and tender, with an internal temperature of about 170° F.

Remove the meat from the smoker and let it sit for 15 minutes at room temperature. Serve pulled into shreds or chopped fine, accompanied by Black Sauce or Moonlite and Moonshine sauce, if you wish.

☆**Serving Suggestion:** Mutton and lamb shoulder taste great chopped and served between a couple of pieces of rye bread with slices of dill pickle and onion—an Owensboro favorite. Top the sandwiches with a dose of spicy Moonlite and Moonshine sauce. Offer a side dish of Kentucky Burgoo and finish the meal with Booker's Bourbon Mint Ice Cream.

BBQ tips With all the alarms raised in recent years about food safety, it pays to be careful in barbecuing. Keep raw meat separate from other food, and wash all cutting boards and knives after using them. If you carry raw meat to the smoker on a plate, don't put anything cooked back on the same plate.

Seva's Sassy Lamb Ribs

*Our masterful meat-cutter and all-around meat author-
ity, Seva Dubuar, introduced us to these ribs. An expert on
lamb, she markets the meat through her Santa Fe–based
company. The "Denver cut" Seva suggests for barbecuing
comes from the middle ribs of a lamb breast.*

FIVE-SPICE RUB

⅓ cup store-bought five-spice powder or make your own by
    grinding together equal amounts of cinnamon sticks, star anise,
    cloves, fennel seeds, and Szechwan peppercorns
⅓ cup brown sugar

4 Denver-cut slabs of lamb ribs, about 1 pound each

West Coast Wonder barbecue sauce (page 300) (optional)

Serves 4

At least 2 hours and preferably the night before
you plan to barbecue, mix together the rub ingredients in a small bowl. Rub the ribs liberally with
about a third of the spice mixture. Place the ribs in a
plastic bag and refrigerate.

Prepare the smoker for barbecuing, bringing the temperature to 200° F to 220° F.

Remove the ribs from the refrigerator. Rub them
thoroughly again with the spice mixture and let them sit
at room temperature for 20 to 30 minutes.

Transfer the meat to the smoker. Cook for 3½ to 4
hours, turning and sprinkling the ribs with the remaining dry rub about halfway through the cooking time.
When done, the ribs should have a thin coating of crispy
spices on the surface and should pull apart easily.

Serve warm with West Coast Wonder, if you wish.

☆**Serving Suggestion:** Add a fruit salad topped with
poppy seed dressing and Sweet Potatoes with Orange-
Pecan Butter.

The most important tip we can give you about meat is to find a high-quality butcher or meat-cutter. Look for a market that cuts and grinds to order, perhaps does some aging, and has people who take an interest in you and what you're cooking. We've always found that the people at a serious meat market are fascinated by barbecuing and eager to help. That's especially true if you sometimes take them a sample of your 'Q' later.

Martini Lamb

This gin-scented dish is an elegant lamb preparation, inspired by a creation of Bon Appétit *columnists Jinx and Jefferson Morgan.*

MARTINI PASTE

½ medium onion, chopped
10 garlic cloves
Juice and zest of 1 lemon

3 tablespoons gin
2 teaspoons kosher salt
¼ cup olive oil

5-pound to 6-pound leg of lamb

MARTINI MOP (OPTIONAL)

1 cup gin
1 cup beef stock
⅔ cup water

Juice of 1 lemon
2 tablespoons olive oil

Serves 6 to 8

The night before you plan to barbecue, prepare the paste. In a food processor, combine the onion, garlic, lemon, gin, and salt and process to combine. Continue processing, pouring in the oil until a thin paste forms.

Generously spread the paste on the lamb. Place the lamb in a plastic bag and refrigerate it overnight.

Prepare the smoker for barbecuing, bringing the temperature to 200° F to 220° F.

Remove the meat from the refrigerator and let it sit at room temperature for about 30 minutes.

If you plan to baste the meat (see chapter 3, "To Mop or Not"), mix together the mop ingredients in a saucepan and warm the mixture over low heat.

Transfer the lamb to the smoker. Cook for 35 to 40 minutes per pound, until the internal temperature of the meat is 145° F, rare to medium-rare. Baste the meat with the mop every 45 to 50 minutes in a wood-burning pit, or as appropriate for your style of smoker.

Remove the lamb from the smoker and let it sit for 10 minutes. Slice the lamb and serve it warm or chilled.

☆**Serving Suggestion:** Have a martini first, to put your taste buds in the right mood. Serve the lamb with Bronzed Garlic, a crusty loaf of bread, Southern Caesar Salad, and Rhubarb Crunch.

BBQ tips Leg of lamb is best when lightly smoked. We like to cook it in a water smoker, but charcoal grills and ovens work well, too. If you're using a wood-burning pit, wrap the lamb in foil after the first hour.

BBQ tips We often use coarse kosher salt in barbecuing, as we do in both of these leg of lamb preparations. Because of its mild flavor, you can spread it generously without overpowering a dish.

Journalists Alexander Sweet and John Knox described a Texas barbecue around 1880 in their book *On a Mexican Mustang through Texas.* "We arrived on the barbecue-grounds at about ten o'clock. More than two thousand people had already arrived, some from a distance of forty to fifty miles,—old gray-bearded pioneers, with their wives, in ox-wagons; young men, profuse in the matter of yellow-topped boots and jingling spurs, on horseback; fair maidens in calico, curls, and pearl-powder, some on horseback, others in wagons and buggies…. A deep trench, three hundred feet long, had been dug. This trench was filled from end to end with glowing coals; and suspended over them on horizontal poles were the carcasses of forty animals,—sheep, hogs, oxen, and deer,—roasting over the slow fire."

Luscious Leg of Lamb

A spinach and goat cheese stuffing might taste good even in a tennis ball, but the combo is always a sure bet inside a tender leg of lamb.

LUSCIOUS PASTE

10 garlic cloves
2 teaspoons kosher salt

1½ tablespoons olive oil

5-pound to 5½-pound boned leg of lamb

FILLING

1 tablespoon olive oil
½ medium onion, chopped
2 garlic cloves, minced
⅓ cup pine nuts or chopped walnuts
1½ pounds spinach, cooked, drained, and chopped

8 ounces mild goat cheese
⅓ cup chopped fresh parsley
¼ cup dried currants or chopped raisins
1 teaspoon anchovy paste (optional)

LUSCIOUS MOP (OPTIONAL)

2½ cups beef stock
½ cup red wine vinegar
2 tablespoons olive oil

1 teaspoon anchovy paste (optional)

Serves 6 to 8

The night before you plan to barbecue, prepare the paste. With a mortar and pestle, or in a mini–food processor, crush or mince the garlic with the salt. Add the olive oil in a stream until a thick paste forms. Rub the paste very lightly over the lamb. Place the lamb in a plastic bag and refrigerate it overnight.

Prepare the smoker for barbecuing, bringing the temperature to 200° F to 220° F.

Remove the meat from the refrigerator and let it sit at room temperature for about 30 minutes.

To make the filling, warm the oil over medium heat in a small skillet. Add the onions and garlic and sauté until softened. Add the pine nuts and continue to cook for another minute or two. Spoon the mixture into a bowl. Add the spinach, cheese, parsley, currants, and the anchovy paste, and blend well. Spread the filling evenly over the lamb. Roll the meat up snugly from one of the long sides, totally enclosing the filling. Tie as needed with kitchen twine to secure.

If you plan to baste the meat (see chapter 3, "To Mop or Not"), mix together the mop ingredients in a saucepan and warm the mixture over low heat.

Warm a heavy skillet over high heat and sear the lamb quickly on all sides. Transfer the lamb to the smoker. Cook for 35 to 40 minutes per pound, until the internal temperature of the meat is 145° F, rare to medium-rare. Baste the meat with the mop after 30 and 60 minutes in a wood-burning pit, or as appropriate for your style of smoker.

Remove the lamb from the smoker and let it sit for 10 minutes. Slice the lamb and serve it warm.

☆**Serving Suggestion:** Start off with a Warm Mushroom Salad, and serve the lamb with steamed asparagus dressed with olive oil, garlic, and lemon. Try Wild Huckleberry Pie with Coconut Crumble for dessert.

BBQ tips   Some people barbecue at temperatures as high as 250° to 300°. We don't recommend it as a general rule, but it works fine for some food, particularly large cuts of meat that don't require long cooking for tenderness, such as leg of lamb.

Racial integration in the South began at the barbecue pit. African-Americans owned and operated many of the original Bar-B-Q joints, but the food attracted everyone in town, even when churches, schools, and other restaurants were strictly segregated.

Minted Chops

MUTTON AND LAMB RUB

¼ cup ground black pepper
2½ tablespoons brown sugar
2 tablespoons salt

1½ tablespoons garlic powder
1½ teaspoons ground allspice

8 lamb loin chops, each weighing about 5 ounces and cut 1 inch thick
Garlic-flavored oil

MINTED MOP AND/OR SAUCE

1 cup brewed mint tea made with 2 mint tea bags
¼ cup mint jelly

4 teaspoons garlic-flavored oil
Fresh mint sprigs, for garnish

Serves 4

Prepare the smoker for barbecuing, bringing the temperature to 200° F to 220° F.

An hour before you plan to barbecue, combine the rub ingredients in a small bowl. Coat the chops with a thin layer of oil and then massage them with the rub. Let them sit at room temperature for 30 minutes while you prepare the mop and/or sauce.

If you are going to baste the meat (see chapter 3, "To Mop or Not"), mix the ingredients together in a saucepan over low heat, keeping the mop warm. If you intend to use the mixture only as a sauce, combine the same ingredients in a saucepan and bring the mixture to a simmer over medium-high heat. Reduce the mixture by half and then keep it warm over low heat.

Transfer the chops to the smoker. Cook them to your desired doneness; after 45 to 55 minutes the chops will be rare, with an internal temperature around 140° F. Baste the chops twice in a wood-burning pit, or as appropriate for your style of smoker.

If you have used the mop, bring the remaining liquid to a vigorous boil and reduce it by half. Serve the chops immediately, drizzled lightly with the reduced sauce and garnished with the mint.

☆**Serving Suggestion:** Serve the lamb with cinnamon-scented rice to soak up the mint sauce and meat juices.

Lamb Chops à la Greek Town

No lamb repertoire is complete without a Greek rendition. This one came to us by way of Chicago's Greek Town, a fun place to eat, if not exactly a barbecue bastion.

GREEK TOWN MARINADE AND OPTIONAL MOP

1 cup olive oil (an inexpensive kind is fine)	1½ tablespoons minced fresh oregano or 2 teaspoons dried oregano
1 cup fresh lemon juice	1 teaspoon salt
5 garlic cloves, minced	
2 bay leaves, crumbled	

8 lamb loin chops, each weighing about 5 ounces and cut 1 inch thick

1 tablespoon Char Crust (optional)
Fresh-ground black pepper
Lemon wedges and sprigs of fresh oregano, for garnish (optional)

Serves 4

About 2 hours before you plan to barbecue, combine the marinade ingredients in a lidded jar. Place the chops in a shallow dish big enough to hold them in a single layer, or in a large plastic bag. Pour the marinade over the chops and refrigerate them.

Prepare your smoker for barbecuing, bringing the temperature to 200° F to 220° F.

Remove the chops from the refrigerator and drain them, reserving the marinade if you intend to baste the meat. Dust the chops with Char Crust, if you wish, and

In the Old South, barbecues were often linked to fancy-dress balls. Scarlett O'Hara and Rhett Butler met at that kind of all-day party in *Gone with the Wind.* Slaves started the cooking the night before in big underground pits, and when Scarlett arrived in the morning she "saw a haze of smoke hanging lazily in the tops of tall trees and smelled the mingled savory odors of burning hickory logs and roasting pork and mutton."

a generous grinding of pepper. Let the chops sit at room temperature for 30 minutes.

If you are going to baste the chops (see chapter 3, "To Mop or Not"), pour the marinade into a saucepan. Bring the mixture to a vigorous boil over high heat and boil for several minutes. Keep the mop warm over low heat.

Heat a heavy skillet over high heat. Sear the chops quickly on both sides. Transfer them to the smoker, and cook to your desired doneness; after 45 to 55 minutes, the chops will be rare, with an internal temperature around 140° F. Baste the chops with the mop twice in a wood-burning pit, or as appropriate for your style of smoker. Serve immediately, garnished with lemon and oregano, if you wish.

☆**Serving Suggestion:** Offer Smoked Olives and cubes of feta cheese for openers. Serve Arty-Rice Salad on the side and Liar's Lime Pie for dessert.

BBQ tips Char Crust, a smoky-flavored dry rub, hails from the Windy City, as does this recipe. Once available only to restaurants, it now appears in some supermarkets and can be mail-ordered from the Char Crust Company, 3015 North Lincoln Avenue, Chicago, Illinois 60657, 312-528-0600. Developed originally for grilled steaks, the rub enhances many meats.

Lamb Burgers with Berry Sauce

Sheila Lukins and Julee Rosso introduced us to grilled lamb burgers in The Silver Palate Good Times Cookbook. *We've taken their wonderful idea and modified it for smoke cooking, which makes the burgers even more succulent.*

BURGER RUB

2 teaspoons garlic powder
2 teaspoons onion powder
1 teaspoon fresh-ground black pepper
1 teaspoon salt

BERRY SAUCE

1¼ cups fresh mint leaves, chopped fine
7 tablespoons raspberry vinegar
1 tablespoon fresh lemon juice
3 tablespoons sugar
Salt and fresh-ground black pepper to taste

2 pounds ground lamb
3 tablespoons raspberry vinegar
3 green onions, sliced thin
2 garlic cloves, minced
Salt and fresh-ground black pepper to taste
8 ounces mild goat cheese

BURGER MOP (OPTIONAL)

½ cup raspberry vinegar
2 tablespoons extra-virgin olive oil

Serves 6

Prepare the smoker for barbecuing, bringing the temperature to 200° F to 220° F.

Combine the rub ingredients in a small bowl. In another bowl, combine the sauce ingredients, stirring until the sugar dissolves.

Mix together the lamb, vinegar, onions, garlic, salt, and pepper in a large bowl. Form the mixture into 12 thin patties. Slice the cheese into 6 equal portions, and cover half the patties with it. Top the cheese with another patty and seal the edges carefully. Sprinkle the burgers lightly with the rub and let them sit at room temperature for 20 to 30 minutes.

If you plan to baste the burgers (see chapter 3, "To Mop or Not"), combine the mop ingredients in a small saucepan and warm over low heat.

Transfer the burgers to the smoker. Cook until lightly browned and medium-rare, about 40 minutes, or to your desired doneness. Dab the burgers with the mop once or twice in a wood-burning pit, or as appropriate in your style of smoker. Serve the burgers hot, with the Berry Sauce spooned over them or on the side.

Up and At 'Em Lamb Sausage

While good any time of day, these sausages make a hearty breakfast meal, perfect on mornings when you're firing up the pit for a long spell of smoking. After tossing on a beef brisket or pork shoulder, barbecue a few of these to fortify you for the day.

Juice and zest of 1 orange
1½ pounds mildly seasoned bulk lamb sausage

SWEET SENSATION RUB

Zest of 1 orange, dried and crumbled (about 1½ teaspoons)
1½ teaspoons ground cinnamon
1½ teaspoons paprika
1 teaspoon ground chipotle chile powder, preferably, or ½ teaspoon cayenne

1 teaspoon sugar
½ teaspoon ground coriander
½ teaspoon salt

UP AND AT 'EM MOP (OPTIONAL)

6 tablespoons orange juice
1 tablespoon sherry or cider vinegar

1 tablespoon oil, preferably canola or corn

Makes six 4-ounce patties

The country's first drive-in restaurant sold barbecue to newly mobile Americans in the early years of the automobile. Opened in 1921 in Dallas, Texas, the Pig Stand expanded into a national chain by the next decade. Waiters with white shirts and black bow ties ran to meet approaching cars and tried to jump on the running board before they stopped, giving rise to the term *carhop*.

Prepare the smoker for barbecuing, bringing the temperature to 200° F to 220° F.

Mix the orange juice and zest into the sausage. Form the sausage into 6 thick patties. Combine the dry rub ingredients in a small bowl and sprinkle the patties lightly with the dry rub. Let the patties sit at room temperature for about 15 minutes.

If you intend to baste the sausages (see chapter 3, "To Mop or Not"), mix together the mop ingredients in a small pan. Warm the mop liquid over low heat.

Transfer the patties to the smoker. Cook for 50 to 60 minutes, until the sausages are richly browned and cooked through. Mop them every 20 minutes in a wood-burning pit, or as appropriate in your style of smoker. Serve hot.

☆**Serving Suggestion:** When you need an elegant breakfast, pair the sausage with a variation on eggs Sardou, a fancy concoction first popularized by Antoine's in New Orleans. Top poached eggs with artichoke hearts, ham, and as many anchovies as you can handle, and then spoon Hollandaise sauce over the whole cholesterol-laden extravaganza. Serve with some fruit-filled muffins.

BBQ tips Kansas City's Baron of Barbecue, Paul Kirk, teaches classes on the barbecue craft around the country. Don't miss him if he's in your area. One of the keys to his success, Kirk says, is taking notes on everything he does. As the Baron emphasizes, it's the only sure way you can learn from experience.

If you're looking for a special way to celebrate Labor Day weekend, head down to the World Championship Barbecue Goat Cook-Off in Brady, Texas. You might want to try your hand at cooking the local goat in the main competition, or you can just enter the contest for tossing goat patties. In either case, don't miss the big Saturday lunch prepared by Gilbert Currie and his crew, who barbecue up to 150 goats for the crowd.

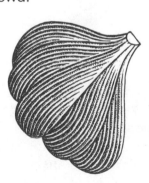

Southwestern Cabrito

A festive food throughout the Southwest, particularly in Spanish-speaking areas, cabrito is milk-fed kid slaughtered between the spring and late summer at an age of 30 to 40 days old and a weight of 10 to 15 pounds. You'll probably have to go directly to a farmer for the meat, but it's worth the trouble.

1 cabrito, preferably 10 to 12 pounds, quartered

SAGE PASTE

3   cups fresh sage leaves
1   *whole bulb* garlic, peeled
2   teaspoons salt

2   cups olive oil (an inexpensive kind is fine)

CABRITO MOP (OPTIONAL)

2   cups chicken or beef stock or beer
1   cup cider vinegar
1   cup olive oil (an inexpensive kind is fine)

¼   cup chopped fresh sage
¼   cup Worcestershire sauce
4 to 6 garlic cloves, minced

Sauce Olé (page 296) or Bar-BQ Ranch Sauce (page 295) (optional)

Serves 8 to 10

The night before you plan to barbecue, prepare the paste in a food processor. First process the sage, garlic, and salt until the sage and the garlic are chopped fine. Add the olive oil in a slow stream, until a thick paste forms. Rub the paste over the cabrito, covering the meat evenly. Place the cabrito in a plastic bag and refrigerate it overnight.

Prepare the smoker for barbecuing, bringing the temperature to 200° F to 220° F.

Remove the cabrito from the refrigerator and let it sit, covered, at room temperature for 30 minutes.

If you plan to baste the meat (see chapter 3, "To Mop or Not"), mix together the mop ingredients in a saucepan and warm the liquid over low heat.

Transfer the cabrito to the smoker. Cook the meat for about 1 hour per pound of weight for each quarter. The skinny forequarters will be done earlier than the meaty hindquarters, which usually take 4 to 5 hours, depending on size. In a wood-burning pit, turn the meat and drizzle the mop over it every 30 minutes. In other styles of smokers, baste as appropriate and turn the meat at the same time.

When the cabrito is done, remove it from the smoker, and let it sit for 10 minutes at room temperature. Slice or shred the meat and serve with Sauce Olé or Bar-BQ Ranch Sauce, if you wish.

☆**Serving Suggestion:** On the side, offer Cowpoke Pintos, Smoked Corn-on-the-Cob, and Mango and Avocado Salad. For dessert, Santa Fe Capirotada caps the meal.

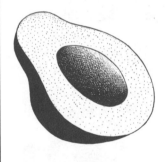

Curried Goat

After goats start eating grass, the flavor of the meat changes and the bony critters get tougher, requiring more complex and spicy preparations than cabrito. This approach, popular in the Caribbean, works particularly well. Your meat market probably doesn't carry goat, but the butcher may be able to direct you to a source.

Despite its relative rarity today, goat was a common barbecue meat in many areas of the South just a generation or two ago. It was usually cooked over an underground pit, often on top of old bedsprings.

CURRY PASTE

4   medium onions, chunked
¾   cup curry powder
1   *whole bulb* garlic, peeled
1   tablespoon salt

1 to 2 fresh habanero or scotch bonnet chiles or 4 to 5 fresh jalapeños, minced
1 cup oil, preferably canola or corn

1 goat, preferably around 25 pounds, quartered

CURRY MOP (OPTIONAL)

2 cups chicken or beef stock or beer

2 cups cider vinegar

1½ cups oil, preferably canola or corn

1 cup water

2 tablespoons curry powder

Jamaican Barbecue Sauce (page 300) or South Florida Citrus Sauce (page 304) (optional)

Serves 14 to 16

The night before you plan to barbecue, prepare the paste in a food processor. First process the onions, curry, garlic, salt, and habanero until finely chopped. Then add the oil, processing until the mixture forms a thick paste. This can be done in two batches if needed.

Wearing rubber gloves, rub the paste over the goat, covering the meat evenly. Place the goat in a plastic bag and refrigerate it overnight.

Before you begin to barbecue, remove the goat from the refrigerator and let it sit, covered, at room temperature for 45 minutes.

Prepare the smoker for barbecuing, bringing the temperature to 200° F to 220° F.

If you plan to baste the meat (see chapter 3, "To Mop or Not"), mix together the mop ingredients in a saucepan and warm the liquid over low heat.

Transfer the goat to the smoker. Cook for about 1¼ hours per pound of weight for each quarter. The forequarters will be done earlier than the hindquarters, which may take 10 hours or longer, depending on size. In a wood-burning pit, turn the meat and drizzle the mop over it every 30 minutes. In other styles of smokers, baste as appropriate and turn the meat at the same time.

When the meat is done, remove it from the smoker, and allow it to sit for 15 minutes before serving. Slice or shred the meat and serve with Jamaican Barbecue Sauce or South Florida Citrus Sauce, if you wish.

✩**Serving Suggestion:** Serve with Sweet Sally's Sweet Potato Salad, Barbecued Rice, and some cooling cucumbers mixed with sour cream or yogurt. Dessert can be a platter of fresh fruits, such as mango, pineapple, and papaya slices, flavored with a touch of fresh lime juice.

BBQ tips Always wear rubber gloves when working with chiles as hot as the habanero and its Caribbean cousin, the Scotch bonnet. They make a jalapeño seem as mild as a jelly bean. Even with less fiery chiles, either wear gloves or wash your hands thoroughly after handling them and before touching your eyes or other sensitive spots.

Stuffed Veal Roast

This veal sirloin roast stuffed full of sweet and savory treats makes a splendid special-occasion dish. The idea, though not the recipe, comes from the Kansas City Barbeque Society's The Passion of Barbecue *(Hyperion), a good source for inspiration. You may have to order the roast from your butcher in advance.*

CHERYL'S CIDER SOAK AND OPTIONAL MOP

1½ cups apple cider or juice
¾ cup cider vinegar
½ medium onion, minced
3 tablespoons oil, preferably canola or corn

1½ tablespoons Worcestershire sauce
1 teaspoon ground cinnamon
1 teaspoon dried thyme

1¾-pound to 2-pound sirloin tip veal roast, about 2 inches thick, cut with a pocket for stuffing

Ronald Reagan invited "Honey" Monk to barbecue for world leaders at the 1983 Economic Summit. Owner of the Lexington Barbecue No. 1, Monk said the heads of state weren't as picky or as smart about barbecue as the folks back home in North Carolina.

FILLING

2 slices bacon, chopped
½ tart apple, such as Granny
   Smith, chopped
2 tablespoons minced onion
1 garlic clove, minced
¼ pound ground veal
¼ cup dried bread crumbs
3 dried pitted dates, chopped

3 green onions, sliced
2 tablespoons minced fresh
   parsley
½ teaspoon dried rosemary,
   crushed
Pinch of ground cinnamon
Pinch of dried thyme

Serves 4 to 6

The night before you plan to barbecue, combine the soak ingredients in a lidded jar. Place the roast in a plastic bag and pour the marinade over it, making sure some goes into the roast's pocket. Refrigerate the meat overnight.

Prepare the smoker for barbecuing, bringing the temperature to 200° F to 220° F.

Remove the roast from the refrigerator and drain the marinade, reserving it if you plan to mop the meat. Let the roast sit for 30 minutes at room temperature while you prepare the filling.

In a skillet, fry the bacon over medium heat until browned and crispy. Remove the bacon with a slotted spoon, drain it, and place it in a medium bowl. Add the apple, onion, and garlic to the skillet and sauté until soft. Spoon the mixture into the bowl. Stir in the remaining filling ingredients and mix until well combined. Stuff the roast loosely with the filling.

If you are going to baste the meat (see chapter 3, "To Mop or Not"), heat the marinade in a small saucepan. Bring the mop mixture to a boil over high heat and boil for several minutes. Keep the mop warm over low heat.

Warm a heavy skillet over high heat. Sear the meat quickly on both sides. Transfer the roast to the smoker. Cook for 1¾ to 2 hours, mopping every 20 to 30 minutes in a wood-burning pit, or as appropriate for your style of smoker. The roast is best when the internal temperature reaches 145° F to 150° F, or medium-rare.

Remove the roast from the smoker and let it sit at room temperature for 10 minutes before carving. Slice the roast and serve.

☆**Serving Suggestion:** For an elegant dinner, nibble Curry Pecans while sipping Mango-Lime Spritzers. Sit down to cups of creamy corn chowder and then pair the roast with spinach sautéed in olive oil. Small slices of South Georgia Pound Cake topped with fresh strawberries make a tasty conclusion.

Veal Top Chops

TOP CHOP SAGE PASTE

1 cup fresh sage leaves	2 tablespoons dry marsala wine
4 garlic cloves	Juice of 1 lemon
¼ teaspoon salt	3 tablespoons olive oil

4 thick-cut veal loin chops, 8 to 10 ounces each
4 bacon slices, cut into thirds

TOP CHOP MOP (OPTIONAL)

¾ cup dry marsala wine	1½ tablespoons olive oil
¾ cup water	Lemon wedges and sage sprigs,
Juice of 1 lemon	for garnish

Serves 4

At least 2 hours, and preferably 4 hours, before barbecuing, make the sage paste. Combine the sage, garlic, and salt in a food processor and process until the sage is minced. Continue to process, adding the oil in a thin stream until a thick paste forms. Apply the paste thickly to the chops, wrap them in plastic, and refrigerate.

Prepare the smoker for barbecuing, bringing the temperature to 200° F to 220° F.

Remove the chops from the refrigerator and let them sit at room temperature for 20 minutes. Drape the top of each chop with 1 slice (3 pieces) of bacon.

If you plan to baste the meat (see chapter 3, "To Mop or Not"), stir together the mop ingredients in a small saucepan and warm the mixture over low heat.

Transfer the chops to the smoker. Cook for 1¼ to 1½ hours, mopping every 20 to 30 minutes in a wood-burning pit, or as appropriate for your style of smoker. The chops are ready when the internal temperature reaches 150° F, or medium-rare.

Remove the chops from the smoker, discard the bacon, and let the chops sit at room temperature for 5 minutes. Serve hot, garnished with lemon and sage.

Down-on-the-Ranch Venison Pot Roast

Hearty and homey, this venison chuck roast makes a great centerpiece for a casual company dinner.

DOWN-ON-THE-RANCH PASTE

1 medium onion, chunked	4 garlic cloves, minced
1 tablespoon prepared yellow mustard	1 teaspoon kosher salt
1 tablespoon Worcestershire sauce	1 teaspoon fresh-ground black pepper
1 tablespoon brown sugar	¼ cup oil, preferably canola or corn

3-pound venison chuck roast

DOWN-ON-THE-RANCH MOP (OPTIONAL)

1 cup beef stock or beer	¼ cup oil, preferably canola or corn
½ cup water	
¼ cup cider vinegar, preferably unrefined	

14½-ounce can whole tomatoes with juice
1   tablespoon prepared yellow mustard
1   tablespoon Worcestershire sauce

Serves 6

The night before you plan to barbecue, combine the paste ingredients in a food processor or blender until the onion is finely chopped and a thick purée forms. Slather the paste over the venison. Transfer the venison to a large plastic bag and refrigerate it overnight.

Before you begin to barbecue, take the roast from the refrigerator and let it sit, covered, at room temperature for 45 minutes.

Prepare the smoker for barbecuing, bringing the temperature to 200° F to 220° F.

If you plan to baste the meat (see chapter 3, "To Mop or Not"), stir together the mop ingredients in a small saucepan and warm over low heat.

Transfer the roast to the smoker and cook for 3 hours, mopping every 30 minutes in a wood-burning pit, or as appropriate for your style of smoker. Place the roast on a large sheet of heavy-duty aluminum foil and pour the tomatoes over the meat. Spoon the mustard and Worcestershire sauce over the tomatoes. Seal the foil tightly and continue cooking the roast for about 2 more hours, until the meat is falling-apart tender.

Remove the roast from the smoker and let it sit at room temperature for 10 minutes before serving.

The American Royal International Invitation cook-off each October deserves its reputation as the "World Series of Barbecue." Unlike the open competition the following day, all the contestants are winners of major barbecue cook-offs and participate strictly by invitation. The winner must excel in barbecuing six kinds of meat—beef brisket, pork shoulder, pork ribs, sausage, poultry, and lamb.

Wine-Sopped Venison Scallops

These tender slices of venison get sloshed to perfection in a red wine marinade. Be careful not to overcook them.

RED WINE MARINADE

2 cups dry red wine	1½ tablespoons minced fresh
½ cup red wine vinegar	sage leaves or 2 teaspoons
¼ cup oil, preferably canola or	dried sage
corn	2 garlic cloves, minced

1½ pounds venison scallops (from the loin or backstrap), cut against the grain in slices ⅓ inch thick

SOPPED SAUCE

1 cup Red Wine Marinade	1 teaspoon minced fresh sage
1 cup beef stock	leaves or ½ teaspoon dried
¼ cup currant jelly	sage
¼ cup crème de cassis	¼ teaspoon salt or more to taste
1 medium onion, chopped	1 tablespoon butter

Salt and fresh-ground black pepper to taste
1 to 2 tablespoons oil, preferably canola or corn
Fresh sage sprigs, for garnish (optional)

Serves 4

About 2 to 3 hours before you plan to barbecue, combine the marinade ingredients in a food processor. Place the venison in a nonreactive dish or plastic bag and pour all but 1 cup of the marinade over it. Cover the venison and refrigerate it.

Prepare the smoker for barbecuing, bringing the temperature to 200° F to 220° F.

Combine the remaining marinade, stock, jelly, crème de cassis, onion, sage, and salt in a heavy saucepan. Simmer over low heat for about 30 minutes, or until reduced by half. Whisk in the butter. Keep the sauce warm over low heat.

Drain the venison and sprinkle it with salt and pepper. In a heavy skillet, warm the oil over high heat until it almost smokes. Add the venison, a few scallops at a time, and sear it, a matter of just seconds. Repeat with the remaining meat.

Transfer the venison immediately to the smoker. Cook until the meat absorbs the smoke lightly, but is still rare to medium-rare, 20 to 25 minutes.

Serve immediately with the sauce ladled over the venison. If desired, garnish with sage sprigs.

BBQ tips Lean, tender cuts of meat often taste best when seared first before barbecuing. The extra step helps keep the food juicy and creates the best combination of internal and external textures.

Gamy Sausage

1½ pounds ground venison
1½ pounds ground wild boar or pork
1 small red bell pepper, chopped fine
¼ cup dry red wine
¼ cup grated Parmesan cheese
2 garlic cloves, minced

2 yards hog sausage casings

Oil, preferably canola or corn

2 teaspoons dried oregano
2 teaspoons dried basil
2 teaspoons salt
1½ teaspoons fennel seeds
1 to 1½ teaspoons crushed dried red chile of moderate heat, such as chile caribe, or a pinch of cayenne (optional)

Makes about twelve 4-ounce sausages serving 6 or more

At least an evening before you plan to barbecue, start the preparations. In a large bowl, mix together all of the ingredients, except the casings and oil. Refrigerate, covered, overnight.

Prepare the casings, soaking them in several changes of water over several hours. (For more information about

Jimmy Carter knows his barbecue, which is why he hired Sconyers Bar-B-Que of Augusta, Georgia, to cater a down-home lunch on the White House lawn in 1980. Opened in a shack in 1956, the restaurant is now a huge operation, serving up to three thousand people a day. Despite the numbers, Larry Sconyer maintains the quality, perhaps because he is, as his car's license plate says, the "No. 1 Pig."

sausage casings and their stuffing, see the BBQ tips, page 94.)

With the stuffing attachment of a meat grinder, stuff the cold sausage mixture into the casings, making 1-inch-thick links about 5 inches long. With your fingers, twist the casings and then tie off the individual sausages with kitchen twine. Cut between them. If you end up with any air bubbles, prick the casing in those spots with a needle. The sausage is ready to be smoked, but it can be refrigerated for several days or frozen for up to a month.

When you are ready to cook the sausage, prepare the smoker for barbecuing, bringing the temperature to 200° F to 220° F. Rub the sausages lightly with the oil.

Transfer the sausages to the smoker and cook for 2 to 2¼ hours, until the skin of the sausage looks ready to pop. Always err on the side of caution with the timing and cut one of the sausages open to check for doneness before eating any of them. Serve hot.

☆**Serving Suggestion:** Make these sausages a part of a mixed "grill" by serving them with Hill Country Links and Store-Bought Hot Brats. Add some good breads and a selection of hearty side dishes, such as Hot German Potato Salad, Kraut Salad, and Devil-May-Care Eggs. Finish off with The Best Cure for a Southern Summer.

Ragin' Rabbit

A spicy Cajun-style coating keeps this rabbit hopping on your tongue.

CAJUN RAGIN' RUB

1 tablespoon brown sugar	1½ teaspoons celery salt
1 tablespoon ground black pepper	½ to 1 teaspoon cayenne
1½ teaspoons white pepper	½ teaspoon dried thyme
	¼ teaspoon dry mustard

2 rabbits, about 2½ pounds each, quartered
1 tablespoon oil, preferably canola or corn
1 tablespoon Creole mustard

Serves 5 to 6

About 2 to 3 hours before you plan to barbecue, combine the dry rub ingredients in a small bowl. Massage the meat lightly with oil and mustard and sprinkle evenly with the dry rub. Place the meat in a shallow glass ovenproof or other smokeproof dish, cover it, and refrigerate it.

Prepare the smoker for barbecuing, bringing the temperature to 200° F to 220° F.

Remove the rabbit from the refrigerator and let it sit in the dish, covered, at room temperature for 20 to 30 minutes. Cut a yard-long section of cheesecloth and dampen it thoroughly with water. Uncover the dish and drape the top of it loosely with several thicknesses of folded cheesecloth.

Transfer the cheesecloth-covered dish to the smoker. Cook for about 1¼ hours, wetting down the cheesecloth with warm water a couple of times in a wood-burning pit, or with other styles of smokers, any time you raise the lid. The cheesecloth will brown but won't burn if it is kept moist. Remove the cheesecloth from the meat and discard it. Continue smoking until the meat is cooked through but still juicy, an additional 15 to 25 minutes. Serve the rabbit immediately.

☆**Serving Suggestion:** Lead off dinner with Smoked Spud Skins, hot from the smoker. Then serve the rabbit with lightly buttered noodles, Killed Salad, Squash Relish, and, for good measure, Peanut Butter Cake.

BBQ tips The function of the cheesecloth in the Ragin' Rabbit and other recipes is to keep lean meat moist during its slow smoking. You can skip the wrapping in smokers designed for moist cooking, such as water smokers and Cookshack ovens.

☆ Fowl Play ☆

Backyard cooks have heaped a lot of abuse on poor chickens. Wringing one's neck, as our grandmothers did, isn't nearly as nasty as what some people do to the birds over a hot fire on the grill. A dinner that should be juicy and tasty often comes out as dry as a salt lick and as tempting as a honeymoon in Salt Lake City.

The slow-smoking process of real barbecue, in contrast, preserves the succulence of chicken and other fowl, while adding new dimensions of flavor. Once you've tried these recipes, most grilled chickens are going to taste like crowed-out roosters.

Chicken on a Throne

This is an established barbecue classic, maybe the best way of cooking a whole chicken ever invented in America.

WILD WILLY'S NUMBER ONE-DERFUL RUB

6 tablespoons paprika	1 tablespoon chili powder
2 tablespoons ground black pepper	1 tablespoon garlic powder
2 tablespoons salt	1 tablespoon onion powder
2 tablespoons sugar	1 teaspoon cayenne

INJECTION LIQUID

12 ounces beer	¼ cup cider or white vinegar
¼ cup oil, preferably canola or corn	2 teaspoons Wild Willy's Number One-derful Rub

Two 3½-pound whole chickens

THRONE MOP (OPTIONAL)

12 ounces beer	1 tablespoon Wild Willy's Number One-derful Rub
1 cup chicken stock	
½ cup water	
¼ cup oil, preferably canola or corn	

Two 12-ounce cans beer (no bottles please)	¼ cup cider or white vinegar
½ medium onion, chopped	4 garlic cloves, minced

Jalapeach Barbecue Sauce (page 302) or Old-Fashioned High Cholesterol Great-Tasting Southern Sauce (page 293) (optional)

Serves 5 to 6

The night before you plan to barbecue, combine the rub ingredients in a small bowl. In another bowl, combine the ingredients for the injection liquid. Remove the organs from the cavity of the chickens.

With a kitchen syringe, inject about ½ cup of the injection liquid deep into the breast and legs of each chicken

Henry Perry was our kind of pioneer, the founding father of Kansas City barbecue. Slapping together a living during the Depression, he started barbecuing ribs in an outdoor pit along the street, selling slabs wrapped in newspaper. Two Bryant brothers joined Perry in the business in 1931 and eventually turned the makeshift operation into the country's most famous 'Q' joint, Arthur Bryant's.

in several spots. Massage the chickens thoroughly, inside and out, with the remaining injection liquid, working it as far as possible under the skin without tearing the skin. Cover the chickens well with the dry rub, again massaging inside and out and over and under the skin. Reserve at least 1 tablespoon of the rub if you are planning to baste the chickens. Place the chickens in a plastic bag and refrigerate them.

Prepare the smoker for barbecuing, bringing the temperature to 200° F to 220° F.

Remove take the chickens from the refrigerator and let them sit at room temperature for about 30 minutes.

While you wait, open the 2 beer cans and drink half—and only half—of each beer. With a can opener, remove the tops of the half-empty beer cans. Place half of the onion, vinegar, garlic, and reserved rub in each can. Insert the replenished beer cans into the cavities of the chickens, balancing the birds so that they rest upright with their legs bent forward. The cans should sit flat on the grill or on a cooking tray, holding the chickens at attention while their insides are steaming and their outsides are smoking.

If you are going to use the mop (see chapter 3, "To Mop or Not"), combine the ingredients in a saucepan and keep the mixture warm over low heat.

Transfer the chickens to the smoker. Cook for 3½ to 4 hours, mopping every 30 minutes in a wood-burning pit, or as appropriate in your style of smoker. When the chickens are done, their legs will move freely and the internal temperature should be 180° F to 185° F.

Let the chickens sit for 5 to 10 minutes. Remove the skins, carve the chickens, and serve. Offer Jalapeach Barbecue Sauce or Old-Fashioned High Cholesterol Great-Tasting Southern Sauce on the side, if you wish, but be sure to try some of the savory bird unadorned before slathering on the sauce.

BBQ tips You should seldom remove the skin from chickens or other birds before barbecuing them. The skin keeps the meat moist and its fat acts as a natural basting agent. When there is skin on only a portion of the meat, as with a chicken breast, place that side up in your smoker. We remove the skin before serving, just as we trim any remaining layers of fat from other barbecue meats.

Mustard 'n' Lemon Chicken

If you want your chickens sober instead of steamy with beer, stuff their cavities with lemons and onions. The rub adds a tangy mustard taste.

POULTRY PERFECT RUB

6   tablespoons paprika
2   tablespoons ground black pepper
2   tablespoons celery salt
2   tablespoons sugar

1   tablespoon garlic powder
1   tablespoon dry mustard
1   teaspoon cayenne
Zest of 1 to 2 lemons, dried and minced

Two 3½-pound chickens
2   tablespoons butter
1   tablespoon Worcestershire sauce

1   medium onion, cut in thin wedges
1   lemon, cut in thin wedges

LEMON MOP (OPTIONAL)

1½ cups chicken stock
¾ cup fresh lemon juice
¾ cup water
½ medium onion, chopped
½ cup butter
1   tablespoon Worcestershire sauce

1   tablespoon prepared yellow mustard
2   teaspoons Poultry Perfect Rub

Golden Mustard Barbecue Sauce (page 293) or Black Sauce (page 297) (optional)

Serves 5 to 6

Arthur Bryant became so legendary in barbecue circles that he rated an obituary in *The New York Times* titled simply, "Arthur Bryant, Barbecue Man." Raised in poverty in East Texas, he bought his famous Kansas City joint from his older brother Charlie in 1946. From then until his death in 1982, the "Barbecue Man" cooked almost daily on his white-tiled pits. Calvin Trillin called Arthur Bryant's the best restaurant in the world, but Bryant himself thought of his place as just the "House of Good Eats."

The night before you plan to barbecue, combine the rub ingredients in a small bowl.

Remove the organs from the cavity of each chicken.

In a small saucepan, melt the butter and stir in the Worcestershire sauce. Massage the chickens thoroughly with the butter mixture, inside and out, working the mixture as far as possible under the skin without tearing it. Cover the chickens well with the dry rub, again massaging inside and out and over and under the skin. Reserve about one-third of the rub. Place the chickens in a plastic bag and refrigerate them.

Prepare the smoker for barbecuing, bringing the temperature to 200° F to 220° F.

Remove the chickens from the refrigerator and rub them again with the dry rub, reserving at least 2 teaspoons of the mixture if you plan to baste the birds. Let the chickens sit at room temperature for about 30 minutes, and then insert the lemon and onion slices into their cavities.

If you are going to use the mop (see chapter 3, "To Mop or Not"), mix together the ingredients in a saucepan. Keep the mop warm over low heat.

Place the chickens in the smoker, breast down. Cook for 3½ to 4 hours, basting the birds with the mop every 30 minutes in a wood-burning pit, or as appropriate in your style of smoker. Turn the birds breast side up about halfway through the cooking time. When the chickens are done, their legs will move freely and the internal temperature should be 180° F to 185° F.

Let the chickens sit for 5 to 10 minutes. Remove the lemons and onions from the cavities, remove the skins, carve the chicken, and serve. Offer Golden Mustard Barbecue Sauce or Black Sauce on the side, if you wish.

☆**Serving Suggestion:** Accompany the chicken with your favorite fresh green vegetable and either Mamie's

Macaroni and Cheese or Boarding House Macaroni Salad. How about Becky's Pineapple Cake for dessert?

BBQ tips You have more control over your cooking temperature in a log-burning pit than in other kinds of smokers, but the mechanisms of control are not always well explained in the owner's manual. First in importance is the size and intensity of the fire. In an efficient, well-constructed pit you seldom need more than three logs burning at once, or more than a small flame going. The air intake control is a close second in significance. You open it to increase the draft—which stirs the flame and raises the heat—or close it to dampen the blaze and reduce the temperature. The out-take adjustment on the smoke stack is most useful in reigning back a fire that's gotten too hot. Unless that happens, leave it fully open to keep the smoke circulating freely. If it's shut down for an extended period, food will get sooty.

BBQ tips Perfectionists may want to truss stuffed whole chickens. The birds will look a bit more shapely coming out of the smoker, but the extra step isn't needed for taste.

Lyndon Johnson loved his barbecue. From the moment he took office as president, Johnson used barbecue parties to coddle political allies and cajole adversaries. His favorite pitmaster was Walter Jetton, who told about what he doled in the 1965 *LBJ Barbecue Cook Book.*

Fancy Chicken with Cheese

A creamy goat cheese under a chicken's skin helps to keep the meat moist and adds its own delightful flavor. Try this when you need to impress someone who looks down their nose at barbecue.

3½-pound whole chicken
2 to 3 ounces fresh mild goat cheese

1 tablespoon prepared pesto
8 to 10 basil leaves

FANCY MOP (OPTIONAL)

1 cup chicken stock
½ cup white wine
½ cup water

2 tablespoons olive oil
1 tablespoon prepared pesto

Serves 3

The night before you plan to barbecue, remove the organs from the cavity of the chicken. Massage the chicken thoroughly with the cheese and pesto, inside and out, working them as far as possible under the skin without tearing it. Insert the basil leaves under the skin, placing them as evenly as possible over the chicken. If you wish, truss the chicken. Place the chicken in a plastic bag and refrigerate it overnight.

Prepare the smoker for barbecuing, bringing the temperature to 200° F to 220° F.

Remove the chicken from the refrigerator and let it sit at room temperature for about 30 minutes.

If you plan to baste the chicken (see chapter 3, "To Mop or Not"), mix together the mop ingredients in a saucepan. Keep the mop warm over low heat.

Transfer the chicken to the smoker, breast down. Cook for 3½ to 4 hours, basting the chicken with the mop every 30 minutes in a wood-burning pit, or as appropriate for your style of smoker. Turn the bird breast side up about halfway through the cooking time. When the chicken is done, its legs will move freely and the internal temperature should be 180° F to 185° F.

Let the chicken sit for 5 to 10 minutes. Remove the skin, carve the chicken, and serve it.

☆**Serving Suggestion:** Lead off by nibbling Smoked Olives. Accompany the chicken with pasta tossed with good olive oil and steamed zucchini, followed by Texas Peach Cobbler.

BBQ tips Different kinds of smokers require different levels of attention during the start-up process. With self-sufficient models that don't need much tending, such as an electric water smoker, you can adjust the order of recipe steps to preheat the smoker while you go about the final food preparations.

Finger Lickin' Fried Smoked Chicken

When eating out in Kansas City, it can be tough to decide between the world-class barbecue and the superlative fried chicken served at places like Stroud's. This technique, first suggested by Bobby Seale, is an at-home compromise between the two down-home dishes, one that bathes the birds in smoke before finishing them in a crunchy coating.

3½ to 4 pounds chicken parts	1 teaspoon fresh-ground black pepper
Buttermilk to cover, about 3 cups	1½ cups all-purpose flour
1½ tablespoons Tabasco or other hot pepper sauce	1½ pounds solid shortening (3 cups), preferably Crisco
2 to 3 teaspoons salt	3 tablespoons bacon drippings

Serves 4

As a leader of the Black Panther Party, Bobby Seale didn't agree with President Lyndon Johnson about anything except barbecue. In 1988 Seale wrote a tribute to the 'Q' he loved at his uncle's restaurant in Liberty, Texas, and showed how to duplicate it on a grill using marinades flavored with liquid smoke. *Barbeque'n with Bobby* (Ten Speed Press) is a gem, for tips and tales alike.

At least 3 hours, and up to 12 hours, before you plan to barbecue, place the chicken in a shallow dish. Pour the buttermilk and Tabasco over the chicken. Turn the chicken in the buttermilk to coat it well. Cover the dish and refrigerate it.

Prepare the smoker for barbecuing, bringing the temperature to 200° F to 220° F.

Drain the chicken, reserving the marinade. Allow the chicken to stand at room temperature for about 20 minutes.

Transfer the chicken to the smoker and cook for 35 to 45 minutes, long enough to give the bird some smoky flavor but only to cook it partially.

Return the chicken to the buttermilk bath. Pour the flour into a medium-size brown paper sack and sprinkle in the salt and pepper.

In a 10-inch to 12-inch cast-iron skillet, melt the shortening and bacon drippings over high heat. When small bubbles form on the surface, reduce the heat to medium-high. Drain each piece of the chicken, starting with the dark pieces, and drop them into the bag of seasoned flour. Shake well to coat.

Lower each piece gently into the skillet, skin-side down. Arrange the chicken so that all pieces cook evenly. It's desirable that the pieces fit snugly together, although they shouldn't be sticking to each other. Reduce the heat to medium and cover the skillet. Fry the chicken for 10 to 11 minutes. Reduce the heat to medium-low, uncover the chicken, and turn it over. Fry it, uncovered, for another 10 to 11 minutes, wiping up any grease spatters on your stove as they occur. The chicken will be a rich mahogany brown and should be cooked through and tender inside. Cut into a test piece first, cooking an additional minute or two if needed. Remove the chicken, drain it, and serve it piping hot.

☆**Serving Suggestion:** For an old-fashioned Sunday dinner, add Country Collard Greens, Flash-Fried Okra, garlicky mashed potatoes and gravy, Sweet Potato Biscuits, Squash Relish, and loads of Sunny Sweet Tea. Finish off with Peanut Butter Cake.

Quick Chick

The inspiration for this recipe comes from Dallas pitmaster Obie Obermark, sometimes known in barbecue cook-off circles as "the chicken champion." Our version is different from his, which relies on Obie's special dry rubs. If you want to make it the original way, you can order his spice mixtures by writing P.O. Box 226124, Dallas, Texas 75222-6124, or calling 214-943-9974. Try the Sweet Rub in particular, a consistent contest winner.

SPLIT-SECOND DRY RUB

1 tablespoon paprika	½ teaspoon onion powder
1 teaspoon salt	Pinch cayenne
1 teaspoon sugar	
½ teaspoon fresh-ground black pepper	

6 boneless, skinless, individual chicken breasts, pounded lightly

SPLIT-SECOND MOP

1 cup orange juice	1 tablespoon Worcestershire
3 tablespoons butter	sauce

South Florida Citrus Sauce (page 304) or Bour-BQ Sauce (page 298) (optional)

Serves 4 to 6

Prepare the smoker for barbecuing, bringing the temperature to 200° F to 220° F.

In his delightful *American Taste*, James Villas brags about the barbecue of his native North Carolina. The *Town and Country* editor says that at any of the great joints in the state, "the scene's always about the same: a counter with short stools, plain wooden tables and chairs, paper napkins, plastic forks and iced-tea glasses, bottles of red-pepper vinegar, maybe a little country music on the spanking-new jukebox and an inexpensive portrait of Jesus."

Combine the rub ingredients in a small bowl. Rub the breasts with the mixture and let them sit at room temperature for about 20 minutes.

Combine the mop ingredients in a small saucepan, placing the pan over low heat to melt the butter. Keep the mop warm over low heat.

Drizzle the breasts with about one-third of the mop. Transfer the chicken to the smoker and cook for 25 to 30 minutes, or until cooked through. In a wood-burning pit, turn the breasts after 15 minutes and mop well again. With other smokers, don't worry about turning the breasts or mopping while cooking—just drizzle the breasts with more mop as soon as you remove them from the smoker. Serve immediately, with South Florida Citrus Sauce or Bour-BQ Sauce, if you wish.

☆**Serving Suggestion:** Accompany the chicken with cool Burstin' with Black-Eyed Peas Salad and hot rice. Sweet Potato Pudding makes a fitting finish if you have time to prepare it. Otherwise, offer a plate of fresh fruit.

BBQ tips We always barbecue more than we intend to eat that day. Most smoked food freezes well and can be reheated in a conventional oven without losing much of the original taste.

Chicken-Wrapped Apple Sausage

A revived interest in sausage in recent years has led to an explosion of new varieties, many leaner than the old favorites. We find Bruce Aidells' nationally distributed sausages among the best at balancing heartiness and healthiness, although many markets now make their own fine versions, too. If you can't find an apple-laced chicken sausage, substitute any other made from chicken or turkey.

CHICKEN-APPLE MARINADE

1 cup apple juice
½ cup cider vinegar
2 tablespoons olive oil
2 tablespoons Wild Willy's Number One-derful Rub (page 36) or other savory seasoning blend to taste

1 tablespoon plus 1 teaspoon prepared brown mustard

4 boneless, skinless, individual chicken breasts, pounded thin

1 teaspoon olive oil
4 chicken-apple sausages, such as Aidells'
1½ teaspoons prepared brown mustard
¼ cup minced onion

Additional Wild Willy's Number One-derful Rub or other savory seasoning blend, to taste
1 tart apple, sliced thin
¼ cup chicken stock

Serves 4

About 2 to 3 hours before you plan to barbecue, combine the marinade ingredients in a lidded jar. Place the chicken in a large plastic bag or shallow, nonreactive dish. Pour the marinade over the chicken and refrigerate it.

Prepare the smoker for barbecuing, bringing the temperature to 200° F to 220° F.

Remove the chicken from the refrigerator and let it sit at room temperature for about 20 minutes.

Warm the olive oil in a skillet over medium-low heat. Add the sausages and sauté until just cooked through. Remove the sausages from the skillet, saving the drippings. Cool the sausages briefly, and then rub them with the mustard.

Drain the chicken, reserving 1 cup of the marinade. Arrange a sausage on each chicken breast, sprinkling 1 to 2 teaspoons of the onion over each portion. Wrap the chicken around the sausage, securing each roll with toothpicks. It's not necessary to entirely encase the sausages, but make the rolls as attractive a possible. Sprinkle the tops of the rolls with dry rub.

Transfer the chicken to the smoker and cook until the chicken is cooked through and tender, about 25 minutes.

While the chicken smokes, add the remaining onion and the apple to the pan drippings and sauté over medium heat until both begin to soften. Pour in the stock and the reserved marinade and bring to a boil. Boil for at least 5 minutes, allowing most of the liquid to evaporate.

Remove the chicken from the smoker and arrange each chicken breast on a plate. Spoon equal portions of the apple mixture over the chicken and serve hot.

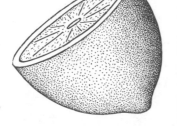

The Choo Chew Bar-B-Q team from Louisville, Kentucky, cooks in a life-size facsimile of a locomotive engine.

Chicken Oregano

OREGANO MARINADE

2 cups olive oil (an inexpensive kind is fine)
1 cup fresh lemon juice
6 to 8 garlic cloves

2 teaspoons salt
¼ cup chopped fresh oregano or 2 tablespoons dried oregano

8 bone-in, skin-on chicken breasts
Fresh oregano sprigs, for garnish (optional)

Serves 6 to 8

About 4 to 8 hours before you plan to barbecue, combine the marinade ingredients in a blender and purée. Loosen the skin of the chicken, and place the chicken in a shallow, nonreactive dish or plastic bag. Pour the marinade over the chicken and refrigerate it, turning once, if needed, to saturate the surface.

Prepare the smoker for barbecuing, bringing the temperature to 200° F to 220° F.

Remove the chicken from the refrigerator and drain the pieces. Let them sit at room temperature for about 20 minutes.

Transfer the chicken pieces to the smoker, skin sides up. Cook the chicken for 50 to 60 minutes, until it is cooked through and the juices run clear when a skewer is inserted into a breast. Remove the chicken from the smoker and serve hot, garnished with oregano sprigs, if you wish.

☆**Serving Suggestion:** Try this simple preparation with Sweet and Sour Cukes, roast potatoes, and Lemon Pudding Ice Cream Pie.

Thunder Thighs

Many dishes from the old South have their origins in Africa, and that's the source of the seasoning combination here, a thunder storm of a mixture.

THUNDER PASTE

1 small onion, chunked	1 teaspoon curry powder
⅓ cup orange juice	1 teaspoon salt
2 tablespoons peanut butter	1 teaspoon brown sugar
1 tablespoon peanut oil	½ teaspoon cinnamon
2 teaspoons ground anise seed	

8 bone-in, skin-on chicken thighs

THUNDER MOP (OPTIONAL)

1   cup chicken stock
½ cup orange juice
¼ cup water

1   tablespoon peanut oil
½ teaspoon curry powder

Serves 3 to 4

The night before you plan to barbecue, combine all the paste ingredients in a food processor or blender. Coat the thighs thickly with the paste, rubbing under and over the skin. Place the chicken in a plastic bag and refrigerate it overnight.

Prepare the smoker for barbecuing, bringing the temperature to 200° F to 220° F.

Remove the chicken from the refrigerator and let it sit at room temperature for about 15 minutes.

If you plan to baste the chicken (see chapter 3, "To Mop or Not"), combine the mop ingredients in a small saucepan and keep the mop warm over low heat.

Transfer the chicken to the smoker and cook for 1½ to 1¾ hours. Mop the thighs every 30 minutes in a wood-burning pit, or as appropriate for your style of smoker.

The chicken is done when it is very tender and the juices run clear when a skewer is inserted into a thigh. Serve the thighs immediately.

☆**Serving Suggestion:** Pair the thighs with Sweet Potatoes with Orange-Pecan Butter, Pickled Okra, and Cracklin' Cornbread. Sip creamy Plumb Loco Coco Punch in place of dessert.

BBQ tips Some people use beer, wine, or other liquids in their water pan or reservoir, or they add slices of apples, onions, or other favorite foods. We usually don't notice any difference in taste, except when we're cooking in a water smoker, which produces more steam than other kinds of barbecue equipment do.

Delectable Drumsticks

Yogurt, like buttermilk, is a miracle marinade, capable of tenderizing anything short of the calluses on a bureaucrat's butt.

DELECTABLE MARINADE

1 cup plain yogurt	¼ cup bourbon
1 cup fresh mint leaves, chopped fine	

8 chicken drumsticks

DELECTABLE MOP (OPTIONAL)

Remaining marinade	2 tablespoons oil, preferably canola or corn
¼ cup bourbon	
¼ cup water	

Lime-Mint Barbecue Sauce (page 304) (optional)

Serves 2 to 4

The night before you plan to barbecue, combine the marinade ingredients in a small bowl. Loosen the skin on the drumsticks, then place the drumsticks in a large plastic bag. Pour the marinade over the drumsticks and refrigerate overnight.

Prepare the smoker for barbecuing, bringing the temperature to 200° F to 220° F.

Remove the chicken from the refrigerator and drain it, reserving the remaining marinade. Let the chicken sit at room temperature for about 15 minutes.

If you plan to baste the chicken (see chapter 3, "To Mop or Not"), combine the mop ingredients in a small saucepan and bring the mixture to a boil, boiling for several minutes. Keep the mop warm over low heat.

Transfer the chicken to the smoker. Cook for 1½ to 1¾ hours, or until the drumsticks are very tender and the juices run clear when a skewer is inserted into one of

Rowdy Southern Swine is a fun-loving barbecue team from Kossuth, Mississippi. In 1993, the group won the Hog Wild cook-off in Corinth, Mississippi, and then took the showmanship competition at Memphis in May with a crowd-rousing skit about the role of the Blues Brothers and barbecue in achieving world peace.

them. Mop the chicken every 30 minutes in a wood-burning pit, or as appropriate in your style of smoker.

Remove the drumsticks from the smoker and serve them immediately, with a dish of Lime-Mint Barbecue Sauce for dipping, if you wish.

☆**Serving Suggestion:** Accompany the drumsticks with white or brown rice, Zooks with Cilantro Sauce, and tangy Corn and Watermelon Pickle-lilli. Santa Fe Capirotada makes an unusual dessert.

Worth-the-Wait Turkey

You may be talking gibberish yourself after a long, long day of barbecuing this bird, but your guests will be talking about the turkey for many more days to come.

Though we love to smoke our own turkeys, we admit to taking a shortcut sometimes when it's cold outside. Greenberg's in Tyler, Texas (903-595-0725), has almost sixty years of experience in smoking turkeys and has perfected the art. You won't find a better commercial holiday bird in the country, and they'll ship them anywhere.

INJECTION LIQUID

½ cup garlic-flavored oil	½ teaspoon cayenne
4 ounces beer	

10-pound to 11-pound turkey

TURKEY PASTE

4 garlic cloves	1 tablespoon kosher salt
1 tablespoon coarse-ground black pepper	Pinch of cayenne
	1 tablespoon garlic-flavored oil

TURKEY MOP (OPTIONAL)

2 cups turkey or chicken stock	¼ cup oil, preferably canola or corn
1 cup water	
8 ounces beer	

Creole Classic Barbecue Sauce (page 299) or Struttin' Sauce (page 290) (optional)

Serves 8 to 10

The night before you plan to barbecue, combine the injection liquid ingredients in a small bowl. With a kitchen syringe, inject the mixture deep into the turkey in a half-dozen places, moving the needle around in each spot to shoot the liquid in several directions. Inject the greatest amount into the breast.

With a mortar and pestle or in a mini–food processor, combine the paste ingredients, mashing the garlic with the pepper, salt, and cayenne. Add the oil to form a thick paste. Massage the turkey with the paste inside and out, working it as far as possible under the skin without tearing the skin. Place the turkey in a plastic bag and refrigerate it overnight.

Before you begin to barbecue, remove the turkey from the refrigerator and let it sit at room temperature for 45 minutes.

Prepare the smoker for barbecuing, bringing the temperature to 200° F to 220° F.

Cut a 4-foot to 5-foot length of cheesecloth and dampen it thoroughly with water. Wrap the bird in the cheesecloth and tie the ends.

Transfer the turkey to the smoker, breast side down (you should be able to feel through the cheesecloth), and cook for 1¼ to 1½ hours per pound, until the internal temperature reaches 180° F. Wet the cheesecloth down with more water at 30-minute intervals in a wood-burning pit, or as appropriate for your style of smoker.

After about 6 hours, remove the cheesecloth, snipping it with scissors if necessary, and discard it. When the cheesecloth is removed, baste the turkey for the remainder of its cooking time, if possible, in your smoker (see chapter 3, "To Mop or Not"). If you plan to baste, combine the mop ingredients in a saucepan and warm the mixture over low heat. Mop every 30 minutes in a wood-burning pit, or as appropriate for your style of smoker.

When the turkey is done, remove it from the smoker and allow it to sit for 15 minutes before carving. Serve

with Creole Classic Barbecue Sauce or Struttin' Sauce, if you wish.

☆**Serving Suggestion:** For a festive meal suitable for a holiday, start with Shrimp Rémoulade. Along with the bird, serve Candied Sweet Potatoes, Peabody-style Stuffed Onions, cornbread dressing, and Buttermilk Biscuits. Load a relish tray with Green Tomato Chowchow, Carolina Jerusalem Artichoke Pickles, Okra Pickles, Bourbon Peaches, or make up a relish tray of store-bought favorites. Offer a scrumptious Black Walnut Cake for dessert.

BBQ tips Injecting an oil mixture is a good way of adding internal moistness and flavor to lean meat. The amounts we recommend in recipes may seem large, but they don't make food greasy. Much of it cooks away.

BBQ tips To make your own garlic-flavored oil, mince a whole bulb of fresh garlic. Place it in a lidded jar and add enough oil to cover the garlic by a couple of inches. Refrigerate for at least a day before using.

Guy Simpson has earned his title as "The Kansas City Rib Doctor," but he can barbecue a lot more than ribs. Our favorite among his specialties is the one Guy calls "roadkill," a consistent award winner at cook-offs. It isn't really roadkill, of course, but he won't say what it is.

Hot Times Jalapeño Turkey Breast

Spanish explorers celebrated a feast of thanksgiving near present-day El Paso back when our Pilgrim mothers and fathers were still boys and girls in England. That's all the excuse you need to add Southwestern flair to your next Thanksgiving meal.

INJECTION LIQUID

⅓ cup oil, preferably canola or corn

⅓ cup pickling liquid from a jar or can of pickled jalapeños

1 teaspoon prepared yellow mustard

5-pound to 7-pound turkey breast

HOT TIMES RUB

2 tablespoons kosher salt	½ teaspoon dry mustard
2 tablespoons brown sugar	½ teaspoon cayenne (optional)
2 teaspoons ground cinnamon	

HOT TIMES MOP (OPTIONAL)

2 cups chicken or turkey stock	¼ cup pickling liquid from a jar
¼ cup oil, preferably canola or corn	or can of pickled jalapeños
	¼ cup jalapeño jelly

Jalapeach Barbecue Sauce (page 302) or Bar-BQ Ranch Sauce (page 298) (optional)

The night before you plan to barbecue, mix together the injection liquid ingredients in a small bowl. With a kitchen syringe, inject all but about 2 tablespoons of the mixture deep into the turkey breast in a half-dozen places, moving the needle around in each spot to shoot the liquid in several directions. Using your fingers, massage the breast with the rest of the liquid, working it as far as possible under the skin without tearing the skin.

Stir together the rub ingredients in a small bowl. Massage the breast well with the mixture, again rubbing it over and under the skin. Place the breast in a plastic bag and refrigerate it overnight.

Prepare the smoker for barbecuing, bringing the temperature to 200° F to 220° F.

Remove the turkey breast from the refrigerator and let it sit at room temperature for about 30 minutes. Cut a 3-foot length of cheesecloth and dampen it thoroughly with water. Wrap the breast in the cheesecloth and tie the ends.

Transfer the breast to the smoker skin side up (you should be able to feel through the cheesecloth) and cook for 1¼ to 1½ hours per pound, until the internal temperature reaches 180° F. Wet the cheesecloth down with

more water at 30-minute intervals in a wood-burning pit, or as appropriate for your style of smoker.

After 4 hours, remove the cheesecloth, snipping it with scissors if necessary, and discard it. When the cheesecloth is removed, baste the turkey for the remainder of its cooking time, if possible in your smoker (see chapter 3, "To Mop or Not"). If you plan to baste, combine the mop ingredients in a saucepan and warm the mixture over low heat. Mop every 30 minutes in a wood-burning pit, or as appropriate for your style of smoker.

When the turkey is done, remove it from the smoker and allow it to sit for 10 minutes before carving. Serve with Jalapeach Barbecue Sauce or Bar-BQ Ranch Sauce, if you wish.

☆**Variation:** If you want a quick glaze for the turkey breast, heat together equal portions of jalapeño jelly and chicken stock. Spoon it over individual slices or offer it on the side.

☆**Serving Suggestion:** For a different spin on a holiday meal, offer Little Devils and Sangrita Marias while everyone gathers. Sit down to Texas Terrine for the first course. Accompany the turkey breast with Drunken Sweet Potatoes, San Antonio Cactus and Corn Salad, spinach sautéed with garlic, and Blue Corn Muffins. Prodigal Pecan Pie makes a great ending.

Two-Steppin' Turkey Legs

6 turkey legs
3 tablespoons Worcestershire
   sauce

1 tablespoon oil, preferably
   canola or corn

TWO-STEPPIN' LEG RUB

2 tablespoons kosher salt
1 tablespoon coarse-ground
   black pepper

1 tablespoon onion powder
1 tablespoon brown sugar
½ teaspoon cayenne

TWO-STEPPIN' LEG MOP (OPTIONAL)

Remaining Two-Steppin' Leg
   Rub
1 cup white vinegar
1 tablespoon Worcestershire
   sauce

1 tablespoon oil, preferably
   canola or corn

Black Sauce (page 297) (optional)

Serves 6

At least 4 hours before you plan to barbecue, and preferably the night before, begin preparations. Loosen the skin on the turkey legs by running your fingers under it as far as possible without tearing the skin.

In a small lidded jar, combine the Worcestershire sauce and oil. In a small bowl, combine the dry spices. Coat your fingers with the wet mixture and rub it well over the legs, getting as much as you can under the skin. Then sprinkle on the dry seasonings liberally, again rubbing as much under the skin as possible. Reserve any remaining dry rub. Place the legs in a plastic bag and refrigerate for at least 4 hours, or overnight.

Prepare the smoker for barbecuing, bringing the temperature to 200° F to 220° F.

Remove the turkey legs from the refrigerator and let them sit at room temperature for about 30 minutes.

If you plan to baste the legs (see chapter 3, "To Mop or Not"), combine the mop ingredients in a small saucepan and warm the mixture over low heat.

Transfer the turkey legs to the smoker. Cook until the legs are very tender and the juices run clear, 3½ to 4 hours. Mop the legs at 45-minute intervals in a wood-burning pit, or as appropriate in your style of smoker. Serve the legs hot, to be eaten with your fingers. Brush on Black Sauce, if you wish.

☆Serving Suggestion: Gobble the legs with down-home fare, such as Devil-May-Care Eggs, Sweet and Sour Cukes, and Buttermilk Onion Rings.

BBQ tips If you're cooking with charcoal, be sure to keep your supply dry. Damp charcoal can be difficult to start, and it burns unevenly. We store our sack of coals in a well-sealed plastic bag, a precaution that's particularly important in a humid climate.

If you live in the Pacific Northwest, you can keep up with regional barbecue news through *Drippings from the Pit*, the quarterly publication of the Pacific Northwest Barbecue Association (4244 134th Avenue SE, Bellevue, Washington 98006).

Quacker 'Q'

If you want to show off like a professional chef, dunk a duck in this marinade, similar to one created by James Beard, the master of American cooking.

4 to 6 duck breasts, about 5 ounces each

JAMES BEARD'S BASIC BARBECUE MARINADE

½ cup soy sauce	1 teaspoon fresh-ground black
½ cup dry sherry	pepper
½ cup strong brewed tea	½ teaspoon ground anise
2 tablespoons honey	½ teaspoon ground cloves
2 tablespoons peanut oil	1 garlic clove, minced

Plum Good Slopping Sauce (page 305) (optional)

Serves 4 to 6

About 3 hours before you plan to barbecue, place the duck breasts in a steamer and steam them for 25 to 30 minutes.

While the breasts steam, mix together the marinade ingredients in a lidded jar. Combine the breasts with the marinade in a shallow, nonreactive dish or plastic bag and refrigerate for 2 hours.

Prepare the smoker for barbecuing, bringing the temperature to 200° F to 220° F.

Remove the breasts from the refrigerator and drain, reserving the marinade if you plan to baste the meat (see chapter 3, "To Mop or Not"). To make the mop, bring the marinade to a boil over high heat in a heavy saucepan. Boil until reduced by about one-third.

Transfer the breasts to the smoker, skin sides up, and cook for 65 to 75 minutes. Mop the breasts immediately and at 30-minute intervals in a wood-burning pit, or as appropriate for your style of smoker.

Let the breasts sit for 5 minutes before slicing the meat on the diagonal. Serve hot or chilled with Plum Good Slopping Sauce, if you wish.

☆**Serving Suggestion:** Serve the duck with Wonderful Watermelon Morsels, Creamy Coleslaw, white or brown rice, and Liar's Lime Pie.

BBQ tips When you barbecue fatty meats, the fat tends to melt away during the cooking process. This general rule doesn't apply to ducks, who shed their excess pounds more reluctantly than a Sumo wrestler. The time-tested method of steaming the birds first keeps you from having to tend the pit all night.

The pit in the name of the Shady Rest Pit-Bar-B-Q in Owensboro, Kentucky, is worth a visit of its own. A splendid piece of barbecue sculpture, the huge, domed brick pit puffs away majestically all day in the take-out area, where the walls are little more than layers of smoke.

Dandy Little Hens

We think Cornish game hens often look more appetizing than they taste, but in this case, the little birds burst with flavor.

DANDY DUNK

1½ cups tequila
1 cup fresh lime juice
¼ cup triple sec or other orange-flavored liqueur
¼ cup minced onion
¼ cup oil, preferably canola or corn

2 tablespoons Worcestershire sauce
Pinch of cayenne or crushed chile de árbol

4 Cornish hens, about 1¼ to 1½ pounds each
Salt and fresh-ground pepper to taste
1 lime, sliced into 4 wedges
1 small orange, sliced

DANDY MOP (OPTIONAL)

Remaining Dandy Dunk
2 tablespoons butter

1 tablespoon triple sec or other orange-flavored liqueur

Sauce Olé (page 296) or South Florida Citrus Sauce (page 304) (optional)

Serves 4

At least 4 hours, and up to 12 hours, before you plan to barbecue, combine the marinade ingredients in a lidded jar. Place the game hens in a shallow, nonreactive dish or plastic bag, pour the marinade over them, and refrigerate. Turn the hens occasionally.

Prepare the smoker for barbecuing, bringing the temperature to 200° F to 220° F.

Remove the hens from the refrigerator. Drain the hens, reserving the marinade if you plan to baste them. Salt and pepper the birds lightly, stuff their cavities with the fruit, and let them sit at room temperature for about 20 minutes.

If you are going to use the mop (see chapter 3, "To Mop or Not"), bring the marinade to a boil over high heat in a small saucepan and boil for several minutes. Stir in the butter and triple sec, and keep the mop warm over low heat.

Transfer the hens to the smoker, breast side down, and cook for 2¼ to 2½ hours. Baste the birds with the mop every 30 minutes in a wood-burning pit, or as appropriate in your style of smoker. Turn the hens over about halfway through the cooking time. When the birds are done, their legs will move freely and the internal temperature should be 180° F to 185° F.

Let the hens sit for 5 to 10 minutes. Remove the skin and slice to serve. Pass a bowl of Sauce Olé or South Florida Citrus Sauce, if you wish.

☆**Serving Suggestion:** Start a summer meal by nibbling on Chicken's Little Livers or guacamole and chips while sipping Firewater. Accompany the hens with Killed Salad and Burstin' with Black-Eyed Peas Salad. A finale of Texas Peach Cobbler should leave your guests smiling.

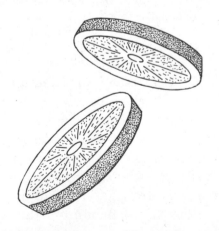

Henry Ford, who revolutionized the American automobile industry, also invented charcoal briquettes. He originally made his cars with lots of wood parts and ended up with a plant full of scraps. Ever the entrepreneur, Ford came up with the idea of charring the discards and compressing them into briquettes, a job he turned over to his brother-in-law, E. G. Kingsford. The new company sold the briquettes only at Ford dealers until the 1950s, when a surge of interest in outdoor cooking prompted grocery stores to start carrying them.

Mushroom-Stuffed Quail

Another miniature fowl, quail has more inherent flavor than Cornish game hens, so it doesn't require as heavy a hand with the seasoning.

¼ cup dried mushrooms, such as morels or cèpes	Salt and fresh-ground black pepper
1 cup warm water	4 garlic cloves, slivered
4 quail	2 bay leaves, halved
1 tablespoon extra-virgin olive oil	

MUSHROOM MOP (OPTIONAL)

Mushroom soaking liquid	2 garlic cloves, minced
½ cup chicken stock	
1 tablespoon extra-virgin olive oil	

Serves 2 to 4

Prepare the smoker for barbecuing, bringing the temperature to 200° F to 220° F.

Combine the mushrooms and water in a small bowl and soak for 30 minutes.

Prepare the quail, cutting off their necks if necessary. Rub the quail with the oil inside and out, and then salt and pepper them liberally. Drain the mushrooms, reserving their liquid if you plan to baste the quail. Stuff each quail with the mushrooms, garlic, and bay leaves. Truss their tiny legs.

If you are going to use the mop (see chapter 3, "To Mop or Not"), pour the mushroom soaking liquid through a fine strainer into a small saucepan. Add the stock, oil, and garlic, and warm the mop over low heat.

Transfer the quail to the smoker, breast side down, and mop them every 20 to 30 minutes in a wood-burning pit, or as appropriate for your style of smoker. The quail are ready when they are well-browned and their legs move easily at the joints, about 1½ to 2 hours. Serve the quail immediately, 1 or 2 to a portion.

Fruited Pheasant

Farm-raised pheasants taste a lot like free-range chickens. This recipe makes the most of that flavor.

PHEASANT MARINADE

4	cups cranberry-apple juice	6	garlic cloves, minced
½	cup balsamic vinegar	1	tablespoon Worcestershire sauce
½	cup oil, preferably canola or corn		
2	pheasants, 2½ to 3 pounds each	1	teaspoon fresh-ground black pepper
2	teaspoons kosher salt		

PHEASANT MOP (OPTIONAL)

Remaining Pheasant Marinade   ½ cup chicken stock

DRESSING

½	cup dried currants	½	teaspoon dried marjoram
½	cup cranberry-apple juice	½	teaspoon dried thyme
3	tablespoons butter	½	cup raw wild rice cooked in chicken stock according to package directions
1	medium onion, chopped		
4	ounces mushrooms, sliced (wild varieties are especially nice)	½	cup raw brown rice cooked in chicken stock according to package directions
½	cup chopped celery	½	cup chicken stock
½	cup pecan pieces		Salt to taste
¼	cup chopped fresh parsley		

Apple City Apple Sauce (page 303) (optional)

Serves 5 to 6

The Beer, Bait 'n Bar-B-Q team from Oklahoma is actually two teams with one name. Gary and Tess Crane used to cook together, but now the husband and wife actively compete against each other in contests. The affable split started when Tess and some women friends went to a cook-off without Gary and came away winners. Tess decided to make the all-female trek an annual adventure, and she kept the family smoker for her group, forcing Gary to build a new one for himself.

The night before you plan to barbecue, combine the marinade ingredients in a lidded jar. Using your fingers, loosen the birds' skins, trying to avoid tearing them. Place the pheasants in a plastic bag and pour the marinade ingredients over the birds. Refrigerate them overnight, turning at least once, if needed, to soak the birds evenly.

Before you begin to barbecue, remove the pheasants from the refrigerator and drain them, reserving the marinade if you plan to baste the birds. Salt and pepper the pheasants inside and out, being sure to rub some under the skin. Let them sit at room temperature for 30 to 45 minutes.

Prepare the smoker for barbecuing, bringing the temperature to 220° F to 220° F.

If you are going to use the mop (see chapter 3, "To Mop or Not"), bring the marinade and stock to a boil in a large saucepan, and boil for several minutes. Keep the mop warm over low heat.

Transfer the pheasants to the smoker, breast side down. Cook for about 3 hours, mopping the birds every 30 minutes in a wood-burning pit, or as appropriate in your style of smoker.

While the pheasants cook, make the dressing. In a small bowl, combine the currants with the cranberry-apple juice and let them steep for about 15 minutes.

Warm the butter in a smokeproof skillet. Add the onion, mushrooms, celery, and pecans. Sauté until the vegetables soften. Mix in the herbs, rices, currants (with any remaining liquid), and chicken stock. Add salt, if needed. Cover the dressing with foil and refrigerate.

After the pheasants have smoked for about 2 hours, transfer the dressing skillet to the smoker. Continue smoking until the pheasants' internal temperatures measure 160° F. The juices will run pink if pierced. The dressing will be ready at the same time as the pheasant. If you want to add a smokier flavor to the dressing, uncover it

193

during the last 15 minutes, adding a little water if the mixture appears dry.

Remove the pheasants from the smoker, tent them with foil, and let them sit for 10 minutes before carving. Accompany the sliced pheasants with the hot dressing and, if you wish, Apple City Apple Sauce.

☆**Serving Suggestion:** Munch on Curry Pecans while waiting for the pheasant. Add a Southern Caesar Salad and meringue-topped 'Nana Pudding to round out the meal.

BBQ tips If you're cooking food in a smoker in a pan or skillet, try to find a container that won't discolor easily from the smoke, such as a cast-iron pot, or something that can be cleaned with relative ease, such as a Pyrex dish. Disposable foil pans are a good option, too. Other utensils may require a lot of scrubbing to remove the dark smoke color, particularly if you're barbecuing in a wood-burning pit.

Rosy Rosemary Quail

A bath in red wine turns these bantam birds a pleasant pink before they brown.

ROSEMARY MARINADE AND OPTIONAL MOP

¾ cup dry red wine
¾ cup red wine vinegar
¾ cup olive oil

12 garlic cloves, minced
1½ teaspoons crushed rosemary

8 quail, butterflied
Salt and fresh-ground black pepper to taste

Serves 4 to 8

About 3 to 4 hours before you plan to barbecue, combine the marinade ingredients in a lidded jar. Arrange the quail in a shallow, nonreactive dish or plastic bag, pour the marinade over them, and refrigerate.

Prepare the smoker for barbecuing, bringing the temperature to 200° F to 220° F.

Drain the quail, reserving the marinade if you plan to baste the birds. Salt and pepper the quail lightly and let them sit at room temperature for about 20 minutes.

If you are going to use the mop (see chapter 3, "To Mop or Not"), bring the marinade to a boil and boil it for several minutes. Keep the mop warm over low heat.

Transfer the quail to the smoker, skin side up, and cook until well-browned and a little crispy, 1½ to 2 hours. Mop every 30 minutes in a wood-burning pit, or as appropriate for your style of smoker. Serve the quail immediately.

☆**Serving Suggestion:** We usually offer Unholy Swiss Cheese and more red wine for openers. With the quail, serve mixed greens dressed with vinaigrette and potato slices sautéed with garlic and thyme. Try a fruity dessert, such as Wild Huckleberry Pie with Coconut Crumble.

BBQ tips If your quail don't come butterflied, the little birds are easy to prepare yourself. Cut through the fragile breast bone, chop off the neck, and flatten as needed.

Chicken Salad Supreme

DRESSING

⅓ cup honey	1 teaspoon dry mustard
¼ cup white vinegar	1 teaspoon grated onion
2 tablespoons fresh lemon juice	½ teaspoon salt
1 tablespoon poppy seeds	1 cup oil, preferably canola or corn

1½ pounds chilled smoked chicken, chunked	½ cup green onions, sliced
¾ cup diced cantaloupe	½ teaspoon minced lemon zest
¾ cup diced honeydew melon	½ cup sliced almonds, toasted

Lettuce leaves
Fresh strawberries and lemon wedges, for garnish

Serves 4 to 6

In a food processor, briefly process the dressing in-gredients, except the oil, until combined. Pour in the oil and continue processing until thick.

In a medium-size bowl, mix the chicken, melons, green onions, and lemon zest with about two-thirds of the dressing. Refrigerate if desired.

Stir the almonds into the salad shortly before serving. Mound the salad on the lettuce leaves and garnish with strawberries and lemons. Spoon additional dressing over the top, if you wish.

☆**Serving Suggestion:** Impress your mom when she comes to visit. Serve a Bronzed Artichoke, followed by this salad and Sweet Potato Biscuits.

Big John Robinson of Peoria, Illinois, ran into financial problems in the 1980s, but he's still a legend in the city. In 1949, he opened a barbecue shack on a downtown sidewalk, buying his meat daily in 15-pound slabs because he didn't own a freezer. By 1974, Big John's 'Q' was Peoria's favorite chow, and the pitmaster was named the state's small-business man of the year.

Hot Browns

Louisville's grand old hotel, The Brown, developed the tasty "Hot Brown" sandwich, which we embellish here by using smoked turkey, preferably our own leftovers.

CHEESE SAUCE

3 tablespoons butter	¼ teaspoon dry mustard
1 tablespoon minced onion	¼ teaspoon paprika
1½ tablespoons all-purpose flour	½ cup grated mild or medium-sharp cheddar cheese (2 ounces)
1 cup whole milk	Salt to taste
1 teaspoon Worcestershire sauce	

4 slices good white bread	4 slices bacon, fried crisp
½ pound sliced or shredded smoked turkey breast, warmed	4 thin slices red-ripe tomato
	1½ tablespoons grated Parmesan cheese

Serves 2

Preheat the oven to 350° F.

Start the cheese sauce by melting the butter over medium heat in a heavy saucepan. Add the onion and sauté briefly until it is softened. Stir in the flour, and continue stirring a minute or two. Add the milk, Worcestershire sauce, mustard, and paprika, and heat until thickened, about 3 to 5 minutes. Turn the heat down to low and sprinkle in the cheese, stirring to melt it evenly. Taste the sauce and add salt if needed. Keep the sauce warm in the top of a double boiler until you are ready to use it.

Toast the bread and cut each slice on the diagonal. Arrange the slices on two plates. Top each plate with half of the turkey and cheese sauce. Arrange the bacon slices, tomato, and sprinklings of Parmesan evenly over both. Pop the plates in the oven for 5 minutes. Serve immediately.

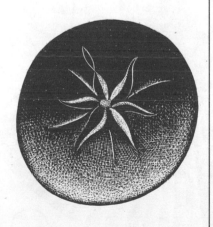

☆ Fishing for ☆ Compliments

Before pork shoulder, long before brisket, fish was America's favorite barbecue fare. When Spanish and British explorers arrived in the New World centuries ago, they found Native Americans smoking their food over wood fires. In the Caribbean, along the East Coast, and all the way over in the Pacific Northwest, different tribes used a similar method of cooking the catch of the day. They didn't offer the Europeans takeout from a "Sandy's Salmon Bar-B-Q" joint, but the natives did share their smoking secrets, and they even gave the newcomers the term *barbecue*.

Today, most smoked fish in markets and restaurants is smoke-cured rather than smoke-cooked in a barbecue manner, but both processes yield delicious results. As the original Americans knew long before Columbus or Sir Walter Raleigh, the fusion of flavors in fish and smoke is a natural bounty.

Kingly Salmon

For thousands of years before the arrival of Europeans, Native Americans in the Pacific Northwest perfected ways to cook salmon, their most abundant food. They boiled the fish in watertight baskets, steamed them in underground rock ovens, and, in their tastiest preparation, smoke-roasted split sides of the salmon over an alder wood fire. To preserve fish for the winter, the Indians smoked their catch until it was fully dehydrated, but during the season, they cooked it similar to this for immediate eating. A butterflied tail section from a Pacific king salmon offers royal flavor, but coho or silver salmon make regal meals, too.

KINGLY RUB

¼ cup dried dill
¼ cup brown sugar
2 teaspoons kosher salt

2 teaspoons fresh-ground black pepper

3-pound to 3½-pound salmon tail section, boned and butterflied

KINGLY MOP (OPTIONAL)

Remaining Kingly Rub
1 cup cider vinegar

¼ cup oil, preferably canola or corn

Serves 8

The night before you plan to barbecue, combine the rub ingredients in a small bowl. Open the salmon flat and massage it well with about two-thirds of the rub, reserving the rest of the mixture. Fold the salmon back into its original shape, place it in a plastic bag, and refrigerate it overnight.

Prepare the smoker for barbecuing, bringing the temperature to 180° F to 200° F.

Remove the salmon from the refrigerator and let it sit at room temperature for 30 minutes.

George Bush likes the barbecue at Otto's in Houston, which honors the ex-president with a photo gallery in a back dining room. Bush can also barbecue for himself, on a fine Pitt's & Spitt's pit that he brought home from Camp David.

If you plan to baste the fish (see chapter 3, "To Mop or Not"), stir the remaining rub together with the other mop ingredients in a small saucepan and warm the mixture over low heat.

Transfer the salmon to the smoker skin side down, placing the fish as far from the fire as possible. Cook for 50 to 60 minutes, mopping it after 10 and 30 minutes in a wood-burning pit, or as appropriate for your style of smoker. The salmon should flake easily when done. Have a large spatula and a platter ready when taking the salmon off the smoker, because it can fall apart easily. Serve hot or chilled.

☆**Serving Suggestions:** Serve with Arty Rice Salad, Smoked Spud Skins, and some crusty bread. Rhubarb Crunch would be wonderful for dessert.

BBQ tips Alder remains the best wood for smoking Pacific salmon. Alder chips are fairly common across the country, but you may have more difficulty finding the wood in chunks or logs. Fruit woods are the best substitute, particularly when mixed with smaller pieces of alder.

Jamaican Jerked Salmon

Jamaicans barbecue with "jerk" seasonings—assertive combinations of allspice, chiles, and other ingredients. Originally, "jerking" preserved meats like pork and chicken, but its popularity today stems from the spicy taste. The rub in this dish will dance on your tongue but won't scorch it, allowing the rich but subtle salmon flavor to shine through.

JERK RUB

1 tablespoon onion powder	1 teaspoon sugar
1 tablespoon dried onion flakes	¾ teaspoon dried thyme
1 teaspoon ground allspice	¾ teaspoon ground cinnamon
1 teaspoon fresh-ground black pepper	¼ teaspoon ground nutmeg
1 teaspoon cayenne	Pinch of dried ground habanero chile (optional)

1½-pound salmon fillet

JAMAICAN BARBECUE SAUCE

1 cup seafood stock	1 tablespoon minced fresh ginger root
2 heaping tablespoons honey	1 tablespoon Jerk Rub
1 tablespoon tamarind concentrate	

Serves 4

About 1½ hours before you plan to barbecue, combine the jerk seasoning ingredients in a small bowl. Rub the salmon thoroughly with a generous portion of the seasoning, reserving at least 1 tablespoon. Wrap the salmon in plastic and refrigerate it.

Prepare the smoker for barbecuing, bringing the temperature to 180° F to 200° F.

Remove the salmon from the refrigerator and let it sit at room temperature for 15 to 20 minutes.

Transfer the salmon to the smoker and smoke it until just cooked through, 45 to 55 minutes. Have a large spat-

The word *barbecue* comes from the Spanish *barbacoa,* the term early explorers in the New World applied to the wood frame Caribbean natives used in their smoke cooking. The Spanish word is probably an adaptation of an unknown Indian word.

ula and a platter ready for taking the salmon off the smoker, since it will be fragile when done.

While the salmon cooks, make the sauce. Combine all the ingredients and bring to a boil over high heat. Reduce the heat and simmer until reduced by one-third; this will take 5 to 10 minutes. Keep warm.

Transfer the salmon to the serving platter. Pour the sauce into a small bowl and pass it separately to spoon over individual portions of salmon.

☆**Serving Suggestion:** Accompany the elegant salmon with Scalloped Green Chile Potatoes and Mango and Avocado Salad. Conclude with South Georgia Pound Cake gilded, if you like, with lemon pudding.

BBQ tips The preferable temperature range for smoking fish is slightly lower than for meat. Our recipes call for a cooking temperature of 180° F to 200° F, but some people like to go down to 165° F.

Stuffed Mountain Trout

The premier freshwater fish for barbecuing, trout relish a swim in the smoke. In this preparation, the bacon does the work of a mop.

TROUT PASTE

4 garlic cloves
Juice of ½ lemon
1 teaspoon Worcestershire sauce
1 teaspoon fresh-ground black pepper

½ teaspoon salt
1 tablespoon oil, preferably canola or corn

Sometimes barbecue inspiration comes from faraway places. Jack and Delores Fiorella, proprietors of the Smoke Shack in Kansas City, decided to add hickory-cooked fish to their extensive menu after a trip along the coast of Yugoslavia, where they found a range of tasty fish dishes.

4 boned trout, approximately
  8 ounces each
8 slices bacon
6 tablespoons chopped onion
6 tablespoons chopped green
  bell pepper

6 tablespoons chopped celery
16 saltine crackers, crushed
6 tablespoons chopped pecans

Serves 4

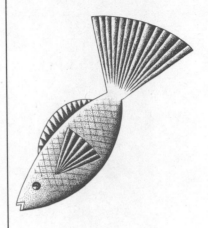

About 1½ hours before you plan to barbecue, prepare the paste by mashing or chopping the garlic in a mortar and pestle or mini–food processor. Mix in the lemon juice, Worcestershire sauce, pepper, and salt. Then blend in the oil to make a paste. Rub the trout inside and out with the paste. Wrap the trout in plastic and refrigerate for about 1 hour.

Prepare the smoker for barbecuing, bringing the temperature to 180° F to 200° F.

Remove the trout from the refrigerator and let them sit at room temperature for about 20 minutes.

In a heavy skillet, fry the bacon over medium heat, removing it from the skillet while still limp. Set the bacon aside. Add the onion, bell pepper, and celery to the bacon drippings and sauté briefly until softened. Remove the mixture from the heat and stir in the cracker crumbs and pecans. Stuff each trout with a portion of this filling. Wrap two slices of bacon around each fish, securing with toothpicks as needed.

Transfer the trout to the smoker. Cook until the bacon is browned and crisp and the fish opaque and easily flaked, 40 to 50 minutes. Serve immediately.

BBQ tips Trout and catfish can take a heavier level of smoke flavor than most fish, making them particularly suitable for log-burning pits.

Mint Trout

Unlike most mops, the one in this recipe can be used in all kinds of smokers because it isn't applied during the cooking process.

MINT PASTE

¾ cup fresh mint leaves
¼ cup kosher salt
¼ cup sugar
2 tablespoons coarse-ground black pepper

2 tablespoons fresh lemon juice
1 tablespoon oil, preferably canola or corn

1½ pounds trout fillets

MINT MOP

1 cup brewed mint tea made from 2 mint tea bags

Mint sprigs, for garnish

Serves 4

The night before you plan to barbecue, prepare the paste by combining the ingredients in a food processor and processing until puréed. Rub the trout fillets with a thick coating of the paste. Wrap the fillets in plastic and refrigerate them.

Prepare the smoker for barbecuing, bringing the temperature to 180° F to 200° F.

Remove the trout from the refrigerator and let them sit at room temperature for approximately 15 minutes.

Transfer the trout, covered with the paste that clings to each fillet, to a small grill rack. Drizzle each fillet with enough mint tea to moisten the coating well and place the fish in the smoker. Cook the trout until opaque and easily flaked, 30 to 45 minutes depending on the size of the fillets. Drizzle with additional mint tea and serve immediately.

☆**Serving Suggestion:** Start with South-of-the-Border Garlic Soup. Pair the fish with Warm Mushroom Salad and steamed asparagus served hot or cold. Finish off with sliced mangoes or papayas sprinkled with rum and lime juice. It's a great combo when you need to impress your boss or main squeeze.

BBQ tips   Several recipes in this chapter suggest using a small grill rack to hold pieces of fish and seafood in a smoker. The mesh on the grate should permit smoke to pass but prevent food from falling through. Nationally distributed brands Griffo Grill and Oscarware both make products that work well.

Peppered Catfish

Most Americans fry their catfish. This will quickly disabuse you of that approach. Plan to make enough to save some for Katzen Dawgs, or for Creamy Catfish Spread.

THREE-PEPPER CATFISH RUB

3 tablespoons coarse-ground black pepper	1 teaspoon onion powder
2 tablespoons kosher salt	½ teaspoon cayenne
1½ tablespoons coarse-ground white pepper	

Six 8-ounce catfish fillets

CATFISH MOP (OPTIONAL)

2 cups seafood or chicken stock	Juice of 3 limes
½ cup oil, preferably canola or corn	1 to 2 tablespoons remaining Three-Pepper Catfish Rub

Golden Mustard Barbecue Sauce (page 293) (optional)

Serves 6

When you're yearning for smoked catfish and you're fresh out of wood, call Betty and Quentin Knussmann at the Pickwick Catfish Farm (901-689-3805) in Counce, Tennessee. You won't find a better mail-order version.

t least 2½ hours before you plan to barbecue, or preferably the night before, mix the rub ingredients together in a small bowl. Cover the catfish lightly and evenly with the rub, reserving at least 1 to 2 tablespoons of the mixture if you plan to baste the fish. Place the fillets in a plastic bag and refrigerate them for 2 hours or overnight.

Prepare the smoker for barbecuing, bringing the temperature to 180° F to 200° F.

Remove the fillets from the refrigerator and let them sit at room temperature for 20 minutes.

If you are going to use the mop (see chapter 3, "To Mop or Not"), mix the ingredients together in a small saucepan and warm over low heat.

Place the catfish in the smoker on a small grill rack as far from the fire as possible. Cook the fish for approximately 1½ hours, dabbing the catfish with the mop every 20 minutes in a wood-burning pit, or as appropriate for your style of smoker. When cooked, the catfish will be opaque and firm, yet flaky. Serve warm. If desired, accompany the catfish with Golden Mustard Barbecue Sauce.

Flounder Surprise

This is a fancy "sandwich" of double-smoked salmon stuffed between two barbecued flounder fillets. Use leftover Kingly Salmon or substitute a store-bought Pacific Northwest–style smoked salmon.

1½ to 1¾ pounds flounder or sole fillets

WILD WILLY'S NUMBER ONE-DERFUL RUB

3 tablespoons paprika	1½ teaspoons chili powder
1 tablespoon freshly-ground black pepper	1½ teaspoons garlic powder
	1½ teaspoons onion powder
1 tablespoon salt	½ teaspoon cayenne
1 tablespoon sugar	

New Yorkers used to barbecue turtles in the eighteenth century, according to food historians Waverley Root and Richard de Rochemont. No wonder they gave up on the 'Q.'

STUFFING

6 to 8 ounces smoked salmon,
    such as Kingly Salmon
    (page 200)
½ cup dry bread crumbs
¼ cup chopped celery

¼ cup chopped onion
1 egg white, lightly beaten
¼ teaspoon paprika
1 to 2 tablespoons milk

SURPRISE MOP (OPTIONAL)

1 cup seafood or chicken stock
3 tablespoons butter
Juice of 1 lemon

Lemon wedges, for garnish
   (optional)

Serves 4

Prepare the smoker for barbecuing, bringing the temperature to 180° F to 200° F.

Cut the flounder into 8 equal portions, about 3 to 4 ounces each. Mix the rub ingredients together in a small bowl and rub the fillets lightly but evenly with the mixture. Let the fillets sit at room temperature for 15 to 20 minutes.

Place the smoked salmon in a food processor. Add the rest of the stuffing ingredients, except the milk, and process together briefly. The stuffing should be thoroughly blended but not puréed to oblivion. Add as much of the milk as is needed to moisten the mixture without making it soupy. Spoon equal portions of the stuffing onto half of the fillets. Top each "stuffed" fillet with one of the remaining fillets.

If you plan to baste the fish (see chapter 3, "To Mop or Not"), combine the mop ingredients in a small saucepan and warm over low heat until the butter melts. Keep the mop warm over low heat.

Transfer the fillets to a small grill rack and place them in the smoker as far from the fire as possible. Cook until the flounder is opaque and flaky and the salmon heated through, 35 to 40 minutes. Mop twice during the cooking process in a wood-burning pit, or as appropriate for your style of smoker. Serve the fish with the lemon wedges, if you wish.

BBQ tips To tell how much smoke flavor you're putting into food, simply check the amount of smoke being vented out of your barbecue equipment. If nothing is coming out, it's time to add more wood.

When Memphis in May competition teams sold barbecue to the public for the first time in 1993, the Paddlewheel Porkers took the "People's Choice" award for the best 'Q.' You can't miss the group at a cook-off. They're the ones who are barbecuing and partying on the huge two-story replica of a Mississippi River paddle boat.

Cuban Snapper

This is a new spin on a dish that's now common in south Florida, where red snapper is often poached or cooked in clay.

3-pound to 3½-pound whole gutted red snapper, sea bass, or other mild-flavored white fish	Juice of 2 lemons Salt and fresh-ground black pepper to taste
1 tablespoon extra-virgin olive oil	

STUFFING

½ cup dry bread crumbs	¼ teaspoon dried oregano
½ medium onion, chopped	¼ teaspoon ground nutmeg
3 tablespoons minced fresh parsley, preferably Italian flat-leaf	¼ teaspoon crushed hot red chile, such as cayenne or chile de árbol
¼ teaspoon dried thyme	Juice of 1 lemon

CUBAN MOP (OPTIONAL)

1 cup fish or seafood stock	2 tablespoons olive oil
¼ cup water	Juice of 1 lemon

AVOCADO SAUCE

2 ripe Hass avocados	3 to 4 tablespoons extra-virgin olive oil
Juice of 2 limes	
2 tablespoons chopped onion	Lemon and lime wedges and parsley sprigs, for garnish
1 teaspoon salt	
Fresh-ground black pepper to taste	

209

Serves 4 to 6

Prepare the smoker for barbecuing, bringing the temperature to 180° F to 200° F.

Rub the snapper inside and out with the oil and half the lemon juice. Sprinkle sparingly with salt and liberally with pepper. Allow the fish to sit at room temperature for about 30 minutes.

In a bowl, mix together the bread crumbs, onion, parsley, thyme, oregano, nutmeg, chile, and lemon juice. Stuff the fish loosely. Place the fish on a greased grill rack or baking sheet.

If you plan to baste the fish (see chapter 3, "To Mop or Not"), mix the mop ingredients together in a small saucepan. Warm the mop over low heat.

Transfer the snapper to the smoker as far from the fire as possible. Cook for about 20 minutes per pound, mopping the fish early and once or twice more in a wood-burning pit, or as appropriate for your style of smoker.

While the fish cooks, prepare the sauce. Peel and chop the avocados. Combine them in a food processor with the lime juice, onion, salt, and pepper. With the processor running, add the oil in a steady stream, until the sauce has the consistency of thin mayonnaise. Spoon the sauce into a small bowl.

Remove the snapper from the smoker with a large spatula and transfer it to a decorative platter. Garnish the snapper with lemons, limes, and parsley. To serve, remove the skin, and cut through the fish, watching for its bones. Serve each portion with some of the stuffing. Pass the sauce separately. Alternatively, skin the top side of the fish, spread a thick layer of the sauce over it, and serve.

☆**Serving Suggestion:** Snack first on Fiesta Salsa and tortilla chips. Accompany the snapper with a mixed green salad and tangy citrus vinaigrette, and top it off with 'Nana Pudding or fresh tropical fruit.

The Owensboro, Kentucky, International Bar-B-Q Festival dates its origin back to the church barbecue picnics that have been a local tradition since 1834. A team from St. Mary Magdalene Catholic Church won the first festival cook-off in 1978 and then claimed its record fifth championship in 1992 in a tight decision over a team from Our Lady of the Lourdes.

Kohala Tuna Steaks

In recent years, Hawaiian chefs have created a sumptuous new regional cuisine, often featuring the local tuna. Here's a smoked version of a Big Island favorite.

KOHALA MARINADE

6 tablespoons melted butter	½ teaspoon dried thyme
6 tablespoons Asian-style sesame oil	1 garlic clove, minced
6 tablespoons rice vinegar	1 crushed Thai, Hunan, or other tiny hot red chile
Juice of ½ lemon	
1½ teaspoons minced fresh ginger root	

4 tuna steaks, each approximately 1 inch thick	Soy sauce
¼ teaspoon kosher salt	West Coast Wonder barbecue sauce (page 300) (optional)

Serves 4

Prepare the smoker for barbecuing, bringing the temperature to 180° F to 200° F.

In a lidded jar, mix together the marinade ingredients. Place the tuna steaks in a shallow, nonreactive dish and pour the marinade over the tuna. Allow the steaks to sit at room temperature for 20 to 30 minutes.

Heat a skillet over high heat and sprinkle in the salt. Drain the tuna steaks. Sear the steaks quickly on both sides.

Transfer the steaks to the smoker. Cook the tuna to desired doneness, 20 to 25 minutes for medium-rare. Avoid overcooking the tuna. Serve hot with soy sauce and, if you wish, a touch of West Coast Wonder barbecue sauce.

☆**Serving Suggestion:** Mix up a salad of thinly sliced snow peas, carrots, red bell peppers, and Napa cabbage or bok choy tossed with a vinaigrette made with Asian-

style sesame oil and rice vinegar. A creamy dessert works best, perhaps Lemon Pudding Ice Cream Pie.

BBQ tips Before you smoke meaty fish steaks, such as tuna and swordfish, it helps to sear them quickly over high heat to seal in their juices and add a light crust.

Tuna Caper

If you prefer Mediterranean to Pacific flavors, this tuna should tantalize.

OLIVE PASTE

¼ cup chopped pitted black olives, preferably kalamata or niçoise
¼ cup extra-virgin olive oil

4 tuna steaks, approximately 1-inch thick
¼ teaspoon kosher salt

2 tablespoons red wine
1 tablespoon capers
1 teaspoon dried thyme
2 garlic cloves, minced

Lemon wedges and basil sprigs, for garnish (optional)

Serves 4

Prepare the smoker for barbecuing, bringing the temperature to 180° F to 200° F.

In a food processor, process the paste ingredients to a thick purée. Rub the paste over the tuna steaks. Transfer the tuna to a plate and allow the steaks to sit at room temperature for about 20 minutes.

Heat a skillet over high heat and sprinkle in the salt. Add the tuna steaks and sear them quickly on both sides.

Transfer the steaks to the smoker. Cook the tuna to desired doneness, 20 to 25 minutes for medium-rare. Avoid overcooking the tuna. Serve hot, garnished with lemons and basil, if you wish.

Rain has always been the bane of barbecuers. In *Gone with the Wind*, Scarlett O'Hara fretted about the weather just before a big Georgia party, saying "There's nothing worse than a barbecue turned into an indoor picnic."

☆**Serving Suggestion:** Serve Unholy Swiss Cheese to start. Accompany the tuna with steamed artichokes, a platter of red-ripe tomatoes and mozzarella dressed with olive oil, and crispy breadsticks. Offer Becky's Pineapple Cake for dessert. For a light meal, the tuna makes a great salad ingredient, used either hot or cold.

Soused Swordfish

If you have any leftovers, these swordfish will have a helluva hangover the next day.

SOUSED MARINADE

¾ cup bourbon
¾ cup seafood or chicken stock
¼ cup oil, preferably canola or corn

3 garlic cloves, minced
1 tablespoon green peppercorns, plus 1 teaspoon of brine

Four 8-ounce to 10-ounce swordfish steaks

BASIC BLACK RUB

1½ tablespoons coarse-ground black pepper

½ tablespoon kosher salt

Serves 4

At least 2, and up to 8, hours before you plan to barbecue, combine the marinade ingredients in a lidded jar. Place the swordfish in a shallow, nonreactive pan or a plastic bag. Pour the marinade over the swordfish and refrigerate it for about 1½ hours.

Prepare the smoker for barbecuing, bringing the temperature to 180° F to 200° F.

Drain the swordfish, reserving about ¾ cup of the marinade. Combine the rub ingredients in a small bowl and sprinkle them lightly but evenly over both sides of the steaks. Let the swordfish sit at room temperature for 15 to 20 minutes.

In a small pan, bring the reserved marinade to a vigorous boil over high heat and boil for several minutes. Keep the liquid warm over low heat.

Heat a heavy skillet over high heat. Place the steaks in the skillet, in batches if necessary, and sear quickly on both sides. Remove the steaks immediately, drizzle the hot marinade lightly over them, and transfer the steaks to the smoker. Cook for 40 to 50 minutes, until the fish is cooked through. Serve the swordfish hot.

☆**Serving Suggestion:** When you need an uptown down-home meal, try these steaks with Barbecued Rice and California Crunch salad. For dessert, we would opt for Long-on-Strawberries Shortcake.

BBQ tips Bourbon is a great marinade ingredient for barbecuing because of its smoky, sweet flavor. It works particularly well with red meat but also enhances some lighter fare, such as meaty swordfish.

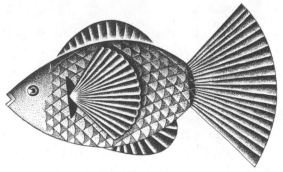

Sherried Grouper

Here's a more delicately inebriated fish, and one that's quick to prepare.

SHERRY MARINADE AND SAUCE

Juice of 2 oranges,
  approximately ⅔ cup
Zest of 1 orange, minced
½ cup sherry
6 tablespoons oil, preferably
  peanut

1 tablespoon Creole mustard
2 garlic cloves, minced
¼ teaspoon salt
¼ teaspoon fresh-ground black
  pepper

Four 6-ounce firm white fish fillets
Chopped parsley, orange slices, and orange zest, for garnish

Serves 4

Prepare the smoker for barbecuing, bringing the temperature to 180° F to 200° F.

Combine all the marinade ingredients in a lidded jar. Lay the fillets in a single layer in a shallow, nonreactive dish or place them in a plastic bag. Pour the marinade over the fillets and let them sit at room temperature for about 30 minutes.

Drain the fillets, reserving the marinade. In a small pan, bring the marinade to a vigorous boil over high heat. Reduce the heat to simmer and cook for several minutes, until the marinade forms a thin sauce. Taste and adjust the seasoning, if needed. Keep the sauce warm over low heat.

Transfer the fillets to the smoker. Cook for 25 to 30 minutes, until the fish is opaque and flaky. Spoon the sauce on a serving platter and top it with the fillets. Garnish the fish with a sprinkling of parsley and a scattering of orange slices and zest. Serve immediately.

California Dreamin' Fish Tacos

Some people dream of sunshine in southern California. We dream of soft tacos overflowing with fish and salsa.

Two 12-ounce to 14-ounce red snapper fillets
1 cup Lawry's Mesquite with Lime Juice Marinade or other commercial mesquite marinade

Juice from 1 lime

TOMATILLO SALSA

3 teaspoons extra-virgin olive oil
1 small red or sweet onion, chopped
1 pound fresh tomatillos, husks removed and chopped, or 2 cups canned tomatillos
2 canned chipotle chiles, minced, or more to taste

1 tablespoon white vinegar
1 teaspoon dried oregano, preferably Mexican
½ cup chopped fresh cilantro
Salt and fresh-ground black pepper to taste

3 tablespoons extra-virgin olive oil
½ pound jícama, peeled and cut in matchsticks
1 small red onion or sweet onion, chopped
1 small red pepper, cut in matchsticks
1 small zucchini, cut in matchsticks

1 roasted green chile, preferably New Mexican or poblano, fresh or frozen, cut in matchsticks (optional)
6 squash blossoms, cut in matchsticks (optional)
⅓ cup chopped fresh cilantro

Warm flour tortillas, preferably no larger than 6 inches in diameter
Lime wedges, for garnish

Serves 4 to 6

Prepare the smoker for barbecuing, bringing the temperature to 180° F to 200° F.
Place the snapper fillets in a nonreactive, shallow dish. Pour the marinade over the fish, add the lime juice, and let the fish sit at room temperature for 30 minutes.

Rich Davis of Kansas City cooks with a conscience. His small, successful chain of K.C. Masterpiece restaurants plants two trees for every one they use in smoking their barbecue.

216

Prepare the salsa while the fish marinates. Warm 1½ teaspoons of the oil in a heavy skillet over medium heat. Add the onion and sauté until softened. Spoon the onion into a bowl. Warm the remaining 1½ teaspoons of the oil in the same skillet over medium-high heat. Add the tomatillos and sauté until lightly browned. Place the tomatillos in the bowl with the onion. Stir in the chipotles, vinegar, and oregano, and refrigerate.

Remove the snapper from the marinade, draining as little of the liquid as possible. Spoon some of the remaining marinade over the fish and place the fillets in the smoker. Cook the snapper until opaque and easily flaked, 45 to 55 minutes.

Remove the fish from the smoker. Let it cool for a couple of minutes while you finish the salsa, stirring in the cilantro and adding salt and pepper to taste. Pour the salsa into a decorative bowl. Flake the fish into bite-size chunks and mound it on one side of a large platter. Cover it with foil.

In a skillet, warm the 3 tablespoons oil over medium heat. Add the jícama, red onion, red pepper, zucchini, and chile, and sauté until the vegetables are crisp-tender. Stir in the squash blossoms and remaining ⅓ cup cilantro and heat through. Spoon the vegetables onto the other half of the platter.

Serve immediately with the tortillas and lime wedges. Spoon some of the fish into the tortillas, along with spoonfuls of the vegetable mixture. Top with salsa and, if you wish, squeezes of lime juice. Fold the tortillas in half and devour.

BBQ tips Our recipes rarely call for commercial marinades, but we're happy to make an exception for Lawry's Mesquite with Lime Juice Marinade in the fish tacos. The sauce works great with many smoked fish dishes.

Jalapeño-Lime Shrimp

Dallas chef Dean Fearing, the genius in the kitchen at the Mansion on Turtle Creek, inspired this fiery Southwestern shrimp treat. It's as classic a combo as Carolina pork and vinegar.

JALAPEÑO-LIME MARINADE

⅓ cup pickled jalapeño slices
¼ cup pickling liquid from jar or can of pickled jalapeños
Juice of 2 limes
4 tablespoons corn oil, preferably unrefined

3 tablespoons minced fresh cilantro
4 green onions, sliced
3 garlic cloves, minced

1 pound large shrimp (24 to 30 shrimp)

JALAPEÑO-LIME MOP

Remaining Jalapeño-Lime Marinade
½ cup seafood or chicken stock
Juice of 1 lime

Slices of fresh red jalapeño or other red chile, for garnish (optional)

Serves 4

Purée the marinade ingredients in a food processor or blender.

Peel the shrimp, leaving the tails on. Clean the shrimp and, if desired, devein them. Place the shrimp in a shallow, nonreactive dish or plastic bag. Pour the marinade over the shrimp and let the shrimp marinate at room temperature for 30 to 40 minutes.

Prepare the smoker for barbecuing, bringing the temperature to 180° F to 200° F.

Drain the shrimp from the marinade, pouring the marinade into a saucepan. Add the stock and additional lime juice to the remaining marinade for the mop. Bring the liquid to a vigorous boil over high heat and boil for several minutes. Keep the mop warm over low heat.

The judging process in a barbecue cooking contest varies considerably depending on the organization that "sanctioned" the event. We're partial to the rules of the International Barbecue Cookers Association (P.O. Box 300556, Arlington, Texas 76007-0556), which emphasizes blind judging and uses a progressive elimination system rather than numerical rankings. The IBCA also insists on evaluating sauces separately from the barbecue, prohibiting any "visible alteration" of food after it is cooked. A $20 membership entitles you to a full packet of materials on sponsoring and judging a barbecue contest.

Place the shrimp on a small grill rack and baste liberally with the mop. Transfer the shrimp to the smoker and place as far from the fire as possible. The shrimp should cook in approximately 25 minutes, but watch them carefully. They are ready when opaque, slightly firm, and lightly pink on the exterior. Remove the shrimp from the smoker and mop them heavily again. Place the shrimp on a platter, scatter the red jalapeños over them, if you wish, and serve.

BBQ tips Shrimp dishes work particularly well in stove-top smokers, making them great winter treats when it's too cold to barbecue outside.

Shrimp Rémoulade

Rémoulade sauce, a Louisiana marvel, is usually served on boiled shrimp. A touch of smoke in the shellfish enhances all the flavors.

1½ pounds medium shrimp

SHRIMP MARINADE

3 tablespoons olive oil
Juice of 1 lemon

2 teaspoons Cajun or Creole seasoning

RÉMOULADE SAUCE

⅓ cup extra-virgin olive oil
2 large celery ribs, chopped
4 green onions, chopped
2 tablespoons Creole mustard
2 tablespoons ketchup
1 tablespoon fresh lemon juice
1 tablespoon capers
1 tablespoon chopped fresh cilantro

2 to 3 teaspoons Tabasco or other hot pepper sauce
1 teaspoon horseradish or more to taste
1 teaspoon paprika
½ teaspoon Cajun or Creole seasoning
½ teaspoon salt or more to taste

Lettuce leaves, for garnish

Serves 4 to 6

Prepare the smoker for barbecuing, bringing the temperature to 180° F to 200° F.

Peel the shrimp, leaving their tails on. In a bowl, toss them with the oil, lemon juice, and seasoning. Let the shrimp marinate at room temperature for 15 to 20 minutes.

While the shrimp marinate, prepare the sauce. Place all the ingredients in a blender or food processor and purée until smooth. Refrigerate until ready to use.

Transfer the shrimp to the smoker and smoke them until just cooked through and lightly fragrant, 15 to 20 minutes. They are ready when opaque, slightly firm, and lightly pink on the exterior. Combine the shrimp with the sauce in a serving dish and chill for 1 to 2 hours. Garnish the dish with the lettuce just before serving.

☆**Serving Suggestion:** Serve as an appetizer preceding Cajun Country Ribs or Creole Crown Roast, or as a light main dish accompanied by Peppery 'Pups.

Eye-Popping Oysters

We've seen these peppery oysters bring jubilation to the most jaded of palates. Crack the peppercorns with a mortar and pestle or use coarse-ground black pepper.

EYE-POPPING MARINADE AND MOP

½ cup bottled clam juice

3 tablespoons fresh lemon juice

3 tablespoons extra-virgin olive oil

1 tablespoon fresh-cracked black pepper

3 to 4 garlic cloves, minced

1 dozen oysters, shucked, with bottom shells and brine reserved

About a dozen ice cubes

Lemon wedges and freshly cracked black pepper, for garnish

Makes 1 dozen

In a lidded jar, combine the clam juice, lemon juice, oil, pepper, garlic, and any oyster brine. Place the oysters in a small bowl or plastic bag. Pour the marinade over the oysters and refrigerate for about 45 minutes.

Prepare the smoker for barbecuing, bringing the temperature to 180° F to 200° F.

Drain the oysters, reserving the marinade for the mop. Arrange each oyster on a half-shell. Bring the marinade to a vigorous boil and boil for several minutes. Reduce the heat and keep the mop warm.

Put the ice cubes in a smokeproof 8-inch-square or 9-by-12-inch baking pan, or in a deep pie pan. Place the oysters on the half-shell on a small grill rack and place the rack over the ice-filled baking pan.

Place the oysters over ice in the smoker as far from the fire as possible. Cook for about 40 minutes, drizzling with the mop once or twice in a wood-burning pit, or as appropriate for your style of smoker. The oysters are done when slightly firm but still plump and juicy. Swab them with the mop when they come off the smoker. Serve the oysters warm with lemon wedges and more pepper.

☆**Serving Suggestion:** Serve as many oysters as you can afford—don't worry, you'll never have any left—with Hand Salad and a lot of Cracklin' Cornbread.

Brined Bluepoints

In contrast to the previous recipe, these firm-textured oysters should dry out during their cooking. Atlantic bluepoints work great this way, but another cold-water oyster can be substituted. The oysters are best smoked a day ahead of serving and their preparation can be spread over two days.

BROWN SUGAR BRINE

¾ cup water
¼ cup kosher salt
3 tablespoons minced onion

3 tablespoons brown sugar
1 teaspoon ground oregano

12 to 18 shucked oysters

BROWN SUGAR RUB

¼ cup kosher salt
2 tablespoons brown sugar

1 teaspoon onion powder
½ teaspoon ground oregano

Extra-virgin olive oil

Makes 12 to 18 oysters

At least 4 hours before you plan to barbecue, begin preparations. Mix the brine ingredients in a large nonreactive bowl, stirring to dissolve. Add the oysters to the liquid and place a plate over them to keep them submerged. Marinate the oysters at room temperature for about 30 minutes.

Rinse the oysters and pat them dry. Transfer them to a platter lined with several thicknesses of paper towels. Allow the oysters to air dry for 1 hour, changing the towels if they become soaked with liquid given off by the oysters.

Combine the rub ingredients in a small bowl. Dunk each oyster lightly in the mixture.

Line the platter with a new batch of paper towels. Return the oysters to the platter. Allow them to air dry for 1 more hour. Rinse the oysters again and pat them

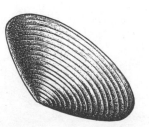

dry. Change the paper toweling on the platter and return the oysters to the platter. Allow the oysters to air dry for 1 more hour. The oysters should have a glossy-looking surface. (The oysters can be covered and refrigerated overnight at this point. Bring them back to room temperature before proceeding.)

Prepare the smoker for barbecuing, bringing the temperature to 180° F to 200° F.

Transfer the oysters to a small grill rack and place them in the smoker as far from the fire as possible. Cook them until somewhat shrunken and dried, yet short of shriveled and toughened, 45 to 55 minutes. Place the oysters in a small bowl and cover them with the oil. Refrigerate overnight or for up to 2 days. Serve at room temperature.

☆**Serving Suggestion:** We prefer the oysters as an appetizer, accompanied by bread or crackers.

A Honey of a Lobster Tail

Honey enhances the already sweet flavor of a juicy Maine lobster tail. In this dish, the smoke is deliciously subtle and light.

A HONEY OF A MARINADE AND OPTIONAL MOP

2 cups seafood stock	2 tablespoons white vinegar
1 cup dry white wine	2 tablespoons kosher salt
½ cup honey	2 bay leaves
¼ cup extra-virgin olive oil	2 teaspoons dried thyme

Four 6-ounce to 7-ounce Maine lobster tails

Serves 4

About 1½ to 2 hours before you plan to barbecue, mix together the marinade ingredients in a saucepan and bring to a boil over high heat. Stir, if

A barbecue competition team composed entirely of Post Office employees, the U.S. Porkmasters cook in a converted mail jeep. There's a charcoal oven under the hood and a smoker in the rear, vented, of course, through the exhaust pipe.

needed, to dissolve the honey and salt. Remove the pan from the heat and let the mixture cool to room temperature.

Immerse the lobster tails in the cooled marinade and refrigerate them for 1 hour.

Prepare your smoker for barbecuing, bringing the temperature to 180° F to 200° F.

Drain the lobster, reserving the marinade if you plan to baste the tails (see chapter 3, "To Mop or Not"). To make the mop, bring the marinade back to a vigorous boil over high heat and boil for several minutes. Keep the liquid warm over low heat.

Transfer the lobster tails to the smoker, placing the lobster as far from the heat as possible. Smoke until just cooked through and tender, 35 to 40 minutes. Mop once or twice in a wood-burning pit, or as appropriate for your style of smoker. Serve the lobster warm or chilled.

☆**Serving Suggestion:** Start a special dinner with 007 Shrimp. Add a green salad with a citrus vinaigrette and Maque Choux Peppers. For a delectable finale, top angel food cake with fresh fruit. For a luscious salad, slice chilled lobster and combine it with mixed greens tossed with a honey-based dressing.

BBQ tips For barbecuing on a covered grill, we like to use a combination of wood chips and chunks. The chips produce more initial smoke but the chunks last much longer. Be sure to replenish the wood as the vented smoke dies out, which may be as often as every 30 minutes if you're using chips alone.

The American Bus Association selected the annual Big Pig Jig in Vienna, Georgia, as one of the Top 100 Events in North America. In addition to a big barbecue cook-off, the week-long October festival features everything from beauty pageants to a hog-calling contest.

Jungle Prince Scallops

A Hawaiian Thai specialty, jungle prince curry tastes as intriguing as it sounds.

1 pound bay scallops
Clam juice or seafood stock (optional)

2 tablespoons peanut oil
1 tablespoon chopped lemongrass, preferably fresh
2 teaspoons minced fresh ginger root
2 garlic cloves, minced
2 teaspoons Thai green curry paste or more to taste

1 cup canned coconut milk (not cream of coconut)
1 tablespoon Asian fish sauce or 2 tablespoons soy sauce
1 cup shredded bok choy or Napa cabbage
½ cup chopped fresh basil

Serves 4

Prepare the smoker for barbecuing, bringing the temperature to 180° F to 200° F.

If the scallops aren't moist and plump, soak them for about 10 minutes in enough clam juice or seafood stock to cover.

Arrange the scallops on a small grill rack or baking sheet. Smoke as far from the fire as possible until just barely cooked through and opaque, 10 to 15 minutes. Remove the scallops from the smoker.

Warm the oil in a skillet over medium heat. Stir in the lemongrass, ginger, garlic, and curry paste and cook for 2 to 3 minutes. Pour in the coconut milk and fish sauce and simmer until reduced by about one-third. Stir in the bok choy and cook for an additional 2 to 3 minutes. Mix in the scallops and the basil, remove from the heat, and serve immediately.

☆Serving Suggestion: Serve over white rice. Add a cool dessert such as Booker's Bourbon Mint Ice Cream.

Scallop and Snapper Ceviche

The citrus juice in traditional ceviche chemically "cooks" the seafood. In this version, we finish the process with smoke, adding another contrasting flavor.

2 oranges, peeled and sectioned
½ pound red snapper, yellowtail snapper, or other firm-fleshed white fish, cut in bite-size chunks
½ pound scallops (small bay scallops can be used as is, larger sea scallops should be halved)
⅓ cup fresh lime juice
1 Hass avocado, cubed
1 tomato, preferably Roma or Italian plum, chopped
¼ cup finely diced red bell pepper
¼ cup finely diced red onion
1 to 2 fresh serranos or about 1 fresh jalapeño, minced
1 to 2 tablespoons extra-virgin olive oil
¼ teaspoon salt

Diced yellow tomato or yellow bell pepper (optional, for more color)
Lime wedges, for garnish

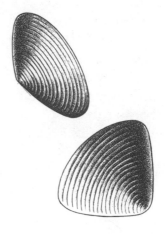

Makes 4 appetizer portions

Squeeze enough orange sections to make 2 tablespoons of juice. Cut the remaining sections in halves or thirds and reserve.

Marinate the snapper and scallops in the lime and orange juices in a nonreactive bowl for 30 to 40 minutes.

While the seafood "cooks," prepare the smoker for barbecuing, bringing the temperature to 180° F to 200° F.

Drain the seafood and arrange it on a small grill rack or in a pie pan. Cook it as far from the fire as possible until warmed through, about 15 minutes. Taste one morsel. If the smoke hasn't yet gently soaked into the snapper and scallops, allow a few more minutes. Be careful to avoid drying out the seafood.

Lightly mix the fish with the orange sections and remaining ingredients in a medium bowl. Refrigerate for up to 30 minutes. Serve in parfait glasses, margarita glasses, or glass bowls to show off the ceviche's colors. Garnish with the limes.

☆**Serving Suggestions:** For a weekend lunch, serve the ceviche with Sweet Potato Biscuits and finish with Santa Fe Capirotada.

Cookin' Clams

Contrary to some claims, the New England clambake was not the first form of barbecue in the country. A traditional clambake uses a wood fire in a pit for cooking, like barbecue, but the clams are steamed with moisture from seaweed rather than smoked. If you would really rather have barbecue, just leave out the wet seaweed.

4 to 5 dozen fresh clams, in   About ½ cup cornmeal
    their shells

Melted garlic butter or Old-Fashioned High-Cholesterol
    Great-Tasting Southern Sauce (page 293) (optional)

Serves 6

Soak the clams in several changes of water, each containing 1 to 2 tablespoons cornmeal, which helps eliminate grit and impurities. This can be done over several hours or overnight. Discard any clams that aren't tightly closed.

Prepare the smoker for barbecuing, bringing the temperature to 180° F to 200° F.

Arrange the clams in a single layer on a small grill rack or baking sheet. Depending on the size of your smoker and cooking implements, this may require cooking in more than one batch. Place the clams as far from the fire as possible. Cook them until the shells pop open, 10 to 15 minutes. Discard any clams that don't open within several minutes of the rest of the batch.

The first Great Yankee Rib Cook-Off made Boston forget about clam chowder for a couple of days in September, 1992. Contestants came from all over, but local chef Marc Rose took the $10,000 grand prize.

Serve the clams immediately, with garlic butter or Old-Fashioned High-Cholesterol Great-Tasting Southern Sauce, if you wish.

☆**Serving Suggestions:** For a Fourth of July feast, complement the clams with Smoky Corn-on-the-Cob, Creamy Coleslaw, and onions and red potatoes boiled with generous spoonfuls of Wild Willy's Number One-derful Rub. Have at least two fruit desserts on hand, perhaps Long-on-Strawberries Shortcake and Wild Huckleberry Pie with Coconut Crumble.

Crab in Garlic Cream

This one is richer than the Rockefeller clan.

GARLIC CREAM

1 tablespoon butter	12-ounce can evaporated milk
3 garlic cloves, minced	½ teaspoon salt or more to taste
1 tablespoon minced onion	½ teaspoon white pepper
1 cup heavy cream	

1½ pounds king crab legs
8 ounces seafood sausage, preferably a link style
Oil, preferably canola or corn

Cooked spinach fettuccine or other noodles

Serves 4 as a main course, 6 as an appetizer

Prepare the smoker for barbecuing, bringing the temperature to 180° F to 200° F.

In a large saucepan, melt the butter over medium heat. Add the garlic and onion and sauté until softened. Add the cream and milk and stir in the salt and pepper. Simmer until reduced by one-third. Keep the sauce warm.Crack the crab legs at the joints and in several other spots. Oil the legs and the seafood sausage. Place the sausage on the smoker. After the sausage has cooked for about 45 minutes, add the crab to the smoker. Cook both for another 15 minutes. The sausage should be cooked through but still succulent and the exposed crab meat should flake easily. Both should have a gentle but distinct smoke taste.

Remove the crab from the shells and slice the sausage into thin rounds. Mix both with the sauce and heat through if needed. Serve the mixture over fettuccine or noodles.

☆**Variation:** Add Cookin' Clams, A Honey of a Lobster Tail, or other smoked seafood to the sauce.

Katzen Dawgs

The name is clever and so is the idea—smoked catfish hush puppies that are superb for appetizers or a main course. Offer a tip of your gimme cap to John Wysor, from the Spoon River Charcuterie in Charlotte, North Carolina, for concocting the original recipe, and another nod to Donna Ellis at Cookshack for making it available. Use your own smoked catfish, which can be cooked up to a couple of days in advance, or buy some from the store.

¾ pound smoked catfish (such as Peppered Catfish, page 206)
½ cup buttermilk
½ cup minced onion
2 tablespoons minced green onion tops
2 eggs
1 tablespoon melted bacon drippings or butter
1 tablespoon fresh lemon juice
1 teaspoon Tabasco or other hot pepper sauce or more to taste
¾ cup yellow cornmeal, preferably stone-ground
¼ cup all-purpose flour
1 tablespoon baking powder
½ teaspoon baking soda
½ teaspoon fresh-ground black pepper
¼ teaspoon salt

Oil for deep-frying, preferably peanut or canola
Tartar sauce or Creole Classic Barbecue Sauce (page 299) (optional)

Bunny Tuttle, of the Kansas City Barbeque Society, and her husband, Rich, have a great approach to family vacations. Several times a year they pack the kids, a tent, and a smoker and take off for a weekend of fun at a barbecue cooking contest. If other families start catching on to the idea, the Disney empire had better beware.

Serves 4 as a main dish or 6 to 8 as an appetizer

Remove the bones from the catfish, if necessary, and chop the fish coarsely. In a bowl, mix the fish, buttermilk, onion, green onions, eggs, bacon drippings, lemon juice, and Tabasco.

Combine the cornmeal, flour, baking powder, baking soda, pepper, and salt in a large bowl. Pour the liquid ingredients into the dry. Stir just to blend.

In a heavy skillet, heat 3 inches of oil to 365° F. Drop heaping tablespoons of the batter into the oil, a few at a time. Don't overcrowd. The hush puppies will rise to the surface as they cook, so turn them if they are browning unevenly. Fry until golden brown on all sides, about 3 minutes. Drain. Serve immediately with tartar sauce or Creole Classic Barbecue Sauce, if you wish.

☆**Serving Suggestion:** For supper, match the Dawgs with Sweet and Sour Cukes and 'Nana Nut Salad. When you want a hearty appetizer, serve the Dawgs as finger food, like Caribbean accras (cod fritters), accompanied by icy drinks such as Cham-gria, Apricoritas, or Derby Day Mint Juleps.

☆ Garden of Eatin' ☆

For some barbecue purists, fish stretches the limits of the 'Q.' Vegetables just go beyond the bounds. You start putting squash in a pit and they'll be dancing in the hog trough with exasperation.

So let 'em. The fact is, some vegetables and even fruits taste great smoked. It may be awhile before you find a yam barbecue festival, or an authentic Bar-B-Q joint featuring pit-smoked apples, but good pitmasters should always be ready to take some liberties in the privacy of their backyard. Try these delicious dishes and they'll probably spark some other licentious ideas.

Vidalias 'n' Georgia BBQ Sauce

Almost the size of footballs, Georgia's famous Vidalia onions are available only in the late spring and early summer, just in time to kick off the barbecue season. When slathered with a mustardy sauce from the same state, smoked Vidalias and other sweet onions become golden orbs of succulence.

3 Vidalia or other large sweet onions Oil, preferably canola or corn

Golden Mustard Barbecue Sauce (page 293) or other mustard-based barbecue sauce

Serves 6

Prepare the smoker for barbecuing, bringing the temperature to 200° F to 220° F.

Slice each onion in half and peel the outer layer. Cut down to, but not through, the base of each onion half in crisscross directions to make an onion "flower." Rub a thin coat of oil over the onions and wrap each half in foil.

Transfer the onions to the smoker and cook for 30 to 35 minutes. Remove the foil or peel it back to form a flat base and brush the onions with a thick coating of barbecue sauce. Continue cooking for an additional 35 to 45 minutes, until the onion is tender. Remove the onions from the smoker and brush with additional barbecue sauce before serving.

☆**Variation:** Instead of topping the onions with a mustard-based barbecue sauce, substitute Pop Mop (page 54) using Dr Pepper, R.C. Cola, or Coke. You'll end up with a sweet caramelized flavor.

"Food like barbecue and chili remains an embarrassment to people who want to think of themselves as living in a big-league city that is sophisticated enough to have an array of Continental restaurants—Continental restaurants that are modeled, an unwary traveler can discover, on the continent of Antarctica, where everything starts out frozen…. [These city dwellers are] afflicted with a disease of the American provinces I have managed to isolate and identify as rubaphobia—not the fear of rubes but the fear of being thought of as a rube." Calvin Trillin, *Alice, Let's Eat*

☆**Serving Suggestion:** Try these when you're preparing traditional barbecued pork, such as The Renowned Mr. Brown, A Perfect Picnic, or Going Whole Hog. They'd be a proud accompaniment to Ginger-Glazed Ham, too.

BBQ tips If you want to experiment with vegetables, keep a couple of general principles in mind. Usually you coat vegetables with oil before putting them in the smoker, to keep them from drying out. That may be all you do, because simple preparations are often the best. You may want to play creatively with dry rubs, pastes, marinades, or mops, but you are less likely to need them than when you barbecue meat.

One of the biggest barbecue events of the year, Kansas City's American Royal cooking contest, got off to a slow start in 1979, when it drew 25 competitors and maybe 2,000 spectators. Today the main cook-off, open to anyone, attracts about 200 teams and close to 50,000 fans.

Peabody-style Stuffed Onions

Best known for the ducks that parade and swim in its lobby, the Peabody Hotel in Memphis also earns lesser kudos for its stuffed onions. If the kitchen smoked them—the dish, not the ducks—the onions might rival the quackers in acclaim.

4 medium onions	Oil, preferably canola or corn
1 tablespoon butter	6 tablespoons Romano or
2 garlic cloves, minced	Parmesan cheese, plus
12 ounces fresh spinach, chopped	additional for sprinkling over the onions
1½ cups cooked rice	½ teaspoon dried sage
1 cup ground ham (leftovers from Ginger Glazed Ham, page 80, are especially flavorful)	¼ teaspoon dried thyme
	Salt and fresh-ground black pepper to taste
	¾ cup chicken broth
1 cup dry cornbread crumbs or other bread crumbs	1 egg, beaten lightly

Serves 8

Prepare the smoker for barbecuing, bringing the temperature to 200° F to 220° F.

Slice the ends off the onions and cut them in half horizontally, but don't remove the skins. Carefully scoop out the centers of the onion halves with a melon baller or spoon, leaving a shell about ⅓ inch to ½ inch thick. Coat the onions with oil.

Transfer the onions to the smoker and cook for 30 to 35 minutes, until softened but not yet tender.

While the onions are cooking, prepare the stuffing. Chop half of the onion center pieces and set them aside. Save the other half for another use.

In a skillet, warm the butter over medium heat. Add the chopped onion and the garlic and sauté for 1 to 2 minutes. Stir in the spinach and cook until limp, adding a tablespoon of water if the mixture begins to stick. Stir in the rice, ham, bread crumbs, cheese, sage, thyme, salt, and pepper, and add as much of the broth as needed to bind the mixture together. It should be moist but not soupy. Mix in the egg.

Remove the onions from the smoker and, when cool enough to handle, peel them. Spoon the stuffing into the onions and sprinkle a bit of Romano or Parmesan over the top of each. Return the onions to the smoker and cook them until they are tender and the stuffing is lightly browned, an additional 20 to 25 minutes. Serve hot.

☆**Serving Suggestion:** These make a good lunch entrée accompanied by a fruit salad, perhaps Mango and Avocado Salad. Serve slices of South Georgia Pound Cake for dessert and, if you like, Booker's Bourbon Mint Ice Cream.

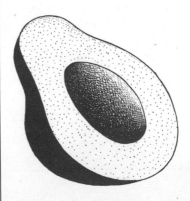

The woodsy flavor you get from grilling vegetables—now a trendy way of cooking them—is deeper and more robust when the food is slow smoked. In addition, you are less likely to dry out or char vegetables in a smoker than on a grill.

Sweet Potatoes with Orange-Pecan Butter

Like onions, sweet potatoes have a natural affinity for smoke. The deep caramel flavor needs no garnish, but we like to gild the lily with the addition of a simple butter sauce.

4   small sweet potatoes   Oil, preferably canola or corn

ORANGE-PECAN BUTTER

4 to 6 tablespoons butter   ¼ teaspoon dry mustard
1   teaspoon honey   Salt and fresh-ground black
Juice and zest of 1 orange   pepper to taste
2   tablespoons chopped pecans

Serves 4

Prepare the smoker for barbecuing, bringing the temperature to 200° F to 220° F.

Scrub the potatoes well, prick them in several spots, and rub a light film of oil over them. Transfer the potatoes to the smoker and cook them until they are soft, about 2 hours. The potatoes can sit for 15 minutes before serving, or you can wrap them in foil to keep warm for up to an hour.

While the potatoes cook, prepare the orange-pecan butter. Melt the butter and honey together in a small saucepan over low heat. Add the remaining ingredients and stir together. Reheat the butter, if necessary, just before serving.

To serve, slit open the top of each of the sweet potatoes and drizzle with the orange-pecan butter. Serve hot.

BBQ tips Try Candied Sweet Potatoes or any favorite sweet potato recipe using smoked spuds. They add a delicious depth to the flavor of most dishes.

Drunken Sweet Potatoes

Tipsy from tequila, these potatoes enhance any Southwest barbecue spread.

¼ cup butter	¼ teaspoon salt
1¼ pounds (about 1 large) grated sweet potato	¼ cup tequila
2½ tablespoons brown sugar	Juice of 2 limes

Serves 4

Prepare the smoker for barbecuing, bringing the temperature to 200° F to 220° F.

In a cast-iron skillet or smokeproof baking dish, melt the butter. Stir in the sweet potatoes and then pat the potatoes down into a thick, even layer. Sprinkle the brown sugar and the salt over the potatoes.

Transfer the potatoes to the smoker and cook for 1 hour. Stir in 3 tablespoons of the tequila and half of the lime juice, pat the potatoes back down again, and continue cooking the potatoes another 50 to 60 minutes, until they are quite tender but crisped a bit around the edges. Remove the potatoes from the smoker and stir in the remaining tequila and lime juice. Serve warm.

☆**Serving Suggestion:** Pair the potatoes with Bona Fide Fajitas and Texas Peach Cobbler.

The Memphis in May World Championship Barbecue Cooking Contest brags of being the biggest event of its kind in the country. Since the first cook-off in 1978, the annual affair has attracted teams from all corners of the globe, including Ireland, France, Estonia, Thailand, and New Zealand. Senator Bob Kerrey of Nebraska took a shot at the title once and Vice President Al Gore has competed regularly.

Scalloped Green Chile Potatoes

A touch of smoke and a kiss of green chile wake up sleepy scalloped potatoes. Use a fresh or frozen chile, because the canned version is pretty drowsy itself.

3 baking potatoes
Oil, preferably canola or corn
¾ cup chopped roasted green
   chile, preferably New
   Mexican, Anaheim, or
   poblano, fresh or frozen
¾ cup grated Monterey jack
   cheese (3 ounces)

⅓ cup chopped red onion
1 cup half-and-half
Salt and fresh-ground black
   pepper to taste
Nutmeg

Serves 6

Prepare the smoker for barbecuing, bringing the temperature to 200° F to 220° F.

Slice the potatoes into chunks about 1 inch thick. Coat each chunk with oil.

Place the potatoes on a small grill rack, transfer them to the smoker, and smoke for 50 to 75 minutes, or until they are partially cooked and well perfumed with smoke. When the potatoes are cool enough to handle, slice them thinly.

Preheat the oven to 350° F and grease a baking dish. Layer one-third of the potatoes with about one-third of the chile, cheese, onion, half-and-half, salt, and pepper. Repeat the layers until all the ingredients are used. Dust liberally with nutmeg.

Bake, covered, for 40 minutes. Uncover the dish and bake for an additional 10 minutes, or until the potatoes are meltingly tender. Serve warm.

Smoked Spud Skins

As potatoes themselves do, the skins step lively after a barbecue bath.

8   baking potatoes
Butter or olive oil
1 to 2 tablespoons Wild Willy's
   Number One-derful Rub
   (page 36), Cajun Ragin' Rub
   (page 38), or other savory
   seasoning blend

¾ cup grated Monterey jack or
   cheddar cheese

Sliced green onions, for garnish
Sauce Olé (page 296) or Creole Classic Barbecue Sauce (page 299)
   (optional)

Serves 4 to 6

Bake or boil the potatoes until tender. Then cut in halves or quarters and scoop out to leave a ¼-inch to ½-inch shell. (Reserve the scooped-out portions for mashed potatoes or another use.)

Prepare the smoker for barbecuing, bringing the temperature to 200° F to 220° F.

Rub the potato skins with a thin coat of butter or oil. Sprinkle the skins, inside and out, with the rub or other dry spice mixture.

Transfer the skins to the smoker and cook for 55 to 65 minutes, until they are browned and crispy. Sprinkle the cheese over the skins and cook for an additional couple of minutes, until the cheese melts. Top with the green onions. Serve piping hot, with Sauce Olé or Creole Classic Barbecue Sauce, if you wish.

Two legendary Texas pitmasters retired in recent years. Sonny Bryan attracted all of Dallas to his Smokehouse shack for three decades. You never knew who you would see eating one of the magnificent brisket sandwiches in his parking lot, dribbling sauce on anything from overalls to designer dresses. "Stubbs" Stubblefield, of Lubbock fame, became the caterer of choice for West Texas musicians and artists. When Jo Harvey and Terry Allen celebrated a big wedding anniversary in Santa Fe, they trucked Stubbs and his pit hundreds of miles to cook the 'Q' and join the fun. Both men made memories.

Bronzed Artichokes

This two-step preparation yields exceptionally tender arti-chokes. You can do the smoking several days in advance of the steaming and serving.

2 medium artichokes   2 teaspoons olive oil
Juice of 1 lemon

Golden Mustard Barbecue Sauce (page 293) or vinaigrette dressing (optional)

Serves 4

At least 3 hours before you plan to eat the arti-chokes, trim the artichokes, cutting off all tough leaf tips. Spread the leaves slightly. Place the arti-chokes in a bowl and add the lemon juice and olive oil. Pour enough water over the artichokes to submerge them. Soak the artichokes for at least 30 minutes, and up to 2 hours.

Prepare the smoker for barbecuing, bringing the temperature to 200° F to 220° F.

Drain the artichokes. Place the artichokes in the smoker and cook for 1½ to 1¾ hours, until the leaves are deeply bronzed and have loosened somewhat.

Remove the artichokes from the smoker and steam them over boiling water until very tender, 25 to 30 minutes. The artichokes can be eaten warm or chilled. Serve whole, accompanied by Golden Mustard Barbecue Sauce or vinaigrette dressing, if you wish.

Abe Davis, a Lebanese immigrant, started selling his barbecue in 1924 at a streetside stand in Clarksdale, Mississippi. His family still runs Abe's in a new, modern building and they still prepare their pork sandwiches in their own distinctive way, smoking the meat first and then grilling it for a crusty finish.

Black-Eyed Pea Cakes

Almost anything flat and porous, from hamburgers to vegetable cakes, is well suited to barbecue.

CAKES

2 cups cooked black-eyed peas, well-drained	1 egg yolk
½ cup saltine-style cracker crumbs	2 teaspoons minced pickled jalapeño
2 tablespoons minced red bell pepper	2 teaspoons mayonnaise
2 tablespoons minced onion	1 teaspoon prepared yellow mustard
1 tablespoon minced fresh parsley	1 garlic clove, minced

Approximately ½ cup saltine-style cracker crumbs
1 tablespoon butter
1 tablespoon oil, preferably canola or corn

Golden Mustard Barbecue Sauce (page 293) or Carolina Red (page 292)

Serves 2 to 3 as a main dish or 4 to 6 as a side dish

In a food processor, purée 1 cup of the peas. Place the puréed peas and whole peas in a bowl and add the remaining cake ingredients. Refrigerate the mixture for at least 1 hour, and up to 24 hours.

Prepare the smoker for barbecuing, bringing the temperature to 200° F to 220° F. Grease a smokeproof baking dish.

Remove the mixture from the refrigerator. It should be moist, but stiff enough to form loose cakes. Place the additional cracker crumbs on a small plate. Make 6 to 8 cakes, dipping each in the cracker crumbs and coating well.

Warm the butter and oil in a skillet over medium-high heat. Fry the cakes for about 30 seconds per side, just long enough to crisp their surfaces.

Roving food writers Jane and Michael Stern vividly remember their first visit to D & H Bar-B-Que in Manning, South Carolina. As they say in their wonderful *Roadfood*, "It was here, twenty years ago, that we detoured from writing a book about truck drivers and ate some of our first genuine southern barbecue. Since then we have spent our life looking for good food, barbecue foremost among our targets; and the hunger inspired by that first real Carolina pig-out has kept us on the road for a million miles."

Transfer the cakes to the smoker and cook for 20 to 30 minutes, until they are firm and heated through. Remove the cakes from the smoker and serve hot, with Golden Mustard Barbecue Sauce or Carolina Red, if you wish.

☆**Serving Suggestion:** The cakes make a satisfying main dish enhanced by a side of Sweet and Sour Cukes. You'll still have room for Black Walnut Cake afterwards.

Powdrell's Barbecue in Albuquerque, New Mexico, has its own distinctive way of spicing up the 'Q.' Order a side of what the legislature named the official state vegetable—chiles—which the kitchen roasts to perfection.

Smoky Corn-on-the-Cob

6 ears of corn, with husks   6 slices bacon
Salt and fresh-ground black
    pepper to taste

Old-Fashioned High-Cholesterol Great-Tasting Southern Sauce
    (page 293) (optional)

Serves 6

Pull back the corn husks enough to remove the silks. Place the corn in a large bowl and cover it with cold water. Soak the corn for at least 30 minutes, and up to 2 hours. Drain the corn.

Prepare the smoker for barbecuing, bringing the temperature to 200° F to 220° F.

Salt and pepper the corn and wrap a piece of bacon around each ear. Rearrange the husks in their original position. Tear 1 or 2 husks into strips and use them to tie around the top of the ears to hold the husks in place.

Place the corn in the smoker and cook until tender, 1 to 1¼ hours. Remove the corn from the smoker and discard the husks and bacon. Serve hot.

☆**Variation:** Instead of wrapping the corn in bacon, try slathering the corn in extra-virgin olive oil, unrefined corn oil, or garlic-flavored oil. All add great taste, too.

Ratatouille

We realized that ratatouille had been adopted as American fare about a decade ago when a cowboy cafe in Cheyenne, Wyoming, offered it to us as the vegetable of the day. We knew the dish still had some territory to cover, though, because the waiter called it "rat tool."

1 whole medium eggplant, sliced thick (do not peel)	2 garlic cloves, minced
2 leeks, halved	¾ cup canned crushed tomatoes
1 green bell pepper	½ cup chicken stock
1 red bell pepper	¼ cup slivered cracked green Greek olives or other green olives with character
1 medium onion, sliced thick	
3 tablespoons extra-virgin olive oil	

Serves 6

Prepare the smoker for barbecuing, bringing the temperature to 200° F to 220° F.

Rub the eggplant, leeks, bell peppers, and onion with oil, reserving about 1 tablespoon of the oil. Place the vegetables in the smoker as far from the heat as possible. Cook for 35 to 45 minutes, until the vegetables are crisp-tender. Remove the vegetables from the smoker and, when cool enough to handle, chop into bite-size pieces.

In a heavy skillet, heat the remaining oil over medium heat. Add the garlic and sauté for 1 minute. Stir in the smoked vegetables and any accumulated juice. Add the tomatoes and chicken stock and simmer the mixture until it's very thick and the vegetables are tender. Stir in the olives and heat through. Serve warm.

☆**Variation:** Ratatouille makes a good soup, too. Purée leftovers with chicken stock and half-and-half in equal parts.

Uncle Billy's SouthSide Barbeque in Portland, Maine, is about as far north as you find barbecue. Nephew Jonny—also known as Jonathan St. Laurent, classically trained as a French chef—does the cooking. He describes his 'Q,' and offers recipes, in the witty and wise *Uncle Billy's Downeast Barbeque Book* (Dancing Bear Books).

Warm Mushroom Salad

Great ideas travel faster than gossip at a church picnic. Pat Wilson, the maker of the Cameron Stove-Top Smoker, passed this on to us after picking it up from Allen Frey, former owner of Aubergine's, a Woodstock, Vermont, restaurant.

12 ounces mushrooms (wild varieties, Portobello in particular, are especially nice)

Salt

DRESSING

¾ cup chopped tomatoes, preferably Romas or Italian plum, or canned crushed tomatoes
⅓ cup extra-virgin olive oil
1 tablespoon balsamic vinegar
1 tablespoon chopped fresh basil

1 tablespoon minced fresh parsley
3 garlic cloves, minced
2 green onions, sliced
Salt and coarse-ground black pepper to taste

Lettuce leaves, for garnish

Serves 4 to 6

Prepare the smoker for barbecuing, bringing the temperature to 200° F to 220° F.

Slice the mushrooms into large bite-size pieces and salt them lightly. Arrange the mushrooms on a small grill rack or a piece of heavy-duty foil.

Place the mushrooms in the smoker and cook for 15 to 20 minutes, until they ooze liquid and are cooked through.

While the mushrooms cook, mix together the dressing ingredients. Add the mushrooms and mix again lightly. Mound on the lettuce leaves and serve warm.

☆**Serving Suggestion:** Make lunch out of the salad or use it as the starter before a full-flavored beef dish.

BBQ tips The Cameron Stove-Top Smoker (see page 14) cooks at a higher temperature than you ordinarily want for barbecue, but it still imparts plenty of smoke flavor to porous foods, such as fish. If you're cooking chicken in this style of smoker, remove the skin and cut the meat into thick strips. For a steak or a similar cut of red meat, smoke it for 15 to 20 minutes and then finish it with high heat over a grill or in a skillet.

BBQ tips The kind of sawdust you use in the Cameron Stove-Top Smoker makes a noticeable difference in the level of smoky flavor you get. Use alder for the lightest touch and pecan or mesquite for the heaviest dose.

Maque Choux Peppers

An assertive Cajun corn dish, maque choux dances a fais do do on the tongue when combined with crimson peppers.

4 medium red bell peppers	1 cup chicken stock
3 tablespoons butter	¼ cup cream or half-and-half
2 tablespoons oil, preferably unrefined corn	Several healthy splashes of Tabasco or other hot pepper sauce
2 cups corn kernels, fresh or frozen	2 cups dry cornbread crumbs or other bread crumbs
1 medium onion, chopped	1 egg white, beaten
½ medium green bell pepper	Salt and fresh-ground black pepper to taste
½ teaspoon white pepper	
Salt to taste	

Serves 4

Slice off the tops of the peppers about ½ inch down from the stems. Remove the seeds and cores from

American jazz and barbecue grew up together in the Kansas City ghettos of the 1920s and 1930s. African-American pace-setters, from Charlie Parker to Charlie Bryant, nourished both, often at the same speakeasies and clubs.

the peppers. If any won't stand upright, slice a little off the bottom, being careful not to cut into the pepper's cavity. Reserve the peppers and their tops.

Melt the butter and oil in a medium skillet. Add the corn, onion, and green bell pepper and sauté over medium heat until fragrant. Add the white pepper and salt. Cover the pan and cook for about 10 minutes. Remove the lid, add the stock, cream, and Tabasco, and continue cooking, uncovered, until about half the liquid has evaporated. Remove the filling from the heat and mix in the cornbread crumbs and egg white.

Prepare the smoker for barbecuing, bringing the temperature to 200° F to 220° F.

Grease a smokeproof baking dish that can hold the peppers snugly upright.

Stuff each bell pepper with a portion of the filling. Replace the tops of the peppers and secure with toothpicks. Arrange the peppers in the prepared dish.

Transfer the peppers to the smoker. Cook until they are tender but still hold their shape, 65 to 75 minutes. Remove the toothpicks and serve the peppers warm.

☆**Serving Suggestion:** The peppers make a hearty meatless main dish, accompanied by Buttermilk Biscuits and a simple green salad. Finish with Peanutty Pie.

BBQ tips Before you begin barbecuing, take a close look at your cooking grate. If you forgot to clean it the last time you used the smoker, scrap the grate thoroughly with a wire brush. Then always spray the surface with a vegetable oil cooking spray to prevent food from sticking to the grate.

Calico Pepper Salad

On a long day of barbecuing, nothing is better for lunch than this colorful salad. It also makes a good side dish with smoked meats.

3 large bell peppers, preferably 1 each of red, yellow, and green	3 garlic cloves
	1 tablespoon oil, preferably canola or corn
1 small onion	1 tablespoon garlic-flavored oil
1 fresh green chile, preferably New Mexican, Anaheim, or poblano (optional)	1 tablespoon minced fresh cilantro
	½ teaspoon ground cumin
1 fresh jalapeño or 1 to 2 fresh serranos	Dashes of red wine vinegar
	Salt to taste

Serves 2 to 3 as a main dish or 4 to 6 as a side dish

Prepare the smoker for barbecuing, bringing the temperature to 200° F to 220° F.

Rub the bell peppers, onion, green chile, jalapeño, and garlic with enough canola or corn oil to coat their surfaces lightly.

Transfer the vegetables to the smoker, as far from the heat as possible. Cook until they are well softened, 25 to 30 minutes for the garlic and 65 to 75 minutes for everything else. Remove each of the vegetables as it is done.

Place the bell peppers, the green chile, and the jalapeño in a plastic bag to steam. Chop the garlic and onion finely and transfer them to a bowl. Remove the peppers from the bag and pull the skin off of each. Slice the bell peppers and green chile into thin ribbons and add them to the garlic and onion. Mince the jalapeño and add about half of it to the bowl.

Stir in the garlic-flavored oil, cilantro, cumin, and a bit of vinegar and salt, and taste. Add more jalapeño or the other seasonings as desired. Serve warm or chilled.

The AutoZone barbecue team is always in the running for showmanship awards. At the Memphis in May contest in 1993, the group staged an elaborate skit about Boris Borscht, a Russian ballet dancer who gets fed up with the food at home and sets out to find real flavor. Boris samples and rejects the cooking of France, Italy, and Mexico. Discouraged, he pins his last hopes on Memphis, where he blows his tutu eating barbecue. Too fat to dance any longer, he starts a new life as Boris Barbecue, "the 'Q' man."

☆**Serving Suggestion:** Pair this with spaghetti tossed with olive oil, garlic, and fresh chopped tomatoes. Round out the meal with Parmesan-topped crusty bread.

BBQ tips It's just as important to keep the inside of your smoker clean as it is the cooking grate. A good scrub after each use insures efficient operation and prevents residue from a previous barbecue from flavoring your next meal. Empty out ashes from the firebox and liquids left in a water pan or reservoir.

Hominy and Summer Squash Nuggets

Here's one example of how barbecue cooking can transform a familiar casserole dish into a new delight. Experiment with other favorite recipes.

2 tablespoons oil, preferably corn or canola
½ medium onion, chopped
1 pound yellow squash, diced
2 tablespoons diced red bell pepper or pimiento
1 to 2 pickled jalapeños, minced
¼ teaspoon dried oregano, preferably Mexican

2 tablespoons milk
1¾ cups hominy (1 can), drained
3 tablespoons sour cream
½ cup grated jalapeño jack or sharp cheddar cheese (2 ounces)
3 to 4 tablespoons crushed corn chips

Serves 4

Prepare the smoker for barbecuing, bringing the temperature to 200° F to 220° F. Grease a smoke-proof baking dish.

In a skillet, warm the oil over medium heat. Add the onion and sauté until it is well softened but not browned. Mix in the squash, bell pepper, jalapeños, and oregano, and continue cooking until the vegetables are limp. Add the milk, reduce the heat slightly, and cover the pan. Simmer the mixture for 15 to 20 minutes, or until the squash is very soft. Remove the pan from the heat and stir in the hominy and sour cream.

Layer half of the vegetable mixture into the prepared baking dish and sprinkle it with half of the cheese. Top with the remaining mixture and cheese. Sprinkle the crushed corn chips over the top. Transfer the dish to the smoker and cook for 40 to 50 minutes, until the mixture is hot, bubbly, and lightly smoky. Serve immediately.

Zooks and Cilantro Sauce

If you have a garden, it probably overproduces zucchini around the height of the barbecue season. We use some of the largest this way.

4 whole zucchini, 6 to 8 ounces each
Oil, preferably canola, corn, or olive

Wild Willy's Number One-derful Rub (page 36) or other savory seasoning blend (optional)

SAUCE

1 cup chopped fresh cilantro
½ cup chopped fresh parsley
2 green onions, chopped
1 garlic clove, minced
½ cup chicken or vegetable stock

¼ cup half-and-half
Juice of 1 lime
Salt and fresh-ground black pepper to taste

Serves 4 or 8

Prepare the smoker for barbecuing, bringing the temperature to 200° F to 220° F.

Rub the zucchini liberally with the oil. Sprinkle with the dry rub, if you wish.

Place the zucchini in the smoker and cook for about 1 hour, or until tender.

Barbecue is a southern specialty even in a northern city like Chicago. The biggest concentration of Bar-B-Q joints is on the tough South Side, where some of the take-out places pass your order under bulletproof glass. Stalwart rib lovers head to Lem's or Leon's, both neighborhood institutions.

While the zucchini cooks, make the sauce. Combine the cilantro, parsley, onions, and garlic in a food processor and process until smooth. Add the stock and half-and-half and process again until combined.

Pour the sauce mixture into a saucepan. Cook it over medium-low heat for about 10 minutes, reducing the liquid by one-quarter. Don't boil the sauce or it will lose the fresh cilantro punch. Remove the sauce from the heat, add the lime juice and salt and pepper to taste, and reserve.

When the zucchini are ready, slice each vegetable in half horizontally. Transfer the zucchini to a serving platter and spoon the sauce over. Serve warm.

Cinnamon-Scented Acorn Squash

1   good-size acorn squash
1   teaspoon oil, preferably canola or corn

CINNAMON BUTTER

4 to 6 tablespoons butter
2   teaspoons brown sugar
1   teaspoon ground canela
    (Mexican cinnamon) or
    cinnamon

½   teaspoon ground dried red
    chile, preferably New
    Mexican or ancho

2 tablespoons chopped walnuts, for garnish

Serves 4

Prepare the smoker for barbecuing, bringing the temperature to 200° F to 220° F.

Cut the squash in half but don't remove the seeds (they help to keep it moist while cooking). Rub the oil over the cut surfaces of the squash and on the outside.

Place the squash in the smoker, cut side down, and cook for about 2 hours, or until tender.

While the squash cooks, melt the butter in a small pan or dish and stir in the sugar, canela or cinnamon, and chile. Keep the butter warm until needed.

Scrape the seeds out of each squash half and cut the halves into quarters. Spoon some of the melted cinnamon butter over each piece of squash and top with a sprinkling of chopped walnuts. Serve hot.

Sausage and Wild Rice Butternut Squash

If you want to win serious carnivores over to squash barbecue, tantalize them with a little pork, too.

1 small butternut squash, under 2 pounds
Oil, preferably canola or corn

DRESSING

2 tablespoons dried currants
Juice of ½ orange
1 tablespoon Worcestershire sauce
¼ pound bulk breakfast-style sausage
½ medium onion, chopped

1 celery rib, chopped
1 cup cooked wild rice
2 teaspoons minced fresh sage or 1 teaspoon dried sage
Pinch of nutmeg
Salt and fresh-ground black pepper to taste

Black Sauce (page 297) (optional)

Serves 4

Prepare the smoker for barbecuing, bringing the temperature to 200° F to 220° F.

Cut the squash in half but don't remove the seeds (they help to keep it moist while cooking). Rub the oil over the cut surfaces of the squash and on the outside.

Place the squash in the smoker, cut side down, and cook for about 1½ hours, until the squash is softened but not yet tender.

While the squash cooks, make the dressing. In a small bowl, combine the currants with the orange juice and Worcestershire and let them steep. Fry the sausage in a heavy skillet, adding the onion and celery after some of the fat has been rendered. Sauté until the sausage is cooked through and the vegetables softened. Mix in the currants with any remaining liquid and the rest of the ingredients.

Remove the squash from the smoker and, as soon as the halves are cool enough to handle, scrape the seeds out of each half. Slice each piece in half again. Mound the hot dressing over the squash and serve, with Black Sauce if you wish.

Cheese-Stuffed Tomatoes

6 ripe medium tomatoes	1 cup rye bread cubes
1 cup grated Gouda or Monterey jack cheese	½ teaspoon caraway seeds Paprika

Serves 6

Slice the tops off the tomatoes and with a spoon, scoop out the seeds, leaving a thick shell. Turn the tomatoes upside-down to drain for 5 minutes.

Prepare the smoker for barbecuing, bringing the temperature to 200° F to 220° F.

Mix together the cheese, bread, and caraway. Stuff the mixture into each of the tomatoes and top each with a liberal dusting of paprika.

Transfer the tomatoes to the smoker and cook for 20 to 30 minutes, until the cheese is melted and the tomatoes are warmed through. Remove the tomatoes from the smoker and serve immediately.

☆**Serving Suggestion:** Serve these on the side with mixed sausages and spicy brown mustard.

Barbecued Rice

1 cup uncooked white rice
1 small green bell pepper, chopped
2 celery ribs, chopped
1 small onion, chopped
2 tablespoons Worcestershire sauce

¼ teaspoon fresh-ground black pepper
Salt to taste
2½ cups chicken or beef stock

1 cup canned French-fried onion rings (optional)

Serves 6

Prepare the smoker for barbecuing, bringing the temperature to 200° F to 220° F.

In a smokeproof dish, combine the rice with the bell pepper, celery, onion, Worcestershire sauce, pepper, and salt. Pour the stock over the rice and cover the dish with foil.

Place the dish in the smoker and cook for about 1½ hours, until most of the liquid is absorbed. Uncover the rice and cook for an additional 15 to 25 minutes, or until the rice is tender and all the liquid is absorbed.

Serve immediately, or cover again and keep warm for up to 1 hour. Stir in the onion rings just before serving, if you wish.

☆**Serving Suggestion:** For a change of pace, serve this rice alongside enchiladas or tacos. Try Liar's Lime Pie for dessert.

Southern Arizona is better known for cactus than ribs, but Jack's Original Barbecue in Tucson has been serving an authentic version of its specialty since the 1950s. The family business offers it all, from peppery links to blackened brisket.

Garlic Cheese Grits

This is an old Southern favorite, reworked for the smoker.

5 cups water	2 cups grated sharp cheddar
1 cup grits (not instant)	cheese (about 8 ounces)
1 teaspoon salt	2 eggs, lightly beaten
2 tablespoons butter	1 teaspoon paprika
½ medium onion, minced	¼ teaspoon Tabasco or other
4 garlic cloves, minced	hot pepper sauce

Serves 6

Prepare the smoker for barbecuing, bringing the temperature to 200° F to 220° F. Grease a 9-by-11-inch smokeproof pan.

In a large saucepan (grits will expand in volume during the cooking), bring the water to a boil. Sprinkle in the salt, then the grits, a handful at a time, stirring constantly. Reduce the heat to a simmer and cook for about 20 minutes, until thickened and soft in texture. Stir the grits occasionally as they cook.

In a small skillet, warm the butter over medium heat. When it is melted, add the onion and garlic and cook until they are well softened. Remove from the heat and reserve.

Remove the grits from the heat and stir in the onion-garlic mixture, cheese, eggs, paprika, and Tabasco. Pour the grits into the prepared pan.

Place the grits in the smoker and cook for 1½ to 1¾ hours, until the mixture is lightly firm and somewhat browned. Remove the grits from the smoker and let sit at room temperature for at least 5 to 10 minutes. Cut into squares or wedges and serve warm or at room temperature.

☆**Serving Suggestion:** Top the grits with Warm Mushroom Salad or Ratatouille and serve with mixed greens.

Barbecuers with bicycles might want to enter the Tour de Pig at the Lexington, North Carolina, Barbecue Festival, held each October. If that doesn't wear you out, you can also compete in the Hawg Run, join the Parade of Pigs, or try to win a year's supply of Pepsi-Cola in the Pig Tales creative writing contest.

Smokin' Waldorf

New York's Waldorf-Astoria Hotel not only created the original Waldorf salad but invented room service to deliver it. Here's a twist, using smoked apples and the tang of lime juice. You can smoke the fruit a day ahead of the salad's preparation if you wish.

2 unpeeled apples
Oil, preferably walnut

2 celery ribs, chopped	⅓ cup plain yogurt
⅔ cup raisins	Juice of 2 limes
⅔ cup chopped walnuts	1 to 2 teaspoons sugar
⅓ cup mayonnaise	

Lettuce leaves, for garnish (optional)

Serves 4

Prepare the smoker for barbecuing, bringing the temperature to 200° F to 220° F.

Coat the apples liberally with the oil and place them in the smoker. Cook for about 1 hour, until the apples are deeply browned and softened. Remove from the smoker and set aside until cool enough to handle. Peel the apples and slice them into bite-size chunks. Combine the apples in a bowl with the celery, raisins, and walnuts.

In a small lidded jar, combine the mayonnaise, yogurt, lime juice, and sugar. Pour over the apple mixture. Mix well and refrigerate for at least 30 minutes.

Serve cool, on top of lettuce leaves if you wish.

☆**Serving Suggestion:** The salad is filling enough for a main course at lunch. Try it with Blue Corn Muffins.

In 1918, Charles "Pappy" Foreman gave up blacksmithing to start barbecuing mutton for the folks of Owensboro, Kentucky. Five generations later the Foreman family continues to serve some of the finest mutton in the country at Old Hickory Bar-B-Q, still located near the site of Pappy's original pit.

Peaches Keen

Some fruits are delicious smoked, particularly peaches, ba-nanas, and apples. We usually cook bananas and apples whole, but prefer peaches halved and flavored with a fruity vinegar.

6 ripe but firm peaches, halved
   but with peel left on
Oil, preferably walnut

2 tablespoons raspberry or
   other fruit vinegar

Serves 6

Prepare the smoker for barbecuing, bringing the temperature to 200° F to 220° F.

Rub the peaches liberally with the oil.

Spoon a teaspoon of vinegar into the cavity of each peach half and transfer them to the smoker. Cook for 35 to 45 minutes, until the peaches are heated through and softened. Remove them from the smoker and serve warm.

Barbecued Bananas

You just might go bananas over these.

4 unpeeled bananas

Oil, preferably canola or corn

Brown sugar and ground cinnamon or caramel sauce, for garnish (optional)

Serves 4

Prepare the smoker for barbecuing, bringing the temperature to 200° F to 220° F.

Rub the bananas with a thin coating of oil.

Place the bananas in the smoker and cook for 50 to 60 minutes, until the bananas are deeply browned and soft. Remove from the smoker and set aside until cool enough

Gary Wells, the father of the Kansas City Barbeque Society, has always insisted that no one should take the organization too seriously. The goal is to have fun. You would know people were getting overly earnest, he has said, when membership in the Society is noted in obituaries.

to handle. Peel the bananas and slice them. Serve them warm, topped with a simple sprinkling of brown sugar and cinnamon or spoonfuls of your favorite caramel sauce.

BBQ tips Weather can affect not only whether you barbecue but also how you do it. A hot sun increases the cooking temperature inside a smoker and a cold, cloudy day decreases it, requiring adjustments in the amount of fuel used or the time allowed for cooking. Wind is also a factor because of the air circulation inside most smokers. On a blustery day, you have to watch the vents and other draft controls carefully to prevent the wind from causing major fluctuations in the cooking temperature.

☆ While You Wait ☆

When you've got hungry folks standing around the fire, and dinner won't be done for a spell, pop one of these dishes in your smoker. They make a super snack or light meal any time of the day, but they're particularly good as late afternoon appetizers with your favorite libation.

Can't Wait Queso

Few things are simpler, or tastier, than a melted cheese starter. This is the barbecue version of a Tex-Mex favorite, queso fundido, *a baked white cheese.*

12-ounce chunk medium
   cheddar cheese or half
   cheddar and half Monterey
   jack
1 to 2 teaspoons Cajun Ragin'
   Rub (page 38), Wild Willy's
   Number One-derful Rub
   (page 36), or other savory
   seasoning blend

1 to 2 pickled or fresh jalapeños,
   sliced

Warm flour tortillas

Serves 2 to 8, depending on hunger levels

Prepare the smoker for barbecuing, bringing the temperature to 200° F to 220° F.
   Place the cheese in a small smokeproof baking dish. Sprinkle it with the rub and the jalapeños. Place the cheese in the smoker as far from the fire as possible. Cook until the cheese melts through, about 1¼ hours. (Avoid overcooking because the cheese becomes rubbery.) Serve immediately with warm flour tortillas. Cut the tortillas in quarters to make them more manageable to eat as finger food.

BBQ tips   For convenience sake, we've featured appetizers that you can cook with other food in spare space in your smoker, but each is also tasty enough to do on its own. If you have equipment that's easy to start and use—such as an electric water smoker, stove-top smoker, or Cookshack oven—these recipes remain a breeze, and they can add a lot of smoky flavor to a non-barbecue meal.

You have to love the logo at Gates & Son's Bar-B-Q in Kansas City. A gent with a big smile, in top hat and tails, struts down the street carrying a cane in one hand and a take-out bag of barbecue in the other.

In Holland, the local Gouda cheese is sometimes smoked and sprinkled with cumin seeds. When we do it in the smoker, as another European variation on the melted cheese theme, we use a tablespoon of cumin seeds plus a tablespoon of minced onion. A Dutch friend who loves barbecue, Peter Noom, gave us the idea.

Unholy Swiss Cheese

In the Alps, melted raclette cheese is a warming snack after a winter afternoon of skiing. This smoked version is worth savoring any time of the year. If you can't find raclette, substitute Gruyère for a similar flavor.

12-ounce chunk raclette cheese
1 tablespoon Dijon mustard, preferably country-style

Boiled new potatoes
Cornichons or other sour pickles and additional Dijon mustard

Serves 2 to 8, depending on hunger levels

Prepare the smoker for barbecuing, bringing the temperature to 200° F to 220° F.

Place the cheese in a small smokeproof baking dish. Smear the mustard over it. Place the cheese in the smoker as far from the fire as possible. Cook until the cheese melts through, about 1¼ hours. (Avoid overcooking because the cheese becomes rubbery.)

Serve immediately on the potatoes, which can be halved, if needed, for easier eating. Accompany the cheese with the cornichons and more mustard.

☆**Serving Suggestion:** If you add a hearty loaf of bread, a green salad, and a bottle of red wine, you've got the makings for a satisfying Sunday night supper.

Nachos Blancos

Gooey with molten strings of mild cheese and punctuated with spicy toppings, an authentic nacho bears little resemblance to the popular ballpark variety awash in an ugly orange sauce. Smoking the nachos adds an extra dimension to the snack, making grocery-store tortilla chips taste of fresh-roasted corn.

Approximately 36 tortilla chips
2 cups grated Monterey jack
  cheese (8 ounces)
⅓ pound sliced bacon or
  chorizo, fried and crumbled
  (optional)

1 medium red onion, chopped
4 to 6 serranos or jalapeños,
  minced

Sour cream, for garnish
Sauce Olé (page 296), for garnish (optional)

Serves 4 to 6

Prepare the smoker for barbecuing, bringing the temperature to 200° F to 220° F.

Arrange the tortilla chips on a foil-covered baking sheet or smokeproof platter. Scatter the cheese, meat, onion, and chiles over the chips.

Place the nachos in the smoker. Cook until the cheese is well melted, 10 to 20 minutes. Serve immediately with sour cream and, if you wish, Sauce Olé.

Curry Pecans

The "smoked" nuts you get on commercial airlines usually rely on liquid smoke or hickory-flavored salt for their flavor. There's a world of difference in the real thing.

CURRY MARINADE

Juice of 2 medium oranges	1 teaspoon sugar
1½ teaspoons curry powder	1 garlic clove, minced
1½ teaspoons Worcestershire sauce	½ teaspoon salt or more to taste

2 cups pecan halves

Makes 2 cups

Combine all the marinade ingredients in a nonreactive bowl. Add the pecans and allow them to sit at room temperature for about 1 hour.

Prepare the smoker for barbecuing, bringing the temperature to 200° F to 220° F.

Drain the nuts. Transfer them to a piece of greased heavy-duty foil just large enough to hold the nuts in a single layer and place the foil in the smoker. Cook the pecans until they are crisp and lightly smoked, 50 to 60 minutes. Serve immediately or keep in a covered jar for several days.

BBQ tips Although the ideal temperature for barbecuing food is between 180° F and 220° F, don't panic if the temperature drifts up to 250° F or down to 160° F. A little time in an extreme range won't hurt most food, but start making adjustments as quickly as possible to get back to the right level.

Little Devils

A Southwest favorite, these nuts are spicy but not as hot as you might guess from the amount of Tabasco used. The smoking process tames some of the sauce's fiery potency.

2 cups raw peanuts   Peanut oil
½ cup (yes, cup) Tabasco or   Salt to taste
   other hot pepper sauce

Makes 2 cups

Combine the peanuts with the Tabasco in a small bowl. Let the nuts sit in the sauce for about 30 minutes.

Prepare the smoker for barbecuing, bringing the temperature to 200° F to 220° F.

Select a smokeproof dish that will hold the peanuts in a single layer. Thickly coat the dish with the oil. Add the peanuts, stir them, and sprinkle with salt.

Place the peanuts in the smoker and cook until the peanuts are well browned and dry, 50 to 60 minutes. Check the nuts toward the end of the cooking time to avoid burning.

Transfer the peanuts to absorbent paper to cool. Serve immediately or keep in a covered jar for several days.

☆**Serving Suggestion:** For a cocktail party with Southwestern flair, serve the Little Devils along with Fiesta Salsa and chips, Nachos Blancos, garlicky guacamole, jícama slices with lime juice, carrot slices marinated in jalapeño pepper pickling liquid, and Turquoise Margaritas or Apricoritas.

The Hogaholics cooking team from Memphis tried to barbecue an elephant in Thailand but found it hard to turn, according to Carolyn Wells in her wonderful book, *Barbecue Greats Memphis Style* (Pig Out Publications). One Hogaholic told Carolyn that the team's secret ingredient is "diluted battery acid, dried in the sun and stored in the basement, guarded by two killer basset hounds."

266

Smoked Olives

While black and green olives are staples on American relish trays, you rarely see them baked, a common preparation in the Mediterranean region. We take the cooking a step further, adding a light taste of smoke.

1 cup black olives with character, such as Greek kalamata or atalanti, drained lightly	2 tablespoons extra-virgin olive oil
	2 tablespoons white wine
1 cup green olives with character, such as Greek cracked, drained lightly	2 garlic cloves, minced
	¾ teaspoon dried oregano
	Fresh-ground black pepper to taste

Makes 2 cups

Prepare the smoker for barbecuing, bringing the temperature to 200° F to 220° F.

Arrange the olives in a shallow smokeproof dish or in a piece of heavy-duty foil molded into a small tray. Add the remaining ingredients.

Place the olives in the smoker and cook until the olives absorb half of the liquid and take on a light but identifiable smoke flavor, 55 to 65 minutes.

The olives can be served immediately or can sit for several hours to develop the flavor further. Refrigerate any leftovers.

Mouthwatering Watermelon Morsels

This is as simple as it is scrumptious, at least if you've got a supply of watermelon pickles on hand. You can find the pickled rinds in Southern supermarkets or you can make your own (see page 350).

Bacon slices, cut into thirds   Watermelon rind pickles

Makes a bunch

Prepare the smoker for barbecuing, bringing the temperature to 200° F to 220° F.

Wrap as many slices of watermelon rind pickles as you desire in a piece of bacon and secure with toothpicks. Transfer the tidbits to the smoker and cook them until the bacon is brown and crisp, 35 to 45 minutes. Serve hot.

☆**Serving Suggestion:** For a summer afternoon soirée with a Southern theme, serve these along with Greens-Stuffed Mushrooms, Sweet Potato Biscuits with ham or turkey slices, Squash Relish, Okra Pickles, and Peanutty Pie made into individual tarts. Accompany the spread with Derby Day Mint Juleps and Sunny Sweet Tea.

Bronzed Garlic

2 large *whole bulbs* garlic,   Olive oil
    skins on

Crusty country-style white bread

Serves 4 to 6

Prepare the smoker for barbecuing, bringing the temperature to 200° F to 220° F.

The New Braunfels Smokehouse (800-537-6932) is one of the best mail-order sources in the country for smoked food. Though the company brine-cures most of its products—using a dry rub only on beef brisket and pork ribs—the food is cooked in a barbecue style rather than smoke-cured. Originally a local brewery in the German-American community of New Braunfels, Texas, the business switched to smoking during Prohibition.

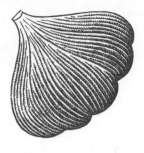

Coat the garlic bulbs well with the oil. Place the garlic in the smoker and cook it until browned and well softened, 40 to 50 minutes.

Pull any loose browned skin from the garlic. Slice a thin layer off the top of each bulb, just deep enough to expose the tops of the individual cloves.

Serve hot accompanied by the bread. To eat, break off the cloves and squeeze the softened garlic onto chunks or slices of bread.

☆**Serving Suggestion:** Use leftover garlic as a spread on sandwiches or mix it into mayonnaise.

Nearly eighty percent of the households in the country own an outdoor grill, according to the Barbecue Industry Association. In 1992, close to half of those households cooked outside in any two-week period in the summer, a jump of ten percent over the past decade.

Fiesta Salsa

Smoky salsas rival barbecue sauces in possibilities. Here's a classic to get you started. If you can't find the smoked jalapeños known as chipotle chiles, smoke 2 or 3 pickled jalapeños for 20 to 30 minutes and substitute them for the chipotles and their adobo sauce.

1 pound red-ripe tomatoes (about 2 to 3 medium)	2 teaspoons adobo sauce from canned chipotles or more to taste
2 teaspoons extra-virgin olive oil	Juice of 1 lime
¼ cup chopped red onion	Salt to taste
2 to 3 garlic cloves, minced	2 to 3 tablespoons chopped fresh cilantro
2 canned chipotle chiles, minced	

Tortilla chips or corn or flour tortillas

Makes about 1½ cups

Prepare the smoker for barbecuing, bringing the temperature to 200° F to 220° F.

Coat the tomatoes with 1 teaspoon of the oil. Transfer the tomatoes to the smoker. Cook them until they are very soft and the skins are ready to split, 45 to 55 minutes. Set the tomatoes aside until cool enough to handle. Coarsely chop the tomatoes with their peels.

Transfer the tomatoes, peels, and any juice to a blender. Add the remaining oil, onion, garlic, chipotles, adobo sauce, and lime juice and purée. Pour into a small serving bowl, add salt to taste, and refrigerate for at least 45 minutes.

Stir in the cilantro just before serving. Serve with tortilla chips or tortillas.

BBQ tips You can create smoked salsas from many combinations of vegetables—or even fruits—by keeping in mind a couple of key principles. For contrasting flavors, avoid smoking everything you plan to throw into the mix. Add a little more lime or other acid than you do in traditional recipes, to balance the assertive smoke taste.

Better-Than-Store-Bought Bacon-Horseradish Dip

Tired of sneaking into supermarkets to buy that ersatz version of bacon-horseradish dip with fake bacon, pseudo sour cream, and enough preservatives to keep Dick Clark young another half-century?

1 cup sour cream	Oil, preferably canola or corn
1 tablespoon plus 1 teaspoon prepared horseradish	3 to 4 slices bacon, chopped
1 slice from a medium onion, about ⅓ inch thick	2 ounces fresh mild goat cheese, at room temperature

Potato chips or carrot sticks

Makes about 1½ cups

Prepare the smoker for barbecuing, bringing the temperature to 200° F to 220° F.

Spoon the sour cream and 1 tablespoon of the horseradish into a smokeproof baking dish. Rub the onion slice with the oil. Place the sour cream and onion in the smoker side-by-side and cook for 30 to 40 minutes. The sour cream should be runny but not separated, and the onion well softened but not cooked through.

While the sour cream and onion cook, fry the bacon in a small skillet. Drain the bacon.

Stir the cheese into the sour cream until well combined. Chop the onion and crumble the bacon. Mix into the sour cream. Add as much of the remaining teaspoon of horseradish as desired. The smoked horseradish will mellow in flavor, and any added at the end creates a pleasantly pungent bite. Serve with potato chips or carrot sticks.

If you're looking for saucy ribs in Memphis, head for Gridley's. It's a chain operation these days, with several look-alike locations, but the pitmasters can mass-produce a mighty tasty product.

Creamy Catfish Spread

Any time we smoke catfish we save some for this spread, one of the tastiest appetizers you can pop between your lips.

8 ounces Peppered Catfish (page 206) or store-bought smoked catfish	2 teaspoons minced onion
	1½ teaspoons brandy
	1 teaspoon fresh lemon juice
4 ounces cream cheese, at room temperature	¼ teaspoon Tabasco or other hot pepper sauce
2 tablespoons butter	Salt and fresh-ground black pepper to taste
1 to 1½ tablespoons milk	

Cucumber rounds, crackers, or crusty country-style white bread

Makes approximately 2 cups

Flake the catfish, discarding any skin and bones. Combine the fish and remaining spread ingredients in a food processor and process until well mixed. Pack the spread into a small serving bowl and refrigerate, covered, for at least 30 minutes.

Serve with cucumber rounds, crackers, or bread.

Drop-Dead Trout Spread

HORSERADISH PASTE

2 teaspoons fresh lemon juice
½ teaspoon horseradish

Salt and fresh-ground black
 pepper to taste

1 trout (about 8 ounces)
3 ounces cream cheese, at
 room temperature
3 tablespoons minced onion
3 tablespoons pecan pieces,
 toasted
1 tablespoon fresh lemon juice

1½ teaspoons Creole mustard
1 teaspoon white wine
 Worcestershire sauce
Several drops Tabasco or other
 hot pepper sauce
Salt to taste

Zucchini rounds, crackers, or breadsticks

Makes about 2 cups

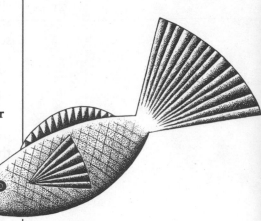

Prepare the smoker for barbecuing, bringing the temperature to 200° F to 220° F.

In a small bowl, combine the paste ingredients. Rub the trout inside and out with the paste and let the fish sit at room temperature for 20 to 30 minutes.

Transfer the trout to the smoker. Cook the fish until it's opaque and flakes easily, 35 to 45 minutes. Allow the trout to cool for at least 15 minutes.

Flake the fish, discarding any skin and bones. Place the fish and remaining ingredients in a food processor and process until well mixed. Pack the spread into a small serving bowl and refrigerate, covered, for at least 30 minutes.

Serve with zucchini rounds, crackers, or breadsticks.

BBQ tips   We always throw a couple of onions on the smoker whenever we're barbecuing. The smoke mellows their pungency but heightens their taste. Use them as a substitute for raw onion in this or any other recipe.

The Meridian, Texas, National Championship Barbecue Cook-off features a charitable fundraising event called Cow Patty Bingo. You buy a ticket for one of a hundred grids marked off in a pen. A cow is placed in the enclosure, and when nature takes its course, the square blessed with the majority of the first cow patty wins the prize.

East Carolina University in Greenville, North Carolina, hosts the annual Carolina Barbecue Championship Cook-Off. It's held in April in conjunction with the Great Pirate Purple/Gold Pigskin Pig-Out Party. If you flunk out of the cook-off, you can try your skill in a golf tournament or at the dunking booth.

Heavenly Hearts

14-ounce can artichoke hearts
1 cup mayonnaise
¾ cup grated Parmesan or Romano cheese
1 teaspoon white or cider vinegar

½ teaspoon dried basil
1 garlic clove, minced
¼ cup fresh bread crumbs

Melba toasts, crackers, or crusty country-style white bread

Serves 4 to 6

Prepare the smoker for barbecuing, bringing the temperature to 200° F to 220° F.

Drain the artichoke hearts and slice them into quarters.

In a shallow, smokeproof dish, mix the artichokes with the mayonnaise, cheese, vinegar, basil, and garlic. Top the mixture with the bread crumbs.

Transfer the dish to the smoker and cook the artichoke mixture for 25 to 35 minutes, until the cheese and mayonnaise are melted together. Serve immediately.

Greens-Stuffed Mushrooms

Southerners have always loved greens with smoked food, a pairing that reaches a peak of perfection in this appetizer.

12 to 16 large white mushrooms
2 tablespoons butter
2 tablespoons oil, preferably corn or canola
¼ cup chopped onion
2 tablespoons minced red bell pepper
2 garlic cloves, minced
12 ounces mustard greens or kale, chopped fine

½ cup chicken stock
1 teaspoon prepared yellow mustard
Salt and fresh-ground black pepper to taste
4 ounces cream cheese, at room temperature
6 tablespoons dry bread crumbs
Romano or Parmesan cheese

Serves 4 to 6

repare the smoker for barbecuing, bringing the temperature to 200° F to 220° F.

Stem the mushrooms and hollow them out. Chop the stems and trimmings and reserve.

Warm the butter and oil in a skillet. Add the mushroom caps and sauté over medium-low heat for 2 to 3 minutes, turning frequently. Remove the partially cooked mushroom caps from the pan and set them aside. Add the onion, bell pepper, garlic, and greens to the skillet. Sauté the mixture for 2 to 3 minutes. Mix in the stock, mustard, salt, and pepper and simmer, covered, for about 5 minutes. Remove the pan from the heat. Immediately stir in the cream cheese followed by the bread crumbs.

Stuff the mushroom caps, mounding the filling high. Sprinkle with the Romano cheese.

Place the mushrooms on a small grill rack or baking sheet and transfer them to the smoker. Cook them until the filling browns on top and the mushrooms are tender, about 20 to 30 minutes. Serve hot.

☆**Serving Suggestion:** The mushrooms make a good side dish, too, especially with pork.

Wild Wings

When in doubt, wing it.

WILD WINGS SAUCE

1 cup beer
¼ cup unsulphured dark molasses
¼ cup creamy peanut butter
¼ cup Worcestershire sauce

1½ tablespoons chili powder
Juice of 1 lime
½ teaspoon dry mustard
¼ teaspoon ground anise seeds
¼ teaspoon salt

1½ dozen uncooked chicken wings

Makes 3 dozen pieces

In Henderson, Kentucky, they mix their meat with music at the W.C. Handy Blues and Barbecue Festival in June.

Combine the sauce ingredients in a large, heavy pan. Simmer over medium heat for 15 to 20 minutes, until reduced by about one-third. The sauce can be made a day or two ahead.

Prepare the smoker for barbecuing, bringing the temperature to 200° F to 220° F. Grease a large smokeproof baking pan or dish.

With a cleaver or butcher knife, remove the chicken wing tips. Then cut each wing in half at the joint.

Transfer the wing sections and the sauce to the baking dish. Place the dish in the smoker and cook the chicken for 1¼ to 1½ hours, stirring the wings once or twice. The chicken should be cooked through and tender, and the sauce reduced to a thick glaze. Serve hot.

BBQ tips For other quick off-the-pit nibbles, try smoked sliced link sausage accompanied by a stout mustard and Bar-BQ Ranch Sauce, smoked bite-size cubes of chicken with Jamaican Barbecue Sauce, or smoked shrimp skewered with jalapeño-stuffed or onion-stuffed green olives. Another good starter is a block of cream cheese covered with Lime-Mint Barbecue Sauce and served with crackers.

Chicken's Little Livers

FRUITY MARINADE AND MOP

¼ cup raspberry vinegar or
  other fruit vinegar
¼ cup chicken stock
¼ cup oil, preferably canola or
  corn
⅓ medium onion, chopped

1 garlic clove, minced
¼ teaspoon ground ginger
¼ teaspoon salt (less if stock is
  salted)
¼ teaspoon fresh-ground black
  pepper

12 chicken livers, trimmed of any membrane
4 slices bacon, cut into thirds

Makes 1 dozen

At least an hour, and up to 2½ hours, before you plan to barbecue, combine the marinade ingredients in a lidded jar. Place the chicken livers in a shallow, nonreactive bowl. Pour the marinade over the livers and marinate for up to 2 hours in the refrigerator.

Prepare the smoker for barbecuing, bringing the temperature to 200° F to 220° F.

Drain the livers, reserving the remaining marinade. Wrap each liver in a piece of bacon and secure with a toothpick. Bring the marinade to a vigorous boil and keep it warm over low heat to use as a mop.

Place the livers on a small grill rack, mopping them liberally before placing them in the smoker. Cook for 35 to 45 minutes, until the bacon is crisp. Apply the mop once or twice during the cooking process if you are using a wood-burning pit; in other styles of smokers, mop as soon as you remove the livers. Serve the tidbits piping hot.

The Dreamland Drive-Inn in Tuscaloosa, Alabama, hasn't changed its menu since Big Daddy John Bishop and his wife, Lillie, opened for business in 1958. The only choice is succulent ribs, served by the slab or, for the really hungry, in a full barbecue dinner that also includes pickles, potato chips, and white bread.

Chicken from Hell

These potent stuffed chiles will spice up anyone's life.

1 large boneless, skinless, individual chicken breast, pounded thin and sliced in 12 sections
1 tablespoon oil, preferably canola or corn
2 tablespoons Wild Willy's Number One-derful Rub (page 36), Southwest Heat (page 39), or other savory seasoning blend

12 large fresh jalapeños or yellow güero chiles
½ medium onion, in slivers
6 slices bacon, halved

Boydesque Brew (page 291) or other barbecue sauce (optional)

Makes 1 dozen

About 1½ hours before you plan to barbecue, toss the chicken with the oil in a small bowl. Sprinkle dry rub over it and stir to coat. Refrigerate, covered, for 1 hour.

Prepare the smoker for barbecuing, bringing the temperature to 200° F to 220° F.

Split the jalapeños along one side and seed them. Stuff a section of chicken breast and a sliver or two of onion in each, wrap with a half piece of bacon, and secure the tidbit with a toothpick.

Place the chicken in the smoker and cook for 30 to 40 minutes, until the bacon is crisp.

These are extremely hot when served with the jalapeño still in place, so proceed cautiously. Tender-mouths may find the chicken plenty potent eaten alone or perhaps with a barbecue sauce, such as Boydesque Brew.

☆**Variation:** The preparation works with game birds, too. Substitute dove or quail breast for chicken, if you wish.

007 Shrimp

A true "seafood cocktail," these shrimp are enhanced by James Bond's favorite drink, the vodka martini.

1 pound large shrimp (24 to 30)

JAMES BOND'S BASIC BARBECUE MARINADE

1½ cups vodka
½ cup dry vermouth
**3 tablespoons oil, preferably
    canola or corn**

3 tablespoons minced onion
Juice of 1 large lemon

Lemon wedges, for garnish

Serves 4 to 6

Prepare the smoker for barbecuing, bringing the temperature to 180° F to 200° F.

Peel the shrimp, leaving the tails on. Clean and, if desired, devein them. Place the shrimp in a shallow, non-reactive dish or plastic bag.

In a lidded jar, combine the marinade ingredients. Pour the marinade over the shrimp and let the shrimp marinate at room temperature for 30 minutes.

Drain the shrimp and arrange them on a small grill rack. Place in the smoker as far from the fire as possible. The shrimp should be done in 20 to 25 minutes, but watch them carefully. They are ready when opaque, slightly firm, and lightly pink on the exterior. Serve them hot or chilled, garnished with lemon.

Until recently at Kreuz Market in Lockhart, Texas, "diners" ate standing, cutting their hunks of meat with a knife chained to a counter. The restaurant has some tables now, but you still place your order at the pit and by the pound, eat off the butcher paper, and get nothing with the meat except a choice of white bread or saltine crackers. A separate serve-yourself station sells onions, pickles, and Big Red, the soft drink of choice. If you want barbecue sauce you'd better sneak it in, because they don't abide it here.

Scallops on a Stick

1 pound sea scallops, cut in bite-size pieces if needed

SCALLOP MARINADE

¼ cup sake or dry sherry   2 teaspoons brown sugar
2 tablespoons peanut oil

10-ounce can water chestnuts, drained and blanched
4 to 6 green onions, sliced in ¾-inch lengths

Plum Good Slopping Sauce (page 305) or West Coast Wonder
   barbecue sauce (page 300) (optional)

Serves 4 to 6

Prepare your smoker for barbecuing, bringing the temperature to 180° F to 200° F.

Place the scallops in a plastic bag or shallow dish. Combine the marinade ingredients and pour the mixture over the scallops. Let the scallops sit at room temperature for 20 to 30 minutes.

Thread the scallops on bamboo skewers interspersed with water chestnuts and green onion pieces. Arrange the skewers on a small grill rack or baking sheet. Place in the smoker as far from the fire as possible. Cook until the scallops are cooked through and opaque, about 15 minutes.

Serve immediately, with Plum Good Slopping Sauce or West Coast Wonder barbecue sauce, if you wish.

☆**Serving Suggestion:** Make lunch out of the scallops by serving them with rice. For dessert, serve orange slices zipped up with a sprinkling of triple sec.

Texas Terrine

A great way to use leftovers, this glorified meat loaf relies on already smoked meat. Unlike many of our appetizers, it keeps well for several days.

1¼ pounds smoked meat, preferably 2 or 3 meats, such as brisket, pork shoulder, ham, chicken, or turkey
3 ounces pork fat
2 tablespoons butter
1 medium onion, minced
2 garlic cloves, minced
¾ cup fresh cornbread crumbs or other bread crumbs
¼ cup minced fresh cilantro
2 to 3 tablespoons milk
1½ tablespoons jalapeño mustard or other hot spicy mustard

1 tablespoon Worcestershire sauce
1 tablespoon chili powder
Salt and fresh-ground black pepper to taste
1 egg
⅓ cup chopped, roasted green New Mexican, Anaheim, or poblano chiles, preferably fresh or frozen

Toasted cornbread slices, crackers, or crusty country-style white bread

Bar-BQ Ranch Sauce (page 295) or Jalapeach Barbecue Sauce (page 302) (optional)

Serves 8 or more

Preheat the oven to 325° F.

In a food processor or meat grinder, mince or grind the meats and pork fat together. Transfer the meat to a bowl.

Warm the butter in a small skillet over medium heat. Add the onion and garlic and sauté briefly until softened. Spoon the mixture over the meat. Add the bread crumbs, cilantro, milk, mustard, Worcestershire sauce, and chili powder, mixing well. Taste the mixture, adding salt or pepper if needed, and mix in the egg.

At cooking competitions sanctioned by the Kansas City Barbeque Society, the judges take an oath about their job. It goes something like, "I solemnly swear to objectively and subjectively evaluate each barbecue meat that is presented to my eyes, my nose, and my palate. I accept my duty so that truth, justice, excellence in Barbecue and the American Way of Life may be strengthened and preserved forever."

Pat half the meat into a 7-by-3-inch loaf pan. Scatter the chiles over the loaf and top with the rest of the meat. Pat the meat down firmly.

Bake the terrine in a water bath for 70 to 75 minutes. Let the terrine cool at room temperature for 20 minutes.

Cover the terrine with foil and weight it down with a couple of bottles of barbecue sauce or cans from your pantry. Refrigerate the meat for at least 2 hours, but preferably longer. Like a meat loaf, the terrine improves with age for a few days.

Serve chilled with toasted cornbread, crackers, or other bread. If you want to offer sauce on the side, the most compatible choices are Bar-BQ Ranch Sauce and Jalapeach Sauce.

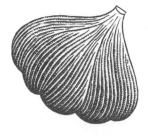

South-of-the-Border Garlic Soup

Some of the finest Mexican dishes are soups that feature ajo, *or garlic. We drew on that tradition in developing this preparation, where the garlic is mellowed dramatically by smoking. Like any soup, it tastes much better with home-made stock.*

2   *whole bulbs* garlic
Oil, preferably canola, corn, or peanut

1½ tablespoons oil, preferably
    peanut
1   medium onion, sliced thin
1   medium tomato, chopped
8   cups chicken stock,
    preferably homemade
1 to 2 dried chipotle chiles

Lime slices, for garnish

Juice of 1 lime
1   ripe avocado, cubed
1   tablespoon minced fresh
    cilantro or more to taste
2   corn tortillas, cut into
    matchsticks

Serves 6

Prepare the smoker for barbecuing, bringing the temperature to 200° F to 220° F.

Rub the unpeeled garlic bulbs with a thin coating of oil and transfer them to the smoker. Cook the garlic until the peel is well browned and the cloves feel quite soft, about 1 hour. When the garlic is cool enough to handle, peel all the cloves and reserve them.

Heat 1 tablespoon of the peanut oil in large saucepan over medium-low heat. Add the onion to the oil and sauté until it's softened and lightly colored. Spoon the mixture into a blender and add the tomato and reserved garlic. Purée.

Add the remaining ½ tablespoon peanut oil to the saucepan and heat it over medium-high heat. Pour in the blender mixture and sauté it until it begins to dry out and the tomato darkens a shade or two. Add the chicken stock and the chipotle, and reduce the heat to medium. Simmer the mixture for 25 to 30 minutes, remove it from the heat, and add the lime juice.

Divide the avocado, cilantro, and tortillas among individual bowls and pour the hot soup over them. Garnish each bowl with a slice of lime and serve.

☆Serving Suggestion: For a light supper, pair the soup with Can't Wait Queso.

BBQ tips Making your own stock is simple. Start by saving trimmings and bones from raw or cooked poultry and beef—separate from each other, for their different stocks—and collect carrot peels, celery tops, and onion skins together to use in both stocks. Stash the ingredients in the freezer in plastic bags until you've got several pounds. To make a stock, put the ingredients into a stockpot or large saucepan with a little garlic, a few peppercorns, and, if you have it, some parsley. Don't add salt, which can make it difficult to control the saltiness of dishes that use the stock. Cover everything with twice as much water, bring the pot to a boil, and then reduce the heat to low. Simmer slowly for several hours. Leave the pot uncovered, evaporating the liquid and intensifying the taste. We usually cook the stock until about one-third of the original liquid remains, but you can reduce it further for greater richness and simpler storage. When the stock is ready, strain it and freeze it in multiple batches, for easy use later as needed.

The Ridgewood in Bluff City, Tennessee, has gotten its share of good press in the last decade, since Jane and Michael Stern anointed its barbecue as the best in the country. Mrs. Grace Proffitt and her staff serve their luscious pork East Tennessee style, with slices piled on big buns and slathered with a thick, tasty ketchup-based sauce.

Better-Than-French Onion Soup

This soup is particularly splendid when you make its beef stock with barbecued brisket trimmings.

4 medium onions	1 teaspoon dried thyme
Oil, preferably canola or corn	Salt to taste
6 cups beef stock, preferably homemade	¼ teaspoon fresh-ground black pepper
¼ cup dry red wine	
1 tablespoon Memphis Magic (page 294) or other not-too-sweet tomato-based barbecue sauce	
4 slices crusty country-style white bread	
1 cup grated Gruyère cheese	

Serves 4

About 3 hours before you plan to eat the soup, prepare the smoker for barbecuing, bringing the temperature to 200° F to 220° F.

Rub the onions with a thin coating of oil and place them in the smoker. Cook until the skins are well browned and the onions feel soft, about 1½ hours. When the onions are cool enough to handle, peel them and slice them thin.

Place the onions in a saucepan and add the stock, wine, barbecue sauce, thyme, salt, and pepper. Simmer the soup for 45 minutes.

Preheat the broiler. Toast the bread.

Spoon the hot soup into 4 ovenproof bowls. Top each portion of soup with a piece of toast and some of the cheese. Broil briefly until the cheese is melted. Serve immediately.

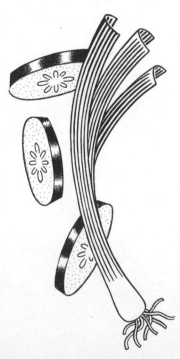

Part Three

★ ★ ★

Great Accompaniments
from Indoors

☆ Barbecue Sauces ☆

Sauces are contentious. Some smart people, such as the pros at the California Culinary Academy, say that sauces define the nature of barbecue. If you don't serve one on your food, they claim, you are "smoke cooking" instead of barbecuing. Other smart people maintain that if something isn't worth eating without a sauce, it doesn't deserve the name barbecue. To them, using a sauce is akin to skinny dipping in your skivvies.

Even if you come down firmly on the side of saucing, you'll soon discover that everyone who agrees with you is talking about a different potion. The styles of barbecue sauce across the country are more numerous and varied than the vices of Washington, D.C. Most regions have a favored style, and within that tradition, each pitmaster has a special twist or two. The only common denominator is a resolute conviction among the inventors and fans that nobody else knows a damned thing about making sauce.

Perhaps everyone is a little right and a little wrong. Most good barbecue doesn't require any sauce to enhance its flavor, but it can often benefit from several different styles of sauce, depending on personal preferences. Our recipes cover the major regional variations and a few offbeat options. Experiment with them to craft your own concoction. Even if you prefer your barbecue bare, you're certain to find that your own sauce is the best one ever brewed.

Struttin' Sauce

Kansas City is the sauce capital of the country, where they practically pave the streets with the stuff. Over the last half-century, local pitmasters perfected a spicy, sweet sauce, thick with tomatoes, that ultimately became the most common and popular style nationally. When you look for a commercial sauce in a supermarket today, Kansas City–style may be the only kind you find. Few of the packaged products, however, rival the originals, still served in Bar-B-Q joints all over town, or good homemade variations on the same theme. This version is modeled on the sauce that Ollie Gates created years ago for his thriving small chain of Gates & Son's restaurants. Like Gates's classic, our rendition will leave you strutting with satisfaction.

1 tablespoon oil, preferably canola or corn	3 tablespoons Worcestershire sauce
1 medium onion, chopped	3 to 4 teaspoons celery salt
2 garlic cloves, minced	1 tablespoon prepared yellow mustard
1 cup tomato purée	
¾ cup cider vinegar	1 tablespoon fresh-ground black pepper
¾ cup water	
6 tablespoons brown sugar	1 tablespoon corn syrup
6 tablespoons chili powder	1 tablespoon pure liquid hickory smoke (optional)
¼ cup tomato paste	

Makes about 2¼ cups

In a saucepan, warm the oil over medium heat. Add the onion and garlic and sauté until they are softened, about 5 minutes. Mix in the remaining ingredients, reduce the heat to low, and cook the mixture until it thickens, approximately 30 minutes. Stir frequently. If the consistency is thicker than you prefer, add a little water. Use the sauce warm or chilled. It keeps, refrigerated, for a couple of weeks.

"Barbecuists put secret ingredients into their sauces for the same reason that dogs piss on trees, to mark out a piece of territory as their own. The secret ingredient is not intended to make the sauce 'better' but to mark it in such a way as to leave no doubt that it's unique—it is peerlessness, not flavor, that makes it perfect. The praise it wants is not culinary exclamation but surrender: 'Damn it, J.D., but I've never tasted the like.'" John Thorne, *Simple Cooking* newsletter, 1988

☆**Serving Suggestion:** To us, many barbecue sauces taste as good, or perhaps even better, on other kinds of food than on real barbecue. Kansas City sauces really shine on barbecued ribs, but they can also enhance grilled hamburgers, baked brisket, fried sausage, boiled crawfish, or even fresh green onions.

Watch out for a new 900 phone number that Otis Boyd plans to offer in the near future for back-yard barbecuers. Along with advice, callers will probably get a packaged dry spice mixture that can be made into a Boyd-style sauce.

Among authentic Kansas City sauces, as opposed to the commercial copycats, the best known nationally are Arthur Bryant's and K.C. Masterpiece. The first, we think, is better in person than in the bottle, and the second is sweet enough to use as a cake frosting.

Boydesque Brew

In a town full of famous brand names, Otis Boyd makes the best unheralded barbecue sauce in Kansas City. This recipe imitates the original, but it's no excuse to skip a visit to the source of inspiration, Boyd 'n' Son Bar-B-Q, where they sell the piquant purée by the bite or the bottle.

¾ cup water
6-ounce can tomato paste
¼ cup white vinegar
½ medium onion, minced
1 tablespoon brown sugar
1 to 2 teaspoons prepared horseradish (optional)
1 teaspoon ground allspice

1 teaspoon celery salt
1 garlic clove, minced
½ teaspoon ground anise seeds
½ teaspoon fresh-ground black pepper
¼ teaspoon ground cinnamon
⅛ teaspoon cayenne

Makes about 2 cups

Mix the ingredients in a saucepan and bring the liquid to a simmer. Reduce the heat to low and cook until the onions are tender and the mixture thickens, 25 to 30 minutes. Refrigerate the sauce overnight to allow the flavors to mingle and mellow.

Use the sauce warm or chilled. It keeps, refrigerated, for a couple of weeks.

Vaunted Vinegar Sauce

If you're one of the millions of Americans who have never tried anything except tomato-based barbecue sauces, a taste of this could be a real revelation. Thin, vinegary sauces of this style are as indigenous to the Southeast as summer humidity and a lot more enjoyable, particularly on pork. A pig couldn't ask for a finer finish.

2 cups cider or white vinegar	1 teaspoon fresh-ground black pepper
2 tablespoons sugar or brown sugar	1 teaspoon cayenne or hot red pepper flakes
2 teaspoons salt	

Makes about 2 cups

Combine all the ingredients in a bowl and stir to dissolve the sugar. Serve at room temperature or chilled. The sauce keeps indefinitely.

This type of vinegar sauce is probably a direct descendant of early English ketchups, which were made with vinegar, mushrooms, and sometimes oysters, but never tomatoes. It can double as a mop, unlike tomato-based sauces, which are rarely applied before the last hour of cooking because they burn.

Carolina Red

The geographic gradation of sauces in North Carolina is fascinating. Toward the eastern shore, pitmasters favor a vinegar style, such as our Vaunted Vinegar Sauce, while their colleagues on the opposite, western border are inclined toward a thick, sweet-sour, ketchup-based sauce. This "Red" from the central Piedmont region is right in-between, blending the best of the rest of the state.

1½ cups cider vinegar	1 tablespoon sugar
½ cup ketchup	1 teaspoon salt
½ teaspoon cayenne or hot red pepper flakes	

Makes about 2 cups

Combine all the ingredients in a bowl and stir to dissolve the sugar. Serve at room temperature or chilled. The sauce keeps indefinitely.

You can't beat the name and you can't beat the sauce, at least if you're partial to pigs and mustard. Maurice's Piggie Park in West Columbia, South Carolina—where uniformed car hops still bring the barbecue to you curbside—sells its "million dollar" sauce by mail order. Call 800-MAURICE for a bottle of the sweet yellow pig potion.

Golden Mustard Barbecue Sauce

In South Carolina and Georgia, mustard-based sauces provide the strongest competition to vinegar mixtures.

1 cup white vinegar	6 garlic cloves, minced
¾ cup prepared yellow mustard	1½ teaspoons salt
½ medium onion, minced	½ teaspoon cayenne
⅓ cup water	½ teaspoon fresh-ground black
¼ cup tomato purée	pepper
1 tablespoon paprika	

Makes about 2 cups

Mix the ingredients in a saucepan and bring the liquid to a simmer. Reduce the heat to low and cook until the onions are tender and the mixture thickens, 20 to 25 minutes. Use the sauce warm or chilled. It keeps, refrigerated, for a couple of weeks.

☆**Variation:** Add a tablespoon or two of mayonnaise or brown sugar for a different level of tang.

Old-Fashioned High-Cholesterol Great-Tasting Southern Sauce

Not so common today, butter-based barbecue sauces frequently flavored pork in the past.

6 tablespoons bacon drippings	2 tablespoons Worcestershire
6 tablespoons butter	sauce
1 medium onion, chopped	2 teaspoons fresh-ground black
½ cup white vinegar	pepper
Juice of 2 lemons	1 teaspoon dry mustard
	1 teaspoon salt

Makes about 2 cups

In a saucepan, melt the bacon drippings and butter over medium heat. Add the onions and sauté for about 5 minutes, or until quite soft. Mix in the remaining ingredients, reduce the heat to low, and simmer for 5 minutes.

Use the sauce warm. It keeps, refrigerated, for at least a week.

☆**Serving Suggestion:** We think the old butter-based sauces are too rich for pork, but this one works well with grilled chicken or steak and with some vegetables, particularly smoked onions and steamed broccoli.

Memphis Magic

The center of mid-South barbecue, Memphis offers a range of sauces that take the high middle ground between Eastern and Western styles. Like this version, they are often medium-bodied mixtures, moderate in sweet, heat, and everything else except taste.

3 tablespoons butter	1 teaspoon salt
¼ cup minced onion	½ teaspoon fresh-ground black pepper
1 cup white vinegar	
1 cup tomato sauce	⅛ teaspoon cayenne
¼ cup Worcestershire sauce	Dash of Tabasco or other hot pepper sauce
2 teaspoons sugar	

Makes about 2 cups

In a saucepan, melt the butter over medium heat. Add the onions and sauté for 6 to 8 minutes, or until the onions begin to turn golden. Stir in the remaining ingredients, reduce the heat to low, and cook until the mixture thickens, approximately 20 minutes. Stir frequently.

Use the sauce warm. It keeps, refrigerated, for a couple of weeks.

Though there's a touch of heresy in the notion, some fine pitmasters use more charcoal than wood in barbecuing pork. In Memphis in particular, many people seem to prefer their pork with just a hint of smoke, supplementing that flavor with a robust sauce. Emily Payne and her daughter-in-law Flora serve their sandwiches that way at Payne's and so does Frank Vernon at the equally good Bar-B-Q Shop.

Our favorite bottled Texas sauce comes from Pitt's & Spitt's, who make and sell "The Best Sauce for the Boss" as a sideline to their pit business. If you can't find it locally, you can order by phone at 800-521-2947.

Bar-BQ Ranch Sauce

A lot of Texans eat their barbecue without a sauce, or with just meat juices laced with cayenne, but others prefer a robust sauce full of Southwestern seasonings.

1 tablespoon oil, preferably canola or corn	⅓ cup unsulphured dark molasses
2 cups chopped onions	¼ cup cider vinegar
2 to 3 minced fresh jalapeños	¼ cup fresh lemon juice
2 to 3 minced fresh serranos	¼ cup chili powder
8 garlic cloves, minced	2 tablespoons prepared yellow mustard
1 cup ketchup	
¾ cup Worcestershire sauce	1½ teaspoons ground cumin
¾ cup strong black coffee	1½ teaspoons salt

Makes about 4 cups

In a saucepan, warm the oil over medium heat. Add the onions, chiles, and garlic, and sauté over medium heat until everything is softened. Mix in the remaining ingredients and bring the sauce to a simmer. Cover and cook for 35 to 40 minutes. Allow the sauce to cool briefly.

Strain the sauce and purée the solids in a food processor. Return the puréed mixture to the sauce, stirring thoroughly. Refrigerate the sauce overnight to allow the flavors to mingle and mellow.

Use the sauce warm or chilled. It keeps for weeks.

☆**Variation:** If you prefer a thinner sauce, water this down to your preferred consistency. It will still pack plenty of pizzazz.

☆**Serving Suggestion:** If you don't want to slop up your 'Q,' use the sauce on potatoes. It makes a good topping on baked spuds, along with other favorite condiments, or stir the sauce into cottage fries or hash browns while they cook to give the potatoes an outdoors ranch flavor.

Sauce Olé

A chunky, salsa-style sauce enhances barbecued pork, smoked turkey, or our Nachos Blancos.

¾ cup canned crushed tomatoes
½ cup water
2 small tomatoes, preferably Romas or Italian plum, chopped
½ medium red onion, chopped
½ cup chopped roasted green chiles, preferably New Mexican, Anaheim, or poblano, fresh or frozen

2 to 3 tablespoons lime juice
2 tablespoons chopped fresh cilantro
1 tablespoon olive oil
½ teaspoon ground cumin
½ teaspoon salt

Makes about 2¼ cups

Combine the ingredients (starting with just 2 tablespoons of lime juice) in a saucepan and bring the mixture to a simmer over medium heat. Cook for approximately 10 minutes, enough to slightly thicken the sauce. The vegetables should soften a little yet still stay crisp-tender. Taste and add the additional lime juice if desired. Refrigerate the sauce for at least 1 hour to allow the flavor to develop.

Serve the sauce chilled. It keeps, refrigerated, for several days.

☆**Variation:** For a green sauce, substitute an equal amount of puréed fresh or canned tomatillos for the canned crushed tomatoes and reduce the amount of lime juice to ½ to 1 tablespoon.

When you're ready to create your own sauce, seek a savory balance of sweet, sour, and spicy flavors. The sweetening can come from regular or brown sugar, honey, maple syrup, molasses, cane syrup, hoisin sauce, or even Coca-Cola. Common sour ingredients include lemon or lime juice, tamarind concentrate, and vinegar—cider, raspberry, wine, white, rice, or sherry, among others. Add onions, garlic, chili powder or chiles, mustard, cumin, ginger, pepper, curry powder, or just about anything else from the spice rack. Salt or salty ingredients such as soy sauce are optional, according to taste. Remember always that a great sauce complements rather than masks the flavor of food.

Two of the mid-South's finest commercial sauces—Wicker's and Corky's—get wide regional distribution and enjoy a limited national market. Outside the area, look for them in specialty stores.

Black Sauce

Around Owensboro, Kentucky, a dark, thin, and tangy sauce like this is usually served on or with the barbecued mutton. It also works well with other dishes, such as our Mustard 'n' Lemon Chicken.

1 cup Worcestershire sauce	1 tablespoon plus 1 teaspoon fresh-ground black pepper
1 cup white vinegar	
2 tablespoons brown sugar	2 garlic cloves, minced
2 tablespoons fresh lemon juice	½ teaspoon ground allspice

Makes about 2¼ cups

Combine the ingredients together in a saucepan and heat over medium heat. Simmer the mixture for about 10 minutes. Serve the sauce hot or at room temperature.

Moonlite and Moonshine

Catherine and Hugh Bosley opened the Owensboro, Kentucky, Moonlite Bar-B-Q in 1963. Lacking restaurant experience, they just pretended they were having company for dinner. These days the company numbers in the thousands on weekends, many making the hour-plus trek from Louisville to load up on the copious buffet. Among the treats, one of our favorites is the vodka-based hot sauce, great on mutton and other red meat. It inspired this fiery concoction of our own.

The original Moonlite Bar-B-Q Very Hot Sauce and hundreds of other fiery sauces and condiments can be ordered from Mo Hotta-Mo Betta in San Luis Obispo, California. Call 800-462-3220 or fax them at 805-545-8349.

¾ cup white vinegar	¼ cup crushed chile caribe or other crushed dried red chile of moderate heat
¾ cup vodka	
½ cup Tabasco or other hot pepper sauce	
	3 tablespoons cayenne
¼ cup water	2 tablespoons ground dried red chile, preferably ancho
¼ cup tomato purée	

Makes about 2½ cups

Combine the ingredients in a saucepan and heat over medium heat. Simmer the mixture for about 20 minutes, until it's thickened a bit.

Serve the sauce warm or chilled, remembering that a little goes a long way. Full of natural preservatives, the sauce keeps indefinitely in the refrigerator.

Bour-BQ Sauce

Another boozy Kentucky inspiration, this sauce uses the state's native whiskey instead of vodka.

¼ cup butter
¼ cup oil, preferably canola or corn
2 medium onions, minced
¾ cup bourbon
⅔ cup ketchup
½ cup cider vinegar
½ cup fresh orange juice

½ cup pure maple syrup
⅓ cup unsulphured dark molasses
2 tablespoons Worcestershire sauce
½ teaspoon fresh-ground black pepper
½ teaspoon salt

Makes about 3 cups

In a saucepan, melt the butter with the oil over medium heat. Add the onions and sauté for about 5 minutes or until they begin to turn golden. Mix in the remaining ingredients, reduce the heat to low, and cook the mixture until it thickens, approximately 40 minutes. Stir frequently.

Serve the sauce warm. It keeps, refrigerated, for a couple of weeks.

Rich Davis and Shifra Stein of Kansas City wrote one of the best barbecue books of recent years, *The All-American Barbecue Book* (Vintage). They present a collection of recipes from pitmasters across the country and give a good overview of differences in regional styles. As you might expect from Davis, the creator of the original K.C. Masterpiece sauce, the information on sauces is particularly strong.

One of Bill Clinton's favorite barbecue sauces comes from McClard's Bar-B-Q in Hot Springs, Arkansas. The McClard family got the recipe in 1928 when they were running a tourist court along the highway. A boarder traded the secrets of the sauce for his $10 monthly rent, inspiring the McClards to fire up their pit for the public. The children and grandchildren of the founders still adhere strictly to the original recipe, now locked in a safe deposit box.

Creole Classic Barbecue Sauce

Snappy as a zydeco band, this sauce features the flavors of Louisiana.

1 tablespoon oil, preferably canola or corn	6 tablespoons Creole mustard, such as Zatarain's
1 medium onion, chopped	3 tablespoons brown sugar
½ medium green bell pepper, chopped	2 tablespoons chili sauce
2 celery ribs, chopped	½ teaspoon Tabasco or other hot pepper sauce
3 garlic cloves, minced	½ teaspoon fresh-ground black pepper
1 cup canned crushed tomatoes	½ teaspoon white pepper
1 cup chicken or beef stock	½ teaspoon cayenne
⅔ cup cider vinegar	Salt to taste
½ cup pecan pieces	

Makes about 3 cups

In a saucepan, warm the oil over medium heat. Add the onion, bell pepper, celery, and garlic and sauté until everything is softened, about 5 minutes. Mix in the remaining ingredients, reduce the heat to low, and cook until the mixture thickens, approximately 30 minutes. Stir frequently. Let the sauce cool briefly. Spoon the sauce into a blender and purée it until smooth. If the consistency is thicker than you prefer, add a little water.

Use the sauce warm or chilled. It keeps, refrigerated, for at least a week.

West Coast Wonder

This Asian-American hybrid works wonders with duck, lamb, fish, and seafood.

1 cup hoisin sauce	2 teaspoons minced fresh
½ cup rice vinegar	ginger root
¼ cup soy sauce	1 teaspoon ground anise seeds
2 tablespoons Dijon mustard	2 garlic cloves, minced

Makes about 1¾ cups

Combine the ingredients together in a saucepan and warm them over low heat for about 10 minutes.

Serve the sauce hot or at room temperature. It keeps, refrigerated, for several weeks.

☆**Serving Suggestion:** Thin the sauce with a little water and use it in a stir-fry with broccoli, green onions, red bell peppers, and sliced water chestnuts.

Jamaican Barbecue Sauce

This light but intensely flavored sauce goes well with salmon and most varieties of white fish. You can find the sweet-sour tamarind concentrate in Caribbean, Latin American, or Asian markets if it's not available in your grocery store.

2 cups seafood stock	2 tablespoons Jamaican Jerk
5 tablespoons honey	Rub (page 40) or other jerk
2 tablespoons tamarind	seasoning
concentrate	
2 tablespoons minced fresh	
ginger root	

Makes about 1¾ cups

Combine the ingredients in a saucepan and bring the mixture to a boil over high heat. Reduce the

Shady Nook BBQ Sauce, made by Chad Everett in Clarksdale, Mississippi, is more than a hundred years old. A German sharecropper developed the recipe in 1873 when he opened a small barbecue stand in a shady nook in Clarksdale. Call 601-624-4985 to find out how to get some.

heat and simmer the sauce until it's reduced by one-third, approximately 10 minutes.

Serve the sauce warm. It keeps, refrigerated, for several days.

☆**Variation:** If you want to pair the sauce with chicken, a delicious combination, substitute chicken stock for the seafood stock. To make the sauce hotter, in true Jamaican fashion, add part of a minced habanero or Scotch bonnet chile. Proceed cautiously, though, because these are the most blistering chiles known.

When you eat Jim Quessenberry's Sauce Beautiful, you glow as brightly as Jim does in the picture on the label. If stores in your area don't carry this classic, cuss them out and then order by mail from 206 East Merriman, Wynne, Arkansas 72396 or call 501-588-4442.

Cinderella Sauce

We developed this originally for our barbecued beef short ribs, but decided it was too good to limit to one dish. It also transforms other mundane cuts of meat, from pork spareribs to chicken drumsticks.

1½ cups ketchup	2 garlic cloves, minced
1 cup beer	2 teaspoons ground cumin
¾ cup cider vinegar	1½ teaspoons ground anise
¼ cup minced fresh cilantro	seeds
3 tablespoons brown sugar	1½ teaspoons salt
2 tablespoons Worcestershire sauce	1 teaspoon Tabasco or other hot pepper sauce

Makes about 2½ cups

Mix the ingredients in a saucepan and bring the liquid to a simmer. Reduce the heat to low and cook the mixture until it thickens, approximately 40 minutes. Stir frequently.

Use the sauce warm. It keeps, refrigerated, for a couple of weeks.

Jalapeach Barbecue Sauce

Fruit flavors are a tasty new fashion in barbecue sauces. This one sizzles with jalapeños and soothes with peaches.

16-ounce can peaches in heavy
    syrup, undrained
¼ cup minced onion
3 tablespoons minced pickled
    jalapeños
2 teaspoons pickling liquid
    from jar or can of pickled
    jalapeños

2 tablespoons peach chutney
2 teaspoons brown sugar
½ teaspoon Worcestershire
    sauce
½ teaspoon salt
¼ teaspoon ground cumin

Makes about 2 cups

Mix the ingredients in a saucepan and bring the liquid to a simmer. Reduce the heat to low and cook the mixture until the onions are tender and the sauce thickens, approximately 25 to 30 minutes.

Use the sauce warm or chilled. It keeps, refrigerated, for a couple of weeks.

☆**Serving Suggestion:** For a different start to the day, serve bacon glazed with the Jalapeach Barbecue Sauce. Bake thick-sliced strips of bacon for about 10 minutes at 350° F. Then brush both sides with the sauce and continue cooking for another 5 to 7 minutes per side.

A professional chef, Karen Putman of Kansas City, brought her expertise to bear in creating the Flower of the Flames Raspberry Bar-B-Q Sauce, one of the most distinctive and flavorful sauces on the market. Write P.O. Box 2182, Shawnee Mission, Kansas 66201 for ordering information. Karen's Flower of the Flames competition team has proven that women can win big on the barbecue circuit, taking more than one hundred awards, including the 1991 Jack Daniel Invitational Grand Championship.

Apple City Apple Sauce

This is our variation on a splendid sauce created by the Apple City BBQuers from Murphysboro, Illinois.

¼ cup butter	2 tablespoons cider vinegar
1 medium onion, minced	2 tablespoons tomato paste
2½ cups apple juice or cider	½ teaspoon chili powder
2 tablespoons unsulphured dark molasses	½ teaspoon cinnamon
2 tablespoons Worcestershire sauce	½ teaspoon salt

Makes about 2½ cups

In a heavy saucepan, melt the butter over medium heat. Add the onion and sauté for a couple of minutes, until the onion is softened. Mix in the remaining ingredients, reduce the heat to low, and cook the mixture until it reduces by about one-quarter, approximately 30 minutes. Stir frequently.

Serve the sauce warm. It keeps, refrigerated, for a couple of weeks.

☆**Serving Suggestion:** The sauce makes a fine glaze for apples. Sauté slices of apples in butter, adding a little apple cider as they soften. Then cover the slices with a few tablespoons of sauce and continue to cook until a glaze forms. We like the apple slices for breakfast or as a side dish with pork later in the day.

A part of Kansas City's big American Royal Barbecue Contest in October, the International Barbecue Sauce Competition attracts some two hundred entries annually for the title "Best Barbecue Sauce on the Planet." Only commercially available sauces qualify. Remus Powers, Ph.B. (Doctor of Barbecue Philosophy), started the event in 1987, originally calling it the "Diddy-Wa-Diddy National Barbecue Sauce Contest."

Lime-Mint Barbecue Sauce

As refreshing as a cool summer shower, this sauce mates well with lamb, salmon, or trout.

¼ cup butter	1 cup fresh lime juice
¼ cup minced celery	Zest of 4 limes
¼ cup minced green onions	¼ cup honey
1 garlic clove, minced	1 tablespoon prepared brown
1½ cups brewed mint tea made	mustard
from 3 mint tea bags	

Makes about 2 cups

In a heavy saucepan, melt the butter over medium heat. Add the onion and sauté for a couple of minutes, until the onion is softened. Mix in the remaining ingredients, reduce the heat to low, and cook the mixture until it reduces by about half, approximately 40 minutes. Stir frequently.

Serve the sauce warm or chilled. It keeps, refrigerated, for a couple of weeks.

South Florida Citrus Sauce

A zingy combo, flavored with citrus and horseradish, this is a winner on chicken, pork, shrimp, and meaty white fish, such as red snapper.

½ cup butter	Juice of 1 medium orange
1 cup cider vinegar	3 tablespoons brown sugar
1 cup tomato purée	1 tablespoon Worcestershire
5 tablespoons prepared	sauce
horseradish	1 teaspoon salt
Juice of 4 limes	

Makes about 2 cups

Mix the ingredients in a saucepan and bring the liquid to a simmer. Reduce the heat to low

Most commercial barbecue sauces are too sweet for our meat. When we use one, we often mix it half-and-half with Lawry's Mesquite with Lime Juice Marinade.

What do we eat? The four best-selling commercial barbecue sauces—Kraft, Bull's Eye, K.C. Masterpiece, and Thick 'N Spicy—are made by food units of the Philip Morris and Clorox conglomerates.

and cook the mixture until it thickens, approximately 40 minutes. Stir frequently.

Serve the sauce warm or chilled. It keeps, refrigerated, for a couple of weeks.

☆**Serving Suggestion:** Try the sauce on chilled boiled shrimp, as a substitute for the standard cocktail sauce.

Plum Good Slopping Sauce

The name lays the claim.

16-ounce to 17-ounce can plums in heavy syrup, undrained
¼ cup minced green onions
1 tablespoon prepared yellow mustard
1 teaspoon unsulphured dark molasses
½ teaspoon ground dried red chile, preferably New Mexican or ancho
¼ teaspoon salt
Dash of Worcestershire sauce

Makes about 2 cups

Mix the ingredients in a saucepan and bring the liquid to a simmer. Reduce the heat to low and cook the mixture until it thickens, approximately 20 minutes. Stir frequently.

Serve the sauce warm or chilled. It keeps, refrigerated, for a couple of weeks.

The Wall Street Journal says the market for commercial, tomato-based barbecue sauces got sluggish in the early 1990s. The newspaper blamed the slump on a trend toward cooking more chicken and fish outdoors. Designed originally for red meat, the usual grocery store sauce seldom does much for lighter fare.

☆ Traditional Side ☆ Dishes and Breads

What pitmasters serve on the side has a lot to do with what they serve in the center, and that has a lot to do with where they happen to be holding forth. Somewhere in the country, someone offers almost anything you can imagine, from pig snouts to tamales.

Our recipes cover the most traditional dishes, plus a few of the most unusual, but we don't always fix them in a purely old-fashioned way. In some cases we've spiced up the preparation a bit to help finish off the flavor of a dish, so that it can stand alone as well as sit on the side. Despite the occasional embellishments, the recipes remain true to their tradition. You'll find them worthy of serving on any barbecue plate, anywhere in the country.

Creamy Coleslaw

The barbecue belt never needed iceberg lettuce. When most of the country started down the road to radicchio in the 1950s, 'Q' lovers remained faithful to America's original crunchy green salad, coleslaw. This is a classic version of the dish, updated for contemporary tastes but still similar to the old cool sla *that many early settlers ate with meat.*

1 cup half-and-half	2 garlic cloves, minced
½ cup sugar	1 teaspoon salt or more to taste
6 tablespoons cider vinegar	1 medium head cabbage, grated
2 tablespoons mayonnaise	2 to 3 carrots, grated

Serves 6 to 8

In a lidded jar, shake together the half-and-half, sugar, vinegar, mayonnaise, garlic, and salt until well blended.

Place the cabbage and carrots in a large bowl, pour the dressing over the vegetables, and toss together. Chill the slaw for at least 1 hour. It keeps well for several days.

Lexington Red Slaw

Coleslaw is so linked to the 'Q,' some pitmasters like to flavor it with a dollop of barbecue sauce. That's particularly popular in the Piedmont region of North Carolina, home of this colorful version.

1 cup mayonnaise	2 to 3 tablespoons sugar
3 tablespoons Carolina Red	1 tablespoon ketchup
(page 292) or other Lexington/	1 tablespoon cider vinegar
Piedmont-style tomato-based	1 teaspoon salt or more to taste
barbecue sauce	1 medium head cabbage, grated

Serves 6 to 8

Lexington, North Carolina, is the only town in the country that has given its name to a type of barbecue. Since the turn of the century—when the burg's first joint opened in a tent across from the courthouse—a succession of pitmasters have maintained a consistent tradition by training their heirs as they cooked. Today as then, the Lexington style is pulled and chopped pork shoulder served with a mild tomato and vinegar sauce, topped off with a mound of red coleslaw made with the same sauce. It's so good that a town of fifteen thousand supports more than a dozen barbecue restaurants.

In a lidded jar, shake together the mayonnaise, barbecue sauce, sugar, ketchup, vinegar, and salt until well blended.

Place the cabbage in a large bowl. Pour the dressing over the cabbage and toss together. Chill the slaw for at least 1 hour. It keeps well for several days.

Brunswick Stew

In *Fading Feast*, a 1979 commemoration of disappearing regional American foods, Raymond Sokolov called Brunswick stew "the most famous dish to emerge from the campfires and cabins of pioneer America." Like many of the other foods Sokolov described, it's ripe for a national revival.

Brunswick stew is as old as barbecue. The first British settlers in the Southeast found Native Americans cooking both kinds of food, and in that region the two are still served together. "A good Brunswick stew," according to one venerable source, "is made of practically everything on the farm and in the woods, including chicken, beef, veal, squirrels, okra, beans, corn, potatoes, tomatoes, butterbeans, vinegar, celery, catsup, sugar, mustard, and enough red pepper to bring tears to your eyes." This version leaves out the squirrel meat—though some swear it's essential for authenticity—and it starts with smoked chicken rather than an uncooked bird.

2½-pound to 3-pound smoked chicken (or substitute the same size uncooked chicken)
1 pound boneless pork loin, cubed
¼ pound sliced bacon, chopped fine
10 cups water
4 large baking potatoes, peeled
3 tablespoons butter
3 medium onions, chopped
Two 10-ounce packages frozen lima beans or 2¼ cups fresh limas

1¼ cups fresh green beans, cut in ¾-inch lengths
5 tablespoons Worcestershire sauce
2 tablespoons prepared yellow mustard
4 teaspoons coarse-ground black pepper
1 tablespoon salt
1 teaspoon cayenne or more to taste

Serves 10 to 12

Place the chicken, pork loin, and bacon in a stock-pot. Pour the water over and bring to a simmer. Cook, uncovered, for 1 hour.

While the meats simmer, slice 3 of the potatoes in thirds and place them in a saucepan with enough water to cover. Bring the potatoes to a boil and cook until soft, about 20 minutes. Drain and mash the potatoes with the butter. Set aside.

Remove the chicken from the pot. When cool enough to handle, discard the skin and bones, and shred the chicken into bite-size pieces.

Return the chicken to the pot along with the mashed potatoes. Cut the remaining potato into bite-size chunks. Add the potato, other vegetables, and seasonings to the pot. Continue to simmer over medium-low heat for 1½ hours, stirring frequently. Add more water if the stew appears dry. The chicken and pork should be tender enough to fall apart, blending with the soft vegetables into a thick ragoût. The stew can be served immediately, but it reheats or freezes well.

☆**Serving Suggestion:** While Brunswick stew accompanies 'Q' in some areas, it also makes a satisfying main dish, especially on a rainy fall evening. We like to offer it with a selection of breads, including Blue Corn Muffins and Sweet Potato Biscuits.

Kentucky Burgoo

The Kentucky equivalent of Brunswick stew, burgoo is a living legacy, a hearty and peppery concoction from the past that's still a passion in the state. Some say the odd name has French or Turkish origins, but one authority suggests that it was just a slurred pronunciation of "bird stew."

The winner of the Kentucky Derby in 1932, a home-state horse, was Burgoo King. The owner named the thoroughbred after a famous Lexington burgoo cook, James T. Looney.

The best restaurant burgoo in the country comes out of the kitchen of George's Bar-B-Q in Owensboro, Kentucky, a cinder-block roadhouse cafe where the food's much finer than the table settings.

2½-pound to 3-pound smoked chicken (or substitute the same size uncooked chicken)
1½ pounds beef or veal shanks
1 pound smoked mutton or lamb (or substitute 1½ pounds uncooked lamb shanks)
12 cups water
1 tablespoon salt
3 cups tomato purée
2½ cups shredded cabbage
3 large baking potatoes, peeled, if you wish, and chopped
2 medium green bell peppers, chopped
2 large onions, chopped
3 to 4 medium carrots, sliced thin
3 large celery ribs, chopped
3 garlic cloves, minced
¼ cup sherry vinegar
1 tablespoon A-1 Steak Sauce
2 teaspoons fresh-ground black pepper
¾ teaspoon cayenne or more to taste
2½ cups sliced okra, fresh or frozen
2 cups corn kernels, fresh or frozen

Serves 10 to 12

Place the chicken, beef or veal shanks, and mutton or lamb in a stockpot. Pour the water over, sprinkle in the salt, and bring the mixture to a simmer. Cook, uncovered, for 1½ hours.

Remove the chicken and meats from the pot. When cool enough to handle, discard the skin, fat, and bones, and shred the chicken and meats into bite-size pieces.

Return the chicken and meats to the pot. Add the remaining ingredients, except for the okra and corn. Continue to simmer over medium-low heat for 2 more hours, stirring frequently. Add the okra and corn and cook for at least 1 more hour, preferably 2. Add more water if the stew appears dry.

As with Brunswick stew, the ingredients should be cooked down and no longer easily identifiable. The stew can be served immediately, but it is even better reheated the following day.

Kansas City Baked Beans

Boston has no monopoly on baked beans. This is how they cook them out west in Kansas City, where barbecue sauce is a key ingredient and a few local "burnt" brisket ends sometimes add a powerful smoky flavor.

1 pound dried navy beans, plus water to cover
6 additional cups water
1 teaspoon salt, plus more to taste
4 slices bacon, chopped
1 medium onion, chopped
2 medium bell peppers, chopped, preferably red and green
1 cup Struttin' Sauce (page 290) or other tomato-based barbecue sauce, or more to taste

1 cup apple cider
⅓ cup dark unsulphured molasses
¼ cup prepared yellow mustard
1 to 2 tablespoons cider vinegar
1 cup shredded Burnt Ends (page 107) (optional)

Serves 6 to 8

Soak the beans for at least 4 hours in water to cover, then drain.

In a large, heavy saucepan, combine the beans with the water. Bring the beans to a boil over high heat, and then reduce to a simmer. Cook slowly, stirring up from the bottom occasionally for at least 2 to 3 hours, depending on the beans. Stir in the salt after the beans have softened. Add more water if the beans begin to seem dry. The beans are ready when they mash easily but still hold their shape. Drain the beans.

Remus Powers's *BBQ Pocket Guide* (Pig Out Publications), a must for Kansas City residents and visitors, is a thorough survey of the local barbecue restaurants, events, products, and more. Known by his mother as Ardie Davis, Powers is a Doctor of Barbecue Philosophy (Ph.B.) and the dean of the College of Barbecue at the Greasehouse University. You can't miss him at a cook-off, attired in a derby and a white apron festooned with barbecue bones.

Preheat the oven to 325° F.

In a skillet, fry the bacon until crisp. Remove the bacon with a slotted spoon and drain it. Add the onion and bell pepper to the rendered bacon drippings and sauté until soft.

Transfer the bacon and the onion mixture to a greased Dutch oven or other baking dish. Mix in the remaining ingredients. Bake, covered, for about 1 hour. Uncover and bake for an additional 15 to 30 minutes. Serve hot. The beans reheat especially well.

Cowpoke Pintos

Meanwhile, down on the ranch, they wouldn't eat a navy bean even if Dolly Parton baked it.

In the chuck-wagon days, cowboys called beans "whistle berries" because of their gas-producing effect. The Coca-Cola in this recipe helps to muffle the whistling, which you can also accomplish with *epazote*, an herb that's sometimes called Mexican tea.

1 pound dried pinto beans, soaked overnight	2 tablespoons Worcestershire sauce
8 cups water, plus more as needed	1 tablespoon ground cumin seeds
12 ounces Coca-Cola	4 garlic cloves, minced
14½-ounce can whole tomatoes, undrained	3 to 4 fresh serranos or jalapeños, chopped
2 medium onions, chopped	1 teaspoon salt or more to taste
3 slices bacon, preferably a smoky slab variety, chopped	1 cup barbecued sausage, sliced (optional)
3 tablespoons chili powder	

Serves 6 to 8

Soak the beans overnight in water to cover. Drain.

In a Dutch oven or stockpot, combine all the ingredients except the salt and sausage. Bring the beans to a boil over high heat and then reduce to a simmer. Cook slowly, stirring up from the bottom occasionally, for at least 2 to 3 hours, depending on your batch of beans. Add more water if the beans begin to seem dry. Stir in the salt and the meat, if desired, in the last 30 minutes of cooking. The beans should still hold their shape but be soft and just a little soupy.

Serve the beans in bowls with a bit of the cooking liquid. The beans reheat especially well.

☆**Serving Suggestion:** With slices of Cracklin' Cornbread and romaine lettuce tossed with the vinaigrette used in Hand Salad, the beans are hearty enough for a weeknight supper.

Flash-Fried Okra

Fried in this old Southern fashion, okra becomes the Cinderella of vegetables, transformed from its humble and homely ways into a majestic mate for the 'Q.'

1 to 1¼ pounds fresh okra pods, preferably under 2½ inches each
Ice water to cover
2 teaspoons salt

2 cups cornmeal, preferably stone-ground
Oil for deep-frying, preferably peanut

Serves 4

Place the okra in a bowl and cover with ice water. Add the salt. Refrigerate for 30 minutes to plump the okra.

Spoon the cornmeal into a medium-size brown paper sack. Drain the okra and cut into thin rounds.

Pour the oil into a heavy saucepan, to a depth of at least 3 inches. Heat the oil to 360° F.

Dredge the okra in the cornmeal and fry until the cornmeal deepens slightly in color, a matter of seconds. Drain the okra and serve it immediately.

Some of the big barbecue competitions are international in scope. That's not enough for Perry, Oklahoma, which hosts Oklahoma Joe's Interplanetary B-B-Q Cook-Off each May. The grand champion team of the galactic event in 1993 was Tim & Todd's Most Excellent Adventure, a crew that spent its spare time launching water balloons into space.

Not Deli Dills

Especially in Arkansas and Mississippi, some pitmasters substitute pickles for okra as their fried green vegetable. The idea may sound strange, but the first bite will delight.

4 large dill pickles, sliced into rounds about ¾ inch thick
1 cup all-purpose flour
1 teaspoon baking powder
Salt and fresh-ground black pepper to taste

1 egg
1 cup buttermilk
Oil for deep-frying, preferably peanut

Serves 6

Blot any moisture from the surface of the pickles.
  In a medium-size bowl, stir together the flour, baking powder, salt, and pepper. Combine the egg and buttermilk in a small bowl, and then pour the mixture into the dry ingredients. Stir just to combine.

Pour the oil into a heavy saucepan, to a depth of at least 3 inches. Heat the oil to 375° F.

Dip the pickles in the batter and fry a few at a time until golden brown, about 2 minutes. Drain the pickles and serve immediately.

Candied Sweet Potatoes

About as down-home as a dish can be, this gooey Southern classic is like a vegetable dessert.

1 cup mini-marshmallows	¼ cup butter
¾ cup bourbon or similar whiskey	¼ cup milk
	¼ cup orange juice
2 to 2½ pounds sweet potatoes (about 3 medium), baked or boiled, still warm	¼ cup brown sugar
	½ teaspoon salt
	½ teaspoon ground cinnamon

Serves 6 to 8

In a small bowl, combine the marshmallows with the bourbon. Soak the marshmallows for 20 to 30 minutes, stirring occasionally.

Preheat the oven to 350° F. Grease a medium-size baking dish.

Peel the sweet potatoes, if needed. In a large bowl, mash or whip the potatoes with the butter. Pour any bourbon not yet absorbed by the marshmallows into the potatoes. Add the remaining ingredients, except the marshmallows, mixing until well incorporated.

Spoon the potatoes into the baking dish. Scatter the marshmallows over the potatoes. Bake, uncovered, for 25 to 30 minutes, until heated through to the ooey-gooey stage. Serve warm.

If some tyrant limited us to a choice of one place in the country to enjoy whole hog barbecue, Sweatman's in Holly Hill, South Carolina, would get our nod. It barely has an address, much less a phone, and it's open only on Friday and Saturday nights, but you can eat as high on the hog as you want. Bub Sweatman, a third-generation pitmaster, serves the whole animal, from the crispy skin to innards made into a heavenly hash.

Country Collard Greens

Another sweetened Southern vegetable dish, these greens may be the perfect accompaniment to barbecue. The combination of the two offers a blend of honey, smoke, and spice that would be the envy of any honky-tonk angel.

3 to 3½ pounds collard greens or kale, tough stems removed and roughly chopped
1 smoked ham hock (about 1 pound)
4 medium onions, chopped
2 medium green or red bell peppers, chopped
⅔ cup cider vinegar, preferably unrefined
1 tablespoon honey
3 garlic cloves, minced
1 tablespoon coarse-ground black pepper
2 teaspoons Tabasco or other hot pepper sauce or more to taste
2 teaspoons celery seeds
8 cups water

Serves 8

Combine all the ingredients in a large pot and bring to a boil. Simmer, covered, for about 2 hours. With a slotted spoon, remove the ham hock. When the hock is cool enough to handle, pick the meat from it in small chunks or shreds and return it to the pot. Reheat the greens briefly, if necessary. Serve warm with some of the liquid, the pot likker. Leftovers keep for several days.

Buttermilk Onion Rings

Barbecue legends, such as Leonard Heuberger of Memphis and Sonny Bryant of Dallas, among others, liked crispy buttermilk-soaked onion rings with their ribs and brisket. Sweet onions are particularly good in this recipe during their short spring season.

3 large onions, preferably sweet onions	2 teaspoons salt
3 to 4 cups buttermilk	2 teaspoons onion powder
1 cup all-purpose flour	2 teaspoons chili powder
1 cup cornmeal	1 teaspoon sugar (if not using sweet onions)

Oil for deep-frying, preferably peanut

Serves 4

Cut the onions into ¼-inch slices. In a nonreactive dish, soak the onions in the buttermilk for 30 to 60 minutes.

In a brown paper sack, combine the flour, cornmeal, salt, onion powder, chili powder, and, if needed, sugar. Drain the onions lightly and dredge them in the seasoned flour.

Pour at least 4 inches of oil into a heavy saucepan. Heat the oil to 375° F. Fry the onions, in batches, for 2 to 3 minutes, or until golden. For the crispiest results, drain on paper towels and spread on a serving platter rather than piling them into a basket, where they could become soggy. Serve immediately.

One of the most legendary Bar-B-Q joints in the country, Leonard's in Memphis got its start in 1922 when Leonard Heuberger opened a small stand and delivered barbecue by bicycle. Heuberger invented the Memphis barbecue sandwich—pork, coleslaw, and red sauce served between a bun—and two Leonard's locations still feature a good version of the original.

The immodest sign out front says it all at Bubba's barbecue joint in Eureka Springs, Arkansas: "It may not look famous, but it is."

Famous French Fries

Anyone can fry potatoes, but few people know how to make great French fries. The secret is a few extra steps, all worth the time in extra flavor. Increase the number of potatoes and other ingredients as needed for additional eaters.

1 to 1½ medium baking
    potatoes
Water
Ice cubes

Peanut oil or lard for deep-frying
Salt and/or Cajun or Creole
    seasoning

Serves 1

Wash the potatoes and, if you wish, peel them. We prefer the peels on, and besides, it's less work. Slice them into fat matchsticks, about ⅜ inch in diameter, and toss them into a bowl of cold water. Soak the potatoes in the water for at least 1 hour and preferably 2, to eliminate much of the starch. Pour off the water, add more cold water to cover, and toss in a half-dozen ice cubes. Soak the potatoes in the ice water to firm them back up, about 30 minutes. Drain them well on a dish towel or sturdy paper towels, drying off each matchstick. Then roll the potatoes up in another dry towel. You want no remaining moisture.

Heat the oil to 340° F in a large heavy saucepan. Add the potatoes in batches and partially fry them for 4 minutes. They should just begin to color. Drain the potatoes. This step can be done up to 30 minutes before eating.

Immediately, or just before serving, reheat the oil to 360° F. Fry the potatoes again for 3 to 4 minutes, or until golden brown. Drain the potatoes again. Sprinkle the salt or seasoning into a brown paper sack, add the potatoes, and shake. Serve the fries hot.

☆**Serving Suggestion:** For "wet fries" at the height of excess, top the fried potatoes with cheese sauce and a dollop of your favorite tomato-based barbecue sauce. (We use Struttin' Sauce.) For extra pizzazz, add a few slices of fresh or pickled jalapeño.

Prize Pilau

Spelled and pronounced a dozen different ways, this chicken-and-rice dish probably landed in Charleston, South Carolina, about 1680 and spread across the South as rice cultivation moved westward. Pilau is unusual for the region because of its French and Spanish overtones, but it's been a favorite in the barbecue belt for more than three centuries. The recipe really benefits from the use of homemade stock.

2½-pound to 3-pound whole chicken
4 cups chicken stock, preferably homemade
4 cups water
1½ teaspoons salt (if the stock is unsalted; otherwise, reduce the salt to taste)
1½ teaspoons fresh-ground black pepper
3 tablespoons bacon drippings or butter

1½ cups chopped green bell peppers
1 cup sliced green onions
1 cup chopped celery
1 teaspoon Worcestershire sauce
1 teaspoon Tabasco or other hot pepper sauce
2 cups uncooked white rice

Serves 6 to 8

Place the chicken in a stockpot. Pour the stock and water over, sprinkle in the salt and pepper, and bring the mixture to a simmer. Cook, uncovered, for 45 to 50 minutes. The chicken should be done, but not falling apart.

Preheat the oven to 350° F.

The official monthly publication of the Kansas City Barbeque Society, the *KC Bullsheet*, is easily worth the $20 membership cost. Write the Society at 11514 Hickman Mills Drive, Kansas City, Missouri 64134, or call 816-765-5801. The motto of the *Bullsheet* is "Barbecue… it's not just for breakfast anymore."

Remove the chicken from the pot. Increase the heat to high and reduce the cooking liquid to 2½ cups. Skim the fat from the cooking liquid. When the chicken is cool enough to handle, discard the skin, fat, and bones, and shred the chicken into bite-size pieces. Reserve both the cooking liquid and the chicken.

In a Dutch oven or other flameproof baking dish, warm the bacon drippings or butter over medium heat. Add the remaining ingredients, except the rice, and sauté until the vegetables are tender.

Stir the rice into the vegetables and pour the cooking liquid over the mixture. Scatter the chicken over the top. Cover the pilau and bake for about 1 hour, or until the liquid is absorbed and the rice is soft. Stir the pilau and serve it warm.

☆**Serving Suggestion:** Although pilau pairs with barbecue in the Carolinas, we find its subtle and distinctive flavors are shown off best when the dish takes center stage. We prefer it as a main dish with Sweet and Sour Cukes or other vegetable salads.

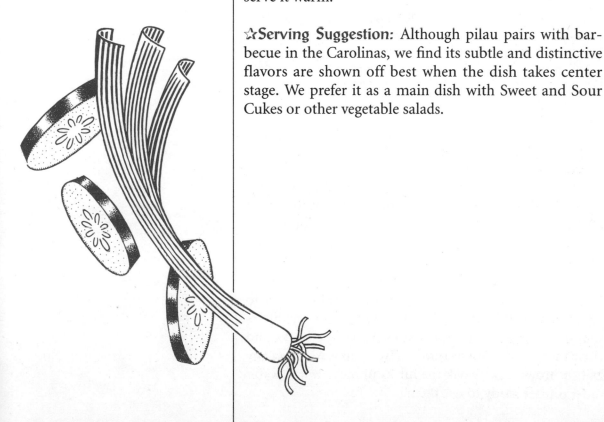

Hot Tamales

By all geographical rights, tamales should be a South-western side dish with barbecue, but it's actually the Mississippi Delta that specializes in them. Only a skinny cousin to a Tex-Mex or New Mexican tamale, they are usually made with yellow cornmeal rather than masa harina.

MEAT FILLING

1 tablespoon bacon drippings
¾ pound ground pork or beef
2 garlic cloves, minced
¼ cup chili powder
¾ teaspoon salt

¼ teaspoon dried oregano, preferably Mexican
¼ teaspoon cumin seeds, toasted and ground
¾ cup beef broth

TAMALES

6-ounce package dried corn husks
4 cups cornmeal, preferably yellow stone-ground
1½ cups beef broth

1¼ cups oil, preferably canola or corn, or solid vegetable shortening
1 cup water or more as needed
1½ teaspoons salt

Makes 24 tamales

In a heavy skillet, warm the bacon drippings over medium heat and add the meat and garlic. Brown the meat, then add the chili powder, salt, oregano, cumin, and broth. Simmer over medium heat for about 20 minutes or until the mixture has thickened but is still moist. Watch carefully toward the end of the cooking time, stirring frequently so it does not burn. Reserve the mixture. It can be made a day ahead.

To prepare the corn husks, soak them in hot water to cover in a deep bowl or pan. After 30 minutes the husks should be softened and pliable. Separate the husks and rinse them under warm running water to wash away any grit or brown silks. Soak the husks in more warm water until you are ready to use them.

Barbecue contest teams compete against each other on all levels, including their names. Some of the winners include Pork, Sweat & Beers (Cordova, Tennessee), ZZ Chop (Irving, Texas), Sow Luau (Memphis), Great Boars of Fire (Cobden, Illinois), Pork Forkers (Columbus, Mississippi), and Hazardous Waist (Collierville, Tennessee).

Pour the cornmeal into another large bowl. Add the broth, oil, water, and salt. Mix with a sturdy spoon, powerful electric mixer, or with your hands until smooth. When well blended, the mixture should have the consistency of a moist cookie dough.

To assemble the tamales, hold a corn husk flat on one hand. With a rubber spatula, spread a thin layer of cornmeal across the husk and top it with about 1 tablespoon of the meat filling. Roll the husk into a tube shape and tie the two ends with strips of corn husk. (It should resemble a party favor.) Repeat the procedure until all the meat and cornmeal mixture are used.

Steam the tamales, standing them on end or crisscrossed over water in a large saucepan or small stockpot. Don't pack the tamales too tightly. Cook the tamales for 50 minutes to 1 hour, until the cornmeal mixture is firm and no longer sticks to the corn husk. Unwrap one tamale to check its consistency.

The tamales should be eaten warm after first removing the corn husk.

☆**Serving Suggestion:** Try the tamales as a main dish served with San Antonio Cactus and Corn Salad and Liar's Lime Pie.

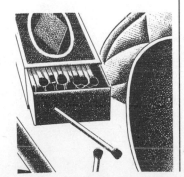

Mamie's Macaroni and Cheese

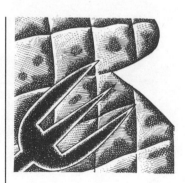

While fettucine, penne, and orzo may be the rage in some American restaurants, modest elbow macaroni still outsells them all. Combined with cheese as a time-honored comfort food, it offers a good foil to the smoky richness of barbecued meats. Cheryl's grandmother, Mamie, perfected this version.

¾ pound elbow macaroni, cooked according to package directions
2 tablespoons butter
3 eggs
1 cup buttermilk
1 cup evaporated milk
1½ teaspoons dry mustard

½ teaspoon Tabasco or other hot pepper sauce
½ teaspoon fresh-ground black pepper
¼ teaspoon salt
2 cups grated sharp cheddar cheese (2 ounces)

Serves 6

Preheat the oven to 350° F. Grease a medium-size baking dish. Toss the warm macaroni with the butter.

In a medium-size bowl, beat the eggs lightly and add the buttermilk, evaporated milk, dry mustard, Tabasco, pepper, and salt. Mix well. Stir in the macaroni and the cheese and pour the mixture into the prepared dish.

Bake, uncovered, for 30 minutes or until the macaroni and cheese is lightly firm and browned. Serve warm. Any leftovers should be reheated gently to avoid developing the consistency of galvanized rubber.

Jeff Smith, the "Frugal Gourmet," is a strong proponent of stove-top smokers such as the Cameron (page 14). He uses the portable indoor contraption in his cookbooks and on his TV show to add smoke flavor to a range of dishes.

Peppery 'Pups

These red pepper hush puppies are a Carolina barbecue specialty. Because of their crunch, they may go better with the 'Q' than with fried fish, the more common mate.

¾ cup cornmeal, preferably white stone-ground
⅓ cup all-purpose flour
¾ teaspoon sugar
½ to 1 teaspoon cayenne
½ teaspoon baking powder

¼ teaspoon baking soda
¼ teaspoon salt
½ cup buttermilk
¼ cup minced onion
1 egg, lightly beaten

Peanut oil for deep-frying

Serves 4 to 6

In a medium-size bowl, stir together the cornmeal, flour, sugar, cayenne, baking powder and soda, and salt. Mix in the buttermilk, onion, and egg.

Put enough oil in a skillet to measure at least 2 inches in depth. Heat the oil to 350° F. Gently spoon in the hush puppy batter by the tablespoon. Try a test pup first. It should quickly puff up and, when done, be deep golden brown on the outside. Cut into the first one to make sure it is cooked through. Adjust the heat if necessary.

Drain the hush puppies and serve hot.

Cracklin' Cornbread

An old Southern favorite, cracklings are crunchy slivers of pork skin or other bits of meat left after fat has been rendered. Using bacon will be easier for most home cooks and will result in a similar flavor.

3 slices bacon, chopped	¾ teaspoon salt
1½ cups cornmeal, preferably stone-ground, such as Arrowhead Mills or Adams	1 teaspoon baking soda
	1½ cups buttermilk
½ cup all-purpose flour	3 eggs, lightly beaten
3 tablespoons sugar	1 cup fresh or frozen corn kernels
1 tablespoon baking powder	2 tablespoons butter, melted

Serves 6 to 8

Preheat the oven to 400° F.

In a cast-iron skillet, fry the bacon over medium-low heat until very crispy. With a slotted spoon, remove the bacon, and drain it. Pour out all but 1 tablespoon of the rendered bacon fat. Keep the skillet warm.

In a medium-size bowl, stir together the cornmeal, flour, sugar, baking powder, salt, and baking soda. Pour in the buttermilk and eggs and mix by hand until lightly but thoroughly blended. Stir in the corn, bacon, and melted butter.

Pour the batter into the warm skillet. Bake for 20 minutes, or until the cornbread's edges are brown and the top has lightly browned. A toothpick inserted in the center should come out clean. Serve warm.

☆**Variation:** The batter, thinned with an additional ¼ to ½ cup buttermilk, can be fried into corncakes, a barbecue accompaniment in some areas of the upper South. For lighter cornbread, eliminate the bacon and substitute 1 tablespoon canola or corn oil for the rendered fat.

Old-fashioned white bread and similar hamburger-style buns are easily the favorite breads to eat with barbecue. The same characteristics that many people disdain—the blandness and sponginess—are a perfect foil for barbecue sauce.

A miraculous product from barbecue country, White Lily flour has been the secret to great Southern biscuits for more than a century. Soft-wheat flours absorb less liquid than all-purpose or hard-wheat flours, creating lighter, flakier biscuits. If you can't find soft-wheat flour, you can order from White Lily in Knoxville, Tennessee, at 615-546-5511.

Buttermilk Biscuits

In contrast to so many commercial versions, a superior biscuit should be a sky-high puff of dough as light as a cumulus cloud. These beauties achieve that ethereal texture and taste, while soaking up barbecue juices with the best of the white breads.

2 cups soft-wheat flour, preferably White Lily, or 1¾ cups all-purpose flour
1½ tablespoons sugar
2 teaspoons baking powder
½ teaspoon baking soda
½ teaspoon salt
3 tablespoons lard, well chilled
2 tablespoons solid vegetable shortening, preferably Crisco, well chilled
1 cup buttermilk, well chilled

Makes about eight 3-inch or twelve to fourteen 2-inch biscuits

Position the baking rack in the middle of the oven and preheat the oven to 450° F. Grease a baking sheet.

Sift together the dry ingredients into a large bowl. Repeat the sifting 3 times. With a pastry blender or large fork, blend in the lard and shortening, working lightly until a coarse meal forms. Pour in the buttermilk and stir together just until a sticky dough forms.

Flour your hands and a pastry board or counter. Turn the dough out and knead it lightly, 4 to 6 times. Pat out the dough to a thickness of about ½ inch. Cut with a 2-inch or 3-inch biscuit cutter or round cookie cutter.

Transfer the biscuits to the baking sheet, arranging so that they just touch each other. Bake for about 10 minutes, or until the biscuits are raised and golden brown. At the halfway point, turn the baking sheet from front to back, to get the most even browning. Serve immediately.

Sweet Potato Biscuits

A lovely shade of orange and very moist, these biscuits stay a little more compact than their buttermilk cousins.

8 ounces cooked sweet potato, well chilled	1½ teaspoons baking powder
⅓ cup buttermilk, well chilled	1 teaspoon sugar
1 cup soft-wheat flour, preferably White Lily, or ⅞ cup all-purpose flour	1 teaspoon chili powder
	½ teaspoon salt
	¼ teaspoon baking soda
	3 tablespoons lard, well chilled

Makes about twelve to fourteen 2-inch biscuits

Position the baking rack in the middle of the oven and preheat the oven to 450° F. Grease a baking sheet.

Purée the sweet potato and buttermilk together in a food processor or blender.

Sift the dry ingredients together into a bowl. With a pastry blender, cut in the lard until the mixture resembles coarse meal. With a spoon or spatula, fold in the sweet potato. Blend together well with the dry ingredients but don't overmix.

On a floured board or counter, knead the dough lightly, about 20 turns of the dough over itself. Pat out the dough to a thickness of about ½ inch and cut with a 2-inch biscuit cutter or round cookie cutter.

Transfer the biscuits to the baking sheet. Bake for about 14 minutes, or until the biscuits are raised and lightly browned on the top edges. At the halfway point, turn the baking sheet from front to back, to get the most even browning. Serve hot.

The biggest challenger to white bread at barbecue joints may be saltine crackers. They are particularly popular in places that serve meat by the pound and don't feature a sauce. Instead of a dainty four-pack you might get with soup in a regular restaurant, the pitmaster is likely to toss you and a mate a full, long bag of crackers directly out of the box.

Blue Corn Muffins

These slightly sweet and delicately flavored muffins are not truly traditional, but they go well with lighter smoked fare, such as fish and fowl. Substitute yellow cornmeal if you can't find the blue variety from the Southwest.

¾ cup butter
⅓ cup sugar
4 eggs
½ cup milk
1 to 2 fresh jalapeños, minced
¾ cup grated mild cheddar
  cheese (3 ounces)
3 ounces cream cheese or fresh,
  mild goat cheese

1 cup all-purpose flour
1 cup blue cornmeal,
  preferably stone-ground
2½ teaspoons baking powder
1 teaspoon salt
2 tablespoons poppy seeds

Makes 1 dozen

Preheat the oven to 375° F. Grease a muffin tin.

Cream together the butter and sugar with an electric mixer or food processor. Add the eggs, milk, jalapeños, and cheeses, mixing well after each addition. Sift together the flour, cornmeal, baking powder, and salt. Spoon the dry mixture into the batter about one-third at a time, again mixing well after each addition. Stir in the poppy seeds at the end.

Spoon the batter into the prepared muffin tins. Bake for 22 to 25 minutes, or until a toothpick inserted in the center comes out clean. Serve warm or at room temperature.

Many Bar-B-Q joints take pride in not cooking anything except their barbecue. In these cases, the side dishes are limited to items that don't require much except cutting—such as onions, tomatoes, avocados, jalapeños, and dill pickles.

Salads and ☆ Relishes ☆

Any pitmasters who limit their accompaniments to traditional barbecue side dishes are being blinded by their own smoke. Many kinds of food go great with barbecue, from down-home picnic specialties to creative, contemporary concoctions. These salads and relishes help to round out a barbecue feast. They complement the smoky taste of the main course while adding other dimensions to the meal.

Southern Caesar Salad

The classic Caesar salad contains some things, such as a coddled egg, that don't seem right at a barbecue. This variation gets extra zing from onions.

SOUTHERN CAESAR DRESSING

1½ cups extra-virgin olive oil

5 to 6 garlic cloves

2 tablespoons fresh lemon juice

2 tablespoons sherry vinegar

1 tablespoon Dijon mustard

1 teaspoon anchovy paste

¼ teaspoon coarse-ground black pepper

2 to 3 medium onions, cut in thick slices

2 to 3 heads romaine, the dark green outer leaves reserved for another purpose

½ cup grated or shredded Romano cheese

Serves 4 to 6

Combine the oil and garlic in a blender or food processor. Strain the oil through a fine sieve and discard the garlic. Pour the oil and remaining dressing ingredients back into the blender or food processor and combine until thick. Set aside.

Place the onions in a shallow dish in a single layer. Pour about ½ cup of the dressing over the onions and allow them to marinate for at least 30 minutes.

Prepare a grill or broiler. Drain the onions and grill or broil them for 8 to 10 minutes, until lightly browned and well softened. Watch them carefully, as they should caramelize lightly but not burn. Toss the onions with a tablespoon or two of dressing and set the onions aside to cool.

In a large bowl, toss the romaine leaves gently with enough dressing to coat, reserving the rest of the dressing for other salads. (Leftover dressing keeps for several weeks.) Transfer the lettuce to a decorative platter and

Something in the origin of the Caesar salad may explain why the classic version is not quite right for barbecue. Caesar Cardini, an Italian chef, created the salad in 1924 in a restaurant he owned in Tijuana, Mexico.

top it with the onion slices. Sprinkle the cheese over the salad and serve.

☆**Serving Suggestion:** On weekends when we're barbecuing for much of the day, we like this for lunch, accompanied by Sweet Potato Biscuits or any good loaf of bread.

The Cowgirl Hall of Fame in Hereford, Texas, has spawned namesake barbecue restaurants in New York City and Santa Fe. Both eateries provide support to the remote museum, though neither caters exactly to a cowgirl clientele.

California Crunch

CALIFORNIA DRESSING

1	ripe avocado, cut in chunks	1	garlic clove, minced
2	tablespoons fresh lemon juice	1	teaspoon chili powder
½	cup sour cream or plain yogurt	½	teaspoon sugar
6	tablespoons oil, preferably canola or corn	¼	teaspoon salt or more to taste
		¼	teaspoon fresh-ground black pepper

1	medium head romaine lettuce, sliced in thick ribbons	1	cup corn chips
2	ripe medium tomatoes, chopped	½	medium onion, cut in very thin rings
1	ripe avocado, sliced	½	cup grated Monterey jack or pepper jack cheese
½	cup black olives, sliced		

Serves 4 to 6

Combine all the dressing ingredients in a blender and purée until smooth.

In a bowl, toss the romaine, tomatoes, avocado, and olives with about half the dressing. Top the salad with the corn chips, onion, and cheese, arranged attractively. Serve immediately with additional dressing on the side. If the dressing thickens, mix a bit of water into it.

Killed Salad

Generations of Southern cooks doused leaf lettuce with a heap of hot bacon drippings, more than a smidgen of sugar, and a splash of vinegar. This is a homey but slightly more sophisticated take on the original idea. Most people know it as a "wilted salad," but some Southerners have always called it "killed salad."

GLAZED BACON

4 slices bacon, preferably a smoky slab variety

1 tablespoon honey

1 tablespoon prepared yellow mustard

Dash of cider vinegar

BACON VINAIGRETTE

Rendered bacon fat plus extra-virgin olive oil to make ½ cup

1 garlic clove, minced

3 tablespoons cider vinegar

1 tablespoon honey

Salt and fresh-ground black pepper to taste

10 to 12 cups torn leaf lettuce

Serves 4 to 6

Preheat the oven to 350° F.

Arrange the bacon in a single layer on a baking sheet with sides. Bake the bacon 10 minutes, and pour off all rendered fat, reserving it.

In a small bowl, mix the honey, mustard, and vinegar together. Spread half the mixture on top of the bacon, and return the meat to the oven for another 7 to 8 minutes. Turn the bacon over and spread it with the remaining syrup mixture. Bake for another 6 to 7 minutes, until the bacon is medium-brown and crispy. Watch carefully for the last few minutes to avoid burning. Cool briefly. Chop or crumble the bacon.

Warm the bacon fat and oil mixture over medium heat in a small skillet. Add the garlic and sauté it briefly. Add

The Dixie Pig in Blytheville is among the oldest restaurants in Arkansas; it opened in a log cabin in 1923. It also has the distinction of serving one of the oddest barbecue dishes in the country, a lettuce and tomato salad topped with a mound of smoky pork and a choice of dressings.

the remaining dressing ingredients and heat through, stirring until the honey dissolves.

Place the greens in a salad bowl and pour the warm dressing over them. Toss lightly. Like cooked spinach, the lettuce will reduce substantially in volume. Sprinkle the bacon over the salad and serve the salad hot or at room temperature.

☆**Serving Suggestion:** Granny served her version of this salad with a Sunday ham and, maybe in the spring, batter-fried mushrooms hunted by the whole family. We like it on summer evenings with crusty rolls and Bourbon Peaches.

Burstin' with Black-Eyed Peas Salad

From the hoppin' John of the deep South to the Texas caviar served in Dallas, the black-eyed pea is featured in some of the favorite dishes of the barbecue belt. While we've never met a black-eyed pea we didn't like, they really shine in this salad.

1 pound black-eyed peas, dried or frozen

4 to 6 cups chicken stock, preferably homemade

1 to 2 teaspoons crab boil seasoning or barbecue dry rub, such as Wild Willy's Number One-derful Rub (page 36)

1 small bell pepper, preferably red, diced fine

6 green onions, sliced

BLACK-EYED PEA VINAIGRETTE

⅓ cup oil, preferably corn or canola

3 tablespoons fresh lime juice

1 tablespoon cider vinegar, preferably unrefined

1 tablespoon tomato-based barbecue sauce

1 to 3 teaspoons brown sugar

1 to 2 pickled jalapeños, minced

2 garlic cloves, minced

1 teaspoon chili powder

1 teaspoon fresh-ground black pepper

1 teaspoon salt, or more to taste

½ teaspoon ground cumin

Serves 4 to 6

In a large saucepan, cover the peas by at least 1 inch with stock, sprinkle in the crab boil seasoning, and bring to a boil over high heat. Reduce the heat to a simmer and cook until the peas are tender, anywhere from 45 minutes to 1½ hours depending on your peas. Frozen peas generally cook faster. Stir occasionally, and add more stock or water if the peas begin to seem dry before they are done.

Drain the peas. In a large bowl, toss them together with the bell pepper and onion.

In a blender or food processor, mix together the vinaigrette ingredients. Pour over the peas.

Refrigerate, covered, for at least 2 hours and preferably overnight. The peas taste best the following day. Serve them chilled.

☆**Serving Suggestion:** Always offer black-eyed peas on New Year's Eve or Day, as solid a guarantee as you can get for good luck in the months ahead. To ring in the year in style, serve the peas with a Creole Crown Roast.

Chief cook Jim Ward designed and built the smoker used by the Porky Pilots, a barbecue contest team composed entirely of Federal Express pilots. The basic concept for the pit, according to Jim, came from the old Southern practice of barbecuing over a slow fire on discarded bedsprings, using a junked car hood for a cover. Back then, he says, when pitmasters didn't have thermometers, they could tell they were cooking at the right temperature if the flies stayed away from the meat.

Hand Salad

At a fancy affair, the hostess would probably call this crudités. *Our version might be a little too crude for her tastes, though.*

BARBECUE VINAIGRETTE

½ cup fresh orange juice
2½ to 3 tablespoons tomato-based barbecue sauce, preferably a variety that isn't overly sweet or flavored with liquid smoke, such as Memphis Magic (page 294)

2 teaspoons Worcestershire sauce
1 garlic clove, minced
½ cup corn oil, preferably unrefined
Salt and fresh-ground black pepper to taste

A batch of easily handled raw vegetables—asparagus stalks, carrot sticks, green onions, cucumber chunks, broccoli florets, summer squash slices, center leaves of romaine, cherry tomatoes
A healthy sprinkling of barbecue dry rub, such as Southwest Heat (page 39) or Cajun Ragin' Rub (page 38), or seasoned salt

Serves 8 to 10

In a food processor, combine the orange juice, barbecue and Worcestershire sauces, and garlic. Drizzle in the oil, continuing to process, until combined. Add salt and pepper to taste.

Arrange the vegetables on a platter. Sprinkle dry rub over them to taste. Pour the salad dressing into a bowl. Serve the veggies as finger food, for people to dunk in the dressing. Leftover dressing keeps for at least a week.

Sweet and Sour Cukes

A cooling combo no matter how hot it gets outdoors.

2   medium cucumbers, peeled
    and chopped
1   medium tomato, chopped
1   medium green bell pepper,
    chopped
1   large onion, chopped

1   cup white vinegar
⅔   cup sugar
½   teaspoon salt
½   teaspoon fresh-ground black
    pepper

Serves 6

In a large bowl, toss the vegetables together. Add the remaining ingredients and stir well. Refrigerate the salad for at least 30 minutes, stirring again before serving. The salad keeps well for a couple of days.

San Antonio Cactus and Corn Salad

A Southwestern delicacy for centuries, prickly-pear cactus deserves to be better known in other regions. Look for it in the Mexican food section of the supermarket in jars labeled nopales *or* nopalitos. *Here succulent strips of the cactus enhance summer sweet corn.*

4   ears corn-on-the-cob,
    smoked, boiled, or roasted
1½ cups nopalitos, drained and
    diced
¾   cup peeled and diced
    cucumber
1 to 2 small tomatoes,
    preferably Roma or Italian
    plum, chopped

2   tablespoons minced fresh
    cilantro
2   tablespoons sliced green
    onions
Lettuce leaves

The Bop-N-Quers contest team from Memphis has a barbecue smoker shaped like a juke box. The group sets up a dance floor in its cooking area and bops away the day while the 'Q' browns.

NOPALITOS DRESSING

3 tablespoons extra-virgin olive oil	1 fresh serrano chile or jalapeño, minced
1 tablespoon fresh lime juice	¼ teaspoon salt

Serves 6

Slice the kernels from the ears of corn. Place the corn in a medium-size bowl and mix in the nopalitos, cucumber, tomatoes, celery, cilantro, and onion.

In a small lidded jar, shake together the dressing ingredients and pour over the vegetables. Serve the salad at room temperature or chilled, on the lettuce leaves.

☆**Serving Suggestion:** The salad can double as a salsa or relish. Try it—without the lettuce—on crisp tortilla chips or warm corn tortillas as an appetizer.

Van's Pig Stand in Shawnee brags of being "the oldest family-owned restaurant in Oklahoma." The Vandegrift clan has a modern building nowadays, but they still cook hogs with the smoke of a hickory fire, just like they did in the 1930s.

Boarding House Macaroni Salad

This is the only kind of pasta salad you should have the nerve to serve with real barbecue.

1 pound macaroni, preferably small elbows or shells, cooked and drained	1 medium green bell pepper, chopped
6 to 8 ounces mild or medium cheddar cheese, cut in small cubes	1 medium onion, chopped
	⅔ cup sweet pickle relish
	¼ cup mayonnaise
1½ cups baby peas, fresh or frozen	¼ cup plain yogurt
	¼ cup chopped pimientos
	White pepper to taste

Serves 6 to 8

In a large bowl, mix together all the ingredients. Refrigerate, covered, for at least 1 hour to develop the flavors. The salad keeps well for several days.

☆**Variation:** Add a minced clove or two of garlic, or some sliced green olives.

Tangy Buttermilk Potato Salad

5 medium baking potatoes, peeled
½ green bell pepper, chopped
6 radishes, grated

4 hard-boiled eggs, grated
⅓ cup chopped sweet pickles
3 tablespoons sweet pickle juice
4 green onions, sliced

BUTTERMILK DRESSING

¾ cup mayonnaise
½ cup buttermilk
2 tablespoons chopped fresh parsley
1 tablespoon plus 1 teaspoon prepared yellow mustard

2 garlic cloves, minced
1 teaspoon fresh-ground black pepper
¼ teaspoon salt, or more to taste

Serves 6 to 8

In a large pan of boiling salted water, cook the potatoes over high heat until tender, 15 to 20 minutes. Drain the potatoes, rinse them in cold water, and drain them again. Set the potatoes aside to cool.

Place the bell pepper, radishes, eggs, pickles, pickle juice, and green onions in a large bowl. Chop the cooled potatoes into bite-size chunks and add them to the bowl, mixing lightly.

In a blender, combine the dressing ingredients. Pour about ¾ of the dressing over the potatoes and stir together until well blended. Add more dressing to taste, or a little more salt to adjust the salad to your liking. Cover and chill for at least 2 hours or, even better, overnight. Serve cold. The salad keeps well for several days.

☆**Variation:** If you can find a "hot and spicy" variety of sweet pickles, try them in the salad for extra punch. Our favorite brand is Jardine's Hot, Sweet, and Spicy Pickles.

Nobody forgets a take-out sandwich from C & K Barbecue in St. Louis. A flattened scoop of potato salad sprawls under the top slice of white bread, making an inherently messy meal into total mayhem. Your meat of choice may be the smoky ribs, but many of the locals prefer "barbe-cued snoots," deep-fried slices of pig snouts as crunchy as cracklin's.

Available widely in supermarkets and specialty stores, the zippy little numbers also can be mail-ordered from the Austin headquarters at 800-544-1880 or 512-444-5001.

Hot German Potato Salad

8 medium red potatoes, peeled if desired	½ teaspoon salt, or more to taste
1½ celery ribs, chopped fine	¼ teaspoon fresh-ground black pepper
½ green bell pepper, chopped fine	¾ cup beer
1 hard-boiled egg, grated	6 tablespoons cider vinegar
⅓ cup chopped fresh parsley	1 tablespoon plus 1 teaspoon sugar
4 slices slab bacon, chopped	1 tablespoon prepared brown mustard
½ medium onion, chopped	
2 teaspoons all-purpose flour	

Serves 6 to 8

In a large pan of boiling salted water, cook the potatoes over high heat until tender, 15 to 20 minutes. Drain the potatoes, rinse them in cold water, and drain them again. Set them aside to cool.

Place the celery, bell pepper, egg, and parsley in a large bowl. Slice the potatoes thick and add them.

Fry the bacon in a skillet over medium heat until browned and crisp. With a slotted spoon, remove the bacon, drain, and reserve it. Add the onion to the warm bacon drippings and cook briefly until softened. Sprinkle in the flour, salt, and pepper and stir to combine. Pour in ½ cup of the beer, the vinegar, the sugar, and the mustard, and bring to a boil. Reduce the heat and simmer for 2 to 3 minutes.

Pour the sauce over the potato mixture and toss to combine. The salad should look moist but not runny. If it seems dry, add some or all of the remaining beer. Taste and adjust the seasoning. The vinegar tang should come

One of the best pits in Virginia is called a "pitt" because the sign painter couldn't spell. You may wonder at first if the same fellow painted the orange and yellow building at Pierce's Pitt Bar-B-Que in Lightfoot, but after one of the succulent pork sandwiches, you'll be an empathetic shade of Day-Glo yourself.

across as assertive but not aggressive. Add the bacon shortly before serving. Serve hot.

☆**Serving Suggestion:** For a hearty lunch while barbecuing, try the German potato salad with the sandwich we call a German burrito—a flour tortilla wrapped around a smoked link sausage and loaded with mustard and onions. Beer would be optional only if you're French.

Sweet Sally's Sweet Potato Salad

The sweet potato makes an attractive alternative to Irish spuds in salads. Our version bathes sweet potato chunks in a zesty dressing featuring chipotle chiles (smoked jalapeños). We got the idea from Sally Martin, an English friend who moved to the Southwest and started putting chipotles in everything short of afternoon tea.

2   large or 4 small sweet potatoes, about 2 pounds total, peeled and cut in bite-size chunks
1   medium bell pepper, preferably red, chopped

1   celery rib, chopped
6 to 8 green onions, sliced thin
2   tablespoons chopped fresh cilantro
Salt and coarse-ground black pepper to taste

CHIPOTLE DRESSING

⅓ cup fresh lime juice
¼ cup canned chipotle chiles
1 tablespoon ketchup

1½ teaspoons Dijon mustard
1 garlic clove, minced
⅓ cup extra-virgin olive oil

Serves 6

In a large pan of boiling salted water, cook the sweet potatoes over medium-high heat until tender, 10 to 12 minutes. Drain the potatoes, rinse them in cold water, and drain them again. Set them aside to cool briefly.

Place the bell pepper, celery, green onion, and cilantro in a large bowl. Add the potatoes, mixing lightly.

Short Sugar's Pit Bar-B-Q in Reidsville, North Carolina, won a Congressional barbecue contest in 1982. Representatives from North and South Carolina got into a spat about which state had the best 'Q' and settled it with a barbecue duel. A dozen of the top joints from each state sent samples to Washington, and a jury of Congressional peers awarded top honors to Short Sugar's—for the pork as well as the name.

Combine all the dressing ingredients, except for the oil, in a food processor and purée together. Drizzle in the oil and continue to process until thick. Pour about three-quarters of the dressing over the potato mixture and toss to combine. The result should look moist but not runny. If it seems dry, add the remaining dressing. Taste and adjust the seasoning. Cover and chill for at least 2 hours or, even better, overnight. Serve cold. The salad keeps well for several days.

Kraut Salad

Paul Bosland, the reigning academic authority on chiles, once specialized in sauerkraut. He changed fields when he decided that kraut wasn't a growth industry. Apparently not enough folks had tried this kind of salad.

16 ounces sauerkraut, preferably not a canned variety
⅔ cup sugar
⅓ cup cider vinegar
½ cup sliced water chestnuts
½ medium onion, chopped
½ small green bell pepper, chopped
½ small red bell pepper, chopped
2 carrots, shredded fine
2 celery ribs, chopped
2 tablespoons oil, preferably canola or corn
1 tablespoon mustard seeds
Dash of ground cloves

Serves 6

Drain the sauerkraut, rinse it, and drain it again. Place the kraut in a large bowl.

In a small saucepan, heat the sugar and vinegar together until the sugar has dissolved. Pour the mixture over the kraut and toss well. Add the remaining ingredients and toss the salad again. Refrigerate, covered, for at least 1 hour. Serve chilled. The salad keeps well for several days.

Arty Rice Salad

2 cups cooked white rice
6-ounce jar marinated artichoke hearts, sliced thin, with marinade
⅓ cup mayonnaise
2 celery ribs, chopped fine
¼ cup sliced pimiento-stuffed green olives
2 tablespoons chopped red bell pepper or pimiento

2 tablespoons minced fresh parsley
3 green onions, sliced thin
1 pickled jalapeño, minced
1 teaspoon curry powder
Pinch of sugar
Lettuce leaves (optional)

Serves 6

In a large bowl, mix the rice with the other ingredients, except the lettuce. Refrigerate, covered, for at least 30 minutes. Serve chilled, on top of the lettuce leaves if desired.

☆**Serving Suggestion:** For a cheery lunch while your meat smokes for dinner, serve the salad mounded in red bell pepper halves and pass Blue Corn Muffins as an accompaniment.

For a different perspective on barbecue secrets, take a look at Matt Kramer and Roger Sheppard's *Smoke Cooking,* published in 1967. It's a terrific resource book, devoted to barbecue cooking methods, but the authors seem completely unaware of real barbecue. They call their technique "smoke roasting" and label it "a revolution in outdoor cooking."

Mango and Avocado Salad

CELERY SEED DRESSING

¼ cup sugar
¼ cup honey
¼ cup white vinegar
2 tablespoons fresh lemon juice
2 teaspoons grated onion
1 teaspoon dry mustard

1 teaspoon paprika
½ teaspoon salt
1 cup oil, preferably canola or corn
2 tablespoons celery seeds

Shredded red cabbage
3 ripe mangoes, sliced
3 ripe Hass avocados, sliced

Serves 6

In a food processor or blender, combine all the dressing ingredients except the oil and celery seeds. Pour in the oil and continue processing until thick and well blended. Spoon in the celery seeds and process just until incorporated.

Make a bed of shredded cabbage on a serving platter. Arrange the mangoes and avocados decoratively on the cabbage. Drizzle some dressing over the salad and serve the salad with the remaining dressing on the side.

The dressing keeps, refrigerated, for a couple of weeks and complements any fruit salad. Process again before using if it separates.

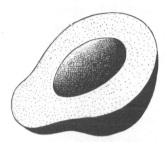

They take pig rustling seriously in Tennessee, according to John Egerton in *Southern Food* (Knopf). Since the early years of statehood, stealing a porker could land you in jail for up to fifteen years, three times longer than the maximum sentence for involuntary manslaughter.

'Nana Nut Salad

We had almost forgotten this childhood favorite until we stumbled onto it recently in the buffet line at the Owensboro, Kentucky, Moonlite Bar-B-Q.

DRESSING

½ cup sugar
1 egg yolk, lightly beaten
3 tablespoons white vinegar

½ cup Miracle Whip salad dressing (not mayonnaise)

6 medium bananas, sliced
½ cup chopped salted peanuts

Additional chopped peanuts, for garnish (optional)

Serves 6

In a small, heavy saucepan, combine the sugar, egg yolk, and vinegar. Warm over low heat, stirring constantly, until the sugar dissolves and the mixture thickens. Remove from the heat and mix in the Miracle Whip.

Combine the bananas and peanuts in a large bowl. Spoon the dressing over the salad and mix well. Top with additional peanuts, if you wish. The salad is best eaten within a couple of hours.

The Bosley family calls their Owensboro barbecue restaurant "Kentucky's Very Famous Moonlite." The acclaim is real, and you'll see why if you try the Moonlite's mountainous buffet, three long tables crowded with coleslaw, gelatin salads, burgoo, green beans, macaroni, cornbread with sorghum, mutton, beef, pork, chicken, and enough desserts to put a dieter into shock. The food is superb and it all costs about the same as a hot dog at Yankee Stadium.

Among the small number of great drive-ins left in the country, the Beacon in Spartanburg, South Carolina, is in a class by itself. It's a better tribute to controlled chaos than central Manhattan, and guiding spirit J.C. Stobel rushes you along with more verve and determination than a New York cabbie. The kitchen cooks everything that's considered edible in the state, but the thousands of people who show up on weekend nights come mainly for the barbecue, heaped on skyscraper sandwiches.

Devil-May-Care Eggs

Despite their own heat, these little numbers will cool you down on a blistering summer day. If you can't find spicy sweet pickles in your area, use regular sweet pickles and up the jalapeño ante.

12 hard-boiled eggs
3 tablespoons mayonnaise
2 tablespoons hot and spicy sweet pickles, chopped
2 tablespoons minced pickled jalapeño
2 tablespoons minced fresh cilantro

1 tablespoon plus 1 teaspoon Dijon mustard
1 tablespoon minced green onion
1 to 2 teaspoons curry powder (optional)
Salt to taste

Cilantro sprigs, for garnish

Makes 24 eggs

Halve the eggs lengthwise. Remove the yolks and place them in a bowl. Reserve the egg whites. Using a fork, crumble the yolks. Stir in the remaining ingredients. Adjust the seasonings to taste.

Spoon the yolk mixture into the egg whites, or, for a more festive look, pipe the mixture with a pastry tube. Refrigerate the eggs, covered, until serving time. Arrange on a platter surrounded by cilantro.

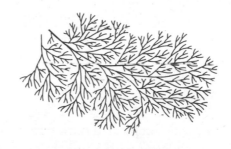

Okra Pickles

2 pounds small whole okra
3 cups vinegar, preferably cider
1 cup water
2 tablespoons pickling salt
2 teaspoons white wine Worcestershire sauce
1 teaspoon Tabasco or other hot pepper sauce

5 small whole dried chiles, preferably cayenne or pequín
5 garlic cloves
5 fresh dill heads
1¼ teaspoons mustard seeds

Makes approximately 5 pints

In a large bowl, soak the okra in cold water for about 1 hour to plump them.

While the okra soaks, sterilize 5 to 6 pint canning jars according to the manufacturer's directions.

Shortly before the okra finishes its bath, combine the vinegar, water, salt, Worcestershire sauce, and Tabasco in a medium-size saucepan and bring the mixture to a boil. Simmer the pickling liquid while you combine the okra and spices in their jars.

With clean hands, snugly pile the okra vertically into the sterilized jars, leaving about ½ inch of space at the top of each jar. Add a chile, garlic clove, dill head, and portion of the mustard seeds to each jar. Arrange the okra and the spices attractively.

Ladle the hot pickling liquid over the okra in each jar, covering the okra but leaving about ½ inch of headspace. Seal.

Process the jars in a boiling water bath for 10 minutes. Let the pickles sit for at least a week, and preferably several weeks, before serving.

☆**Serving Suggestion:** Make the pickled okra part of a dazzling relish tray. Load a platter with a mix of pickles and chowchows, supplementing your homemade goodies with a few store-bought selections, if needed.

Canning requires only a few pieces of equipment, none terribly expensive. The essentials are a big-lidded canning pan or a large stockpot, and canning tongs for gripping jars going in and coming out of steaming water. A wide-mouthed canning funnel is also useful but not a necessity. Use the size jars suggested in recipes, since changes can affect a product's processing time. Let the processed jars cool undisturbed for 12 hours. Check the seals and refrigerate any jars that have not sealed. Store in a cool, dry place.

Carolina Jerusalem Artichoke Pickles

Jerusalem artichokes have nothing to do with the Holy Land or artichokes. These tubers, sometimes known as sunchokes, are kissing cousins to the sunflower. The knobby little fists taste slightly sweet and offer a pleasant crunch. You can find them fresh in well-stocked produce sections from winter through spring.

3 cups cider vinegar	1 medium onion, sliced and pulled into individual rings
⅔ cup water	
⅔ cup light brown sugar	5 small whole dried chiles, preferably cayenne or pequín
1 tablespoon pickling salt	
1 teaspoon whole allspice, bruised	5 whole cloves
½ teaspoon ground turmeric	2 teaspoons mustard seeds
3 pounds Jerusalem artichokes, well scrubbed but unpeeled, sliced about ¼ inch thick	2 teaspoons celery seeds

Makes about 5 pints

Sterilize 5 to 6 pint jars according to the manufacturer's directions.

In a large saucepan, combine the vinegar, water, sugar, salt, allspice, and turmeric. Bring the syrup to a boil and boil for 3 to 5 minutes.

With clean hands, snugly pile the artichoke slices and onion rings into the sterilized jars, leaving about ½ inch of space at the top. Add a chile, a clove, and equal portions of the mustard and celery seeds to each jar.

Ladle the hot pickling liquid over the artichokes, covering the artichokes but leaving about ½ inch of headspace. Seal.

Process the jars in a boiling water bath for 10 minutes. Let the pickles sit for at least a week, and preferably several weeks, before you indulge.

Humphrey Bogart's famous line, "Here's looking at you, kid," is a feeling you can't escape at Roy's in Hutchinson, Kansas, where everyone sits at one big circular table facing each other. A dozen enthusiastic folks chow down on 'Q' at once, producing a chorus of lip-smacking you can hear all the way to Wichita.

Wonderful Watermelon Pickles

Hard to find at a local grocery outside the South, these morsels will make you a believer if you try them once. Just save the rind from the next watermelon you eat and take a little time over the following three days to complete a series of simple steps.

THE FIRST DAY

Rind of one large watermelon, cubed (makes about 16 cups)	¾ cup pickling salt
	1 gallon water

THE SECOND DAY

6 cups sugar	1 tablespoon whole allspice
4 cups white vinegar	4 sticks cinnamon, broken more or less in half
2 cups light brown sugar	
2 lemons, sliced thin	¼ teaspoon mustard seeds
1 tablespoon whole cloves	

Makes about 8 pints

The first day

This is the toughest part of the process. Cut the watermelon rind into manageable chunks. Scrape all the remaining red watermelon meat from the inside of the rind. Then pare off the hard green skin of the outer rind with a small knife. It's not difficult, but it takes a while. Cube the rind into bite-size pieces.

In a large bowl, dissolve the salt in the water. Transfer the rind cubes to the salted water. Find an out-of-the-way corner of your kitchen for the bowl and then weight the rind down with a plate to keep it submerged. Soak the cubes for about 24 hours.

No one has won more barbecue cooking awards than Paul Kirk, the Kansas City Baron of Barbecue. A big winner at the American Royal competition, the Jack Daniel Invitational, and even the Irish Cup International, Kirk generously shares his secrets with others through cooking classes and recipe tips in publications such as the *KC Bullsheet*, the monthly newsletter of the Kansas City Barbeque Society (11514 Hickman Mills Drive, Kansas City, Missouri 64134).

The second day

Combine all the remaining ingredients in a large saucepan and bring them to a boil, simmering the syrup for about 5 minutes.

While the syrup simmers, drain the cubes, rinse them, and drain them again. Rinse the bowl the cubes were soaking in and return the cubes to the bowl. Pour the hot syrup over the cubes, return the bowl to its original resting place, cover it lightly, and let it sit for another 24 hours, more or less.

The third day

Sterilize 5 to 6 pint canning jars according to the manufacturer's directions.

Pour the cubes and syrup into a large pan and bring the mixture to a boil. With a slotted spoon, pack the cubes lightly into the prepared jars, dividing the lemon slices and spices equally among the jars. Pour the syrup over the cubes, covering them but leaving about ½ inch of headspace. Seal.

Process the jars in a boiling water bath for 10 minutes. Allow the pickles to sit for at least 1 week, and preferably several weeks, before serving.

Green Tomato Chowchow

A savory mustard-based relish, chowchow comes in more varieties than the pickup trucks at a honky-tonk.

2 pounds green tomatoes (4 to 5 medium)	2 fresh jalapeños
1½ pounds cauliflower (1 to 1½ heads)	3 tablespoons pickling salt
	2½ cups cider vinegar
1 pound onions, preferably sweet	1½ cups sugar
	2 tablespoons pickling spice
2 large bell peppers, preferably a combination of red and green	1 tablespoon celery seeds
	1 tablespoon mustard seeds
	2 teaspoons dry mustard
	½ teaspoon ground ginger

Makes about 5 pints

Chop all the vegetables in batches in a food processor. Chowchow is generally chopped fine, but stop short of puréeing it. You want some remaining chunkiness and fresh vegetable texture.

Place all the vegetables in a large bowl and sprinkle with the salt. Let the vegetables sit for at least 2 hours and up to 4 hours, stirring occasionally. They will release a good bit of liquid while they rest. Drain them but don't rinse.

Sterilize 5 to 6 pint canning jars according to the manufacturer's directions.

Bring the vinegar, sugar, and spices to a boil in a large pan or stockpot. Reduce the heat and simmer for 10 minutes. Add the vegetables and continue simmering for another 10 minutes. Bring the mixture to a rolling boil and boil for 2 to 3 minutes. Spoon the hot chowchow into the prepared jars, leaving ½ inch of headspace. Seal.

Process the jars in a boiling water bath for 10 minutes. Let the chowchow sit for at least a week, and preferably several weeks, to develop its flavor before serving.

Right along old Route 66, now Interstate 40, in Clinton, Oklahoma, Jiggs Smoke House looks like a frontier cabin painted with smoke. The pitmasters will barbecue anything that moves and sell it to you by the pound, along with jars of chowchow and other superb relishes.

☆**Serving Suggestion:** For our tastes, nothing is better with barbecued meat inside a sandwich than chowchow, which cuts and complements the richness of almost any smoked food.

In a city full of barbecue restaurants, Jim Neely's Interstate won the title of "Best Little Porkhouse in Memphis" in a two-month survey conducted by reporters at the Memphis *Commercial Appeal*. That perked up business, which was mighty slow when Neely opened his place in 1980. Back then, he says, "my wife and I could watch a whole movie between customers."

Squash Relish

Another fine idea from Cajun country, this sweet-sour relish is as zippy as a Justin Wilson quip.

3	quarts water	2½	tablespoons mustard seed
⅔	cup pickling salt	2	cups chopped onions
8	cups chopped yellow squash	2	cups chopped bell peppers,
3	cups sugar		preferably a combination of
2	cups white vinegar		red and green
2½	tablespoons celery seeds	6	green onions, sliced

Makes about 4 pints

Sterilize 4 to 5 pint canning jars according to the manufacturer's directions.

Stir together the water and salt in a large bowl until the salt has dissolved. Add the squash to the brine and soak it for 1 hour. Rinse the squash, drain it, and rinse and drain it again.

In a stockpot, bring the sugar, vinegar, celery seeds, and mustard seeds to a boil. Stir in the squash and other vegetables and bring the mixture back to a boil.

Pack the mixture into the prepared jars, leaving ½ inch of headspace, and seal. Process the jars in a boiling water bath for 10 minutes. The relish is best after it sits for at least 2 weeks.

Corn and Watermelon Pickle-lilli

Cambridge, Massachusetts, chef Chris Schlesinger, a big fan of real barbecue, came up with this unusual relish for his terrific book, The Thrill of the Grill *(Morrow). We've tinkered a bit with the original version. The texture is best when you chop the pickles and vegetables not much larger than the corn kernels.*

2 medium ears of corn, smoked, roasted, or boiled	½ cup cider vinegar
1 cup Wonderful Watermelon Pickles (page 350) or store-bought watermelon pickles, chopped fine	¼ cup brown sugar
	¾ teaspoon chili powder
	½ teaspoon ground cumin
	1 tablespoon minced fresh cilantro
½ medium red onion, chopped	
½ medium red bell pepper, chopped	

Makes about 2 cups

Slice the kernels from the ears of corn. In a medium-size bowl, combine the corn and watermelon pickles.

Place the remaining ingredients, except the cilantro, in a small saucepan and bring the mixture to a boil. Boil for 1 minute and then pour the mixture over the corn and watermelon pickles. Refrigerate the relish for at least 1 hour. Stir in the cilantro just before serving.

☆**Serving Suggestion:** When you've got smoked turkey leftovers, make a sandwich on toasted sourdough with sharp cheddar cheese and this relish.

Piccalilli refers to any one of many highly seasoned relishes. Chowchows are similar, but almost always have mustard among their ingredients.

Chef Schlesinger took a barbecue vacation in 1989, traveling across the country to sample the local 'Q.' He reported in *The Cook's Magazine* that he "ate barbecue in burned-out shacks and McDonald's clones from Texas to Ohio, and it varied wildly in style and quality. The people we met would drive clear across five counties for a taste of their favorite barbecue, and every blessed one of them was an expert."

Bourbon Peaches

2 pounds peeled whole peaches, small to medium in size, ripe yet still firm
2 cups sugar
2 cups water
½ cup bourbon
1 cinnamon stick
8 to 10 peppercorns
2 tablespoons bourbon (optional)

Serves 4 to 6

Combine all the ingredients, except the optional bourbon, in a heavy saucepan. Bring the mixture to a rolling boil over high heat. Boil until the peaches can be pierced easily with a fork, but before they soften, about 5 minutes.

Remove the pan from the heat and let it cool to room temperature. Refrigerate the peaches in the syrup for at least 24 hours. Weight the peaches with a saucer, if necessary, to keep them submerged. Taste the peach syrup and, if desired, add the optional bourbon. Serve chilled or at room temperature. The peaches keep well, refrigerated, for up to a week, and they soften in texture.

When a group of U.S. pitmasters challenged Soviet cooks in a barbecue contest in 1990, the winners were The Wild Boars of Walls, Mississippi, a team headed by Gene and Patti McGee. Estonians hosted the cook-off, but they never stood a chance against the Mississippi masters.

Down-Home
☆ Desserts ☆

Barbecue demands dessert, even if it's no more than a packaged peanut pattie or fried pie picked up at the cash register on the way out of a Bar-B-Q joint. Sweet follows smoke as naturally as amorous eyes track after tight jeans.

The best desserts for a barbecue pig-out are the old American favorites. These are updated recipes for many of the top choices, developed specifically to provide a perfect finish for a hearty, smoky meal.

Prodigal Pecan Pie

Nothing finishes a barbecue meal better than a sinfully rich pecan pie. This recipe is heavily influenced by John Thorne, editor of the wonderful Simple Cooking *newsletter, who came up with the method for making the filling so lusciously dense.*

1 cup dark brown sugar	3 tablespoons dark rum
⅔ cup cane syrup, preferably, or ⅓ cup light corn syrup and ⅓ cup dark unsulphured molasses	½ teaspoon vanilla extract
	½ teaspoon salt
	4 eggs
4 tablespoons butter	2 to 3 tablespoons half-and-half
	2 generous cups pecan pieces

Unbaked 9-inch pie crust
Pecan halves

Serves 6 to 8

Preheat the oven to 350° F.

In a large, heavy saucepan, combine the brown sugar, syrup, butter, rum, vanilla, and salt. Heat to the boiling point, stirring frequently. Boil for 1 minute, stirring constantly. Remove the pan from the heat and let the mixture cool.

In a bowl, beat the eggs with the half-and-half until light and frothy. Mix the eggs into the cooled syrup, beating until well incorporated. Stir in the pecans. Pour the filling into the pie crust. Top with a layer of pecan halves.

Bake for 45 to 50 minutes, until a toothpick inserted into the center comes out clean. Serve warm or at room temperature.

When you're barreling down Interstate 40 between Little Rock and Memphis, treat yourself to a great meal in De Valls Bluff, Arkansas. Start with a pork sandwich at Craig's Bar-B-Q and then wander across the street to that simple building with the hand-painted "Pie Shop" sign. In an annex to her home, Mary Thomas makes some of the best pies in the South, including a pecan delight that she calls a Karo Nut Pie.

Peanutty Pie

Some peanut pies are similar in consistency to a pecan pie. We prefer this creamy, cool style with barbecue.

CRUST

1¼ cups graham cracker crumbs (about 16 crackers)	2 tablespoons sugar
	5 tablespoons butter, melted

FILLING

1 cup whipping cream	1 tablespoon vanilla extract
8 ounces cream cheese, at room temperature	1 cup powdered sugar
1¼ cups creamy peanut butter (don't use a natural or fresh-ground type)	⅓ cup chopped peanuts, preferably honey-roasted
	Chocolate sauce (optional)

Serves 6 to 8

When you're in the mood for a lighter fare to finish a barbecue feed, toss together a platter of juicy seasonal fruit, or turn directly to The Best Cure for a Southern Summer. Consider also a smoked fruit from the Garden of Eatin' chapter, or a sweet beverage from our Cool and Cheery Drinks.

Preheat the oven to 350° F.

In a bowl, stir together the graham cracker crumbs and sugar. Pour in the butter and stir to combine.

Pat the mixture into the bottom and sides of a 9-inch pie pan. Bake for 10 minutes, until lightly set. Put the crust aside to cool.

Whip the cream in a bowl until stiff and reserve it. In another bowl, beat together the cream cheese, peanut butter, vanilla, and powdered sugar. Fold in the whipped cream and blend well. Spoon the filling into the graham cracker crust and sprinkle the peanuts over the pie. Refrigerate, covered, for at least 2 hours, or overnight.

To gild the lily, serve with a spoonful of your favorite chocolate sauce. The pie keeps well for several days.

Run for the Roses Pie

Traditionally served to celebrate the Kentucky Derby, this pie provides a triple crown finish to any barbecue.

1 cup brown sugar	½ teaspoon vanilla extract
⅔ cup cane syrup, preferably, or ⅓ cup light corn syrup and ⅓ cup dark unsulphured molasses	½ teaspoon salt
	4 eggs
	2 to 3 tablespoons half-and-half
3 tablespoons butter	2 cups walnut pieces
3 tablespoons Kentucky bourbon	⅓ cup chocolate chips

Unbaked 9-inch pie crust

Serves 6 to 8

Preheat the oven to 350° F.

In a large, heavy saucepan, combine the brown sugar, syrup, butter, bourbon, vanilla, and salt. Heat to the boiling point, stirring frequently. Boil for 1 minute, stirring constantly. Remove the pan from the heat and let the mixture cool.

In a bowl, beat the eggs with the half-and-half until they are light and frothy. Mix the eggs into the cooled syrup, beating until well incorporated. Stir in the walnuts and the chocolate chips. Pour the filling into the pie crust.

Bake for 45 to 50 minutes, until a toothpick inserted into the center comes out clean. Serve warm or at room temperature.

☆**Serving Suggestion:** On Derby Day serve Almost Owensboro Mutton on sandwiches and a big pot of Kentucky Burgoo. Wash them down with Derby Day Mint Juleps and present this pie for the grand finale.

The pie-eating contest is one of the most appetizing events at the Owensboro, Kentucky, International Bar-B-Q Festival. In 1992, thirteen-year-old Roger Morris took home the $100 prize by holding his breath and scarfing a banana-cream pie in enormous mouthfuls. Still hungry, Roger entered the mutton-eating contest a few minutes later, trying to down an entire barbecue sandwich in one bite.

Wild Huckleberry Pie with Coconut Crumble

You aren't likely to find huckleberries in a grocery store, but they grow wild in many parts of the country and occasionally show up in farmers' markets during summer months. For a reasonable alternative in appearance and taste, substitute blueberries and reduce the amount of sugar.

4 cups huckleberries
⅔ to ¾ cup sugar
3 tablespoons instant tapioca

Juice of 1 lemon
Pinch of nutmeg

Unbaked 9-inch pie crust

⅓ cup all-purpose flour
⅓ cup sugar
3 tablespoons butter, at room temperature

⅓ cup shredded unsweetened coconut

Serves 6 to 8

Preheat the oven to 425° F.

In a large bowl, stir together the huckleberries and enough sugar to make the berries taste sweet with a tart edge. Add the tapioca, lemon juice, and nutmeg. Spoon the fruit into the pie shell.

Bake the pie for 15 minutes, then reduce the heat to 375° F and continue baking for an additional 18 to 20 minutes.

While the pie bakes, mix together the remaining ingredients in a small bowl. Remove the pie from the oven and sprinkle the coconut mixture evenly over the top.

Return the pie to the oven for 25 to 30 more minutes, covering the crust with aluminum foil if it begins to get overly dark. When done, the topping should be crisp and golden brown. Serve warm.

Memphis pitmaster John Willingham tells people that barbecuing is like running for President: "We smoke but don't inhale."

Liar's Lime Pie

When someone serves you a "Key lime pie" these days, what you're actually getting is closer to this liar's version. It can be a great pie, but it's rarely made with the wonderfully distinctive Key limes anymore because Florida's commercial crop was wiped out in a 1926 hurricane. Though you can still find the small, sour gems in the Caribbean and Mexico, most stores in the States carry only Persian limes, which are similar to lemons.

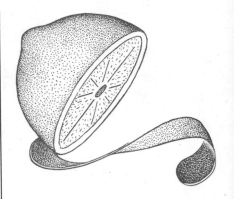

CRUST

1¼ cups graham cracker crumbs (about 16 crackers)

2 tablespoons sugar

2 teaspoons minced lime zest

5 tablespoons butter, melted

FILLING

1 pint heavy cream

14-ounce can sweetened condensed milk

6-ounce can limeade concentrate

6 tablespoons fresh lime juice

2 teaspoons minced lime zest

⅛ teaspoon vanilla extract

Lime slices, for garnish

Serves 6 to 8

Preheat the oven to 350° F.

In a bowl, stir together the graham cracker crumbs, sugar, and lime zest. Pour in the butter and stir to combine.

Pat the mixture into the bottom and sides of a 9-inch pie pan. Bake for 10 minutes, until lightly set. Put the crust aside to cool.

With an electric mixer, whip the cream until very stiff. Add the remaining ingredients, except the lime slices, and continue beating until well combined. Pour the filling into the pie shell. Garnish with the lime slices. Refrigerate the pie for at least 4 hours, and preferably overnight. Serve chilled.

☆**Serving Suggestion:** The creamy pie is perfect after spicy smoked dishes such as Pit Pot Roast or Peppered Catfish.

Molly O'Neill, author of the wonderful *New York Cookbook*, knows her due about the 'Q.' She once wrote in *The New York Times Magazine*, "Barbecue smoke is to the Texas skyline what cathedral spires are to European capitals: sacred things, icons of identity."

Lemon Pudding Ice Cream Pie

LEMON PUDDING

¾ cup sugar	5 egg yolks, lightly beaten
2 tablespoons cornstarch	6 tablespoons fresh lemon juice
⅛ teaspoon salt	Zest of 1 lemon
¾ cup water	2 tablespoons butter

CRUST

1 cup graham cracker crumbs (about 14 crackers)	2 tablespoons sugar
	Zest of 2 lemons
⅓ cup pecan pieces	5 tablespoons butter, melted

4 cups vanilla ice cream, softened

2 tablespoons pecan pieces, for garnish (optional)

Serves 6 to 8

To prepare the pudding, mix together the sugar, cornstarch, and salt in a heavy saucepan. Pour in the water, stirring to combine. Warm the mixture over medium-low heat, stirring constantly until hot but short of boiling. Place the egg yolks, lemon juice, and zest in a small bowl and gradually add about ½ cup of the hot mixture to the yolks. Stir the egg mixture back into the saucepan. Cook slowly and stir constantly, gradually bringing the pudding just to a boil over 7 to 10 minutes. Remove the pudding from the heat and whisk in the butter. The pudding should be somewhat thick but will thicken further while it cools. Refrigerate the pudding for at least 1 hour.

Preheat the oven to 350° F.

To prepare the crust, combine the graham cracker crumbs, pecans, sugar, and lemon zest in a food processor and process until crumbly. Pour in the butter and process just to combine.

Pat the mixture into the bottom and sides of a 9-inch pie pan. Bake for 10 minutes, until lightly set. Put the crust aside to cool.

When both the pudding and pie shell are cool, assemble the pie. Pack about half of the ice cream into the pie shell, smoothing it evenly. Top it with about half the pudding. Place the pie in the freezer for 15 minutes. Remove the pie from the freezer and spoon the remaining ice cream over the pudding, smoothing it again. Decoratively swirl thick spoonfuls of the remaining pudding over the ice cream, leaving some of the ice cream exposed. Sprinkle pecans over the pie, if you wish.

Freeze the pie for 2 hours or longer. Let it sit at room temperature for 5 to 10 minutes before serving.

Pan-Fried Pies

Fried pies are always popular with barbecue. Most versions are deep fried, but we like them cooked this way, which is the leading style around Owensboro, Kentucky.

CRUST

- 2 cups all-purpose flour
- 1 teaspoon salt
- 6 tablespoons lard or solid vegetable shortening, well chilled
- 6 tablespoons butter, well chilled
- 5 to 7 tablespoons ice water

FILLING

- 1½ cups dried peaches
- 1½ cups water
- ½ cup peach jam
- ¼ cup finely minced pecans

Butter for pan-frying

Lindsey's in Little Rock, Arkansas, is known for both its barbecue and its light, flavorful fried fruit pies. Church of God in Christ Bishop D. L. Lindsey opened the restaurant in the mid-1950s, and it has been in his family ever since. You'd better like soda pop with your 'Q,' because there's no beer there.

Serves 8

With a food processor, combine the flour and salt. Add the lard and butter and process until a crumbly meal forms. Pour in the water, a couple of tablespoons at a time, processing until the dough just barely holds together. Form the dough into a ball and wrap it in plastic. Refrigerate the dough for at least 30 minutes, and up to 2 days.

To make the filling, combine the peaches with the water in a heavy saucepan. Simmer the fruit over low heat until it is plump and soft and most of the water is absorbed, about 25 minutes. Add more water if needed.

Drain the peaches and chop them fine. Transfer the peaches to a small bowl. Stir in the jam and the pecans and reserve the mixture.

On a floured pastry board or counter, roll out the dough ¼ inch to ⅛ inch thick. Cut the dough into rounds with a 3-inch biscuit cutter.

Divide the filling among the dough rounds. Moisten the dough's edges with water and fold the pies into half-moons. Crimp the edges with a fork.

Just before serving, melt enough butter in a heavy skillet over medium heat to come up about one-third of the way on the pies. Pan-fry the pies until lightly browned and cooked through on both sides, about 8 to 10 minutes. Serve hot.

☆**Variation:** For crustier pies, deep-fry the little pockets of fruit in 350° F vegetable shortening or oil. If you're watching calories, the pies can be baked instead. Brush the tops with a bit of beaten egg white and bake for 20 minutes at 375° F.

Fruit Pizza

This one is bound to keep your guests smiling to the end.

CRUST

¾ cup butter, at room temperature	½ cup powdered sugar
	1¼ cups all-purpose flour

TOPPING

8 ounces cream cheese, at room temperature
4 ounces almond paste
¼ cup sugar
1 egg
1 teaspoon vanilla extract
½ teaspoon almond extract
3 to 3½ cups colorful mixed fruit (strawberry halves, blueberries, raspberries, kiwi slices, pineapple chunks, apricot halves, orange sections with their membranes removed)

1 cup currant or apricot jelly
1 tablespoon fresh lemon juice
1 tablespoon brandy or triple sec

Serves 8

Preheat the oven to 350° F. Grease a 12-inch pizza pan.

In a food processor or an electric mixer, combine the butter and sugar. Add the flour and mix well. Flatten out the soft dough with your hands and press it into the prepared pan, forming a thin layer.

Bake the crust for 16 to 18 minutes, or until lightly browned and firm.

While the crust bakes, beat together the cream cheese, almond paste, sugar, egg, vanilla, and almond extract with an electric mixer. Pour the mixture over the crust, smoothing it with a spatula.

Bake the pizza for an additional 10 minutes or until the topping is lightly set. Cool the pizza.

The Barbecue Industry Association says that men are more likely than women to do the outdoor cooking in the family, but the women are the ones who decide when and what to cook. There's a point there somewhere.

About 1 to 2 hours before serving, arrange the fruit decoratively over the pizza. In a small, heavy saucepan, heat together the jelly, lemon juice, and brandy until the jelly melts. Brush the jelly mixture over the fruit.

Refrigerate the pizza for 1 to 2 hours. Serve the chilled pizza cut into wedges.

Rhubarb Crunch

Rhubarb offers a tangy contrast to a smoked meal. Food writer Marilynn Marter inspired this homey preparation.

¾ cup all-purpose flour	3 cups chopped rhubarb, fresh
¾ cup rolled oats	or frozen
½ cup brown sugar	½ cup sugar
6 tablespoons butter, melted	1 tablespoon cornstarch
2 teaspoons ground anise seeds	½ cup water
1 teaspoon ground cinnamon	½ teaspoon vanilla extract

Serves 6

Preheat the oven to 350° F. Grease an 8-inch square pan.

In a small bowl, mix together the flour, oats, brown sugar, butter, anise, and cinnamon. Press half of the mixture into the pan, reserving the rest. Place the rhubarb over the crumb mixture.

In a small saucepan, stir together the sugar and cornstarch. Add the water slowly, stirring to avoid lumps. Warm the sauce over medium heat, cooking until it is clear and lightly thickened, 3 to 5 minutes. Remove the sauce from the heat and stir in the vanilla. Pour the sauce over the rhubarb. Top the sauce with the remaining crumb mixture.

Bake for about 55 minutes, or until the rhubarb appears bubbly and the topping crunchy. Serve warm or at room temperature.

Perhaps the fastest-growing barbecue organization in the country, the National Barbecue Association brings together restaurateurs, caterers, equipment manufacturers, sauce makers, and backyard cooks. For a $35 individual membership or a $75 business membership, you receive the monthly newsletter, *Barbecue Today*, and an invitation to a fun-filled annual conference and trade show.

Texas Peach Cobbler

Texans usually like their peach cobblers with an abundance of juicy fruit and a biscuit-like batter topping that's crunchy on the surface and doughy inside.

FILLING

12 to 14 ripe medium peaches (about 3½ pounds), peeled and sliced
¼ cup sugar

1 tablespoon fresh lemon juice
2 teaspoons ground cinnamon
¾ teaspoon ground ginger
¾ teaspoon vanilla extract

BATTER

8 tablespoons butter
1¼ cups all-purpose flour
¾ cup sugar

2 teaspoons baking powder
1 cup milk

Vanilla ice cream or whipped cream (optional)

Serves 8 to 10

Preheat the oven to 350° F.

In a bowl, mix together all the fruit filling ingredients. Set the fruit aside to draw out the juices while preparing the batter. Cobbler filling should be a bit juicier than most pies.

Melt the butter in a 9-by-13-inch baking dish, either in the oven or on the stove.

In another bowl, stir together the flour, sugar, and baking powder and add the milk. Mix until lightly blended. Spoon the mixture evenly over the melted butter. Don't stir it, which eliminates the development of crunchy edges. Pour the peach filling evenly over the batter.

Bake for 45 minutes. As the cobbler cooks, the batter oozes up and around the fruit, crowning the cobbler with a moist golden brown crust. Serve warm. If you're a certified hedonist, top it with vanilla ice cream or whipped cream.

Louie Mueller's in Taylor, Texas, looks and smells barbecue. Almost a century old now, the barn-like building is divided about equally into two areas, one for cooking and the other for eating. A simple counter separates the sections, and behind it sits a huge brick pit with a two-story chimney poking out of the ceiling. You line up at the pit, place your order, and carry your 'Q,' wrapped in butcher paper, to a table.

☆**Variation:** Make a blackberry cobbler by substituting berries for the peaches and eliminating the ginger. Add ¼ teaspoon nutmeg, if you wish.

☆**Serving Suggestion:** Stage a Texas ranch-style barbecue. Put out plentiful quantities of Little Devils in bowls and pass Chicken from Hell. The centerpiece has to be Braggin'-Rights Brisket, supplemented, if you like, by Hill Country Links. Round out the meal with Cowpoke Pintos, Creamy Coleslaw, a tray of pickled jalapeños and onion slices, and this juicy cobbler. Offer beer by the keg and Turquoise Margaritas by the pitcher.

Long-on-Strawberries Shortcake

While summer strawberries are always good over short-cake, the treat is twice as good with fruit in the cake, too.

CAKE

2 cups cake flour, sifted	3 eggs, separated
1 tablespoon baking powder	¾ cup water
½ teaspoon salt	¼ cup crushed fresh ripe strawberries
1 tablespoon poppy seeds	
1½ cups sugar	1 teaspoon almond extract
¾ cup butter, at room temperature	

TOPPING

1 cup whipping cream	2 pints fresh ripe strawberries, sliced
⅓ cup powdered sugar	

Serves 8 to 10

P reheat the oven to 350° F. Grease and flour two 9-inch round cake pans. Cut waxed paper or parchment circles to fit the pans, place in the pans, and grease and flour them again.

Leo and Son Barbeque in Oklahoma City features a banana strawberry cake guaranteed to sweeten anyone's disposition. All the regular barbecue dinners—no extra plates, please—come with macaroni salad, baked beans, iced tea, and a big slice of the fruity, sugar-glazed cake.

Sift together the flour, baking powder, and salt into a bowl. Stir in the poppy seeds.

With an electric mixer, cream together the sugar and butter. Add the egg yolks, beating well after each addition. Combine the water, crushed strawberries, and almond extract. Add the fruit and liquid to the butter mixture in thirds, alternating with the dry ingredients. Continue beating the batter until all ingredients are well incorporated.

With the mixer, beat the egg whites until stiff. Fold them into the batter.

Pour the batter into the prepared pans and bake for 20 minutes, or until a toothpick inserted in the center comes out clean. Cool the layers for about 5 minutes before removing them from the pans. Cool the layers on cake racks.

Prepare the fruit topping while the cake cools. Whip the cream and 1 tablespoon of the sugar. Refrigerate until ready to use. Combine the sliced strawberries with the remaining sugar, a tablespoon or two at a time, to desired sweetness.

To assemble the cake, transfer one layer to a serving plate. Top with half the berries and spread half the whipped cream over them. Repeat with the remaining ingredients. Serve immediately.

Still largely accurate, the 1988 *Real Barbecue* by Greg Johnson and Vince Staten (Harper & Row) is a first-rate guide to one hundred of the top barbecue joints in the country. The authors logged forty thousand miles researching the book and estimated that they ate two hundred pounds of barbecue and consumed some 629,200 calories.

Peanut Butter Cake

A recipe from Southern food authority Nathalie Dupree inspired our version of this cake-eaters' cake.

CAKE

2 cups cake flour	⅓ cup butter, at room
1¼ teaspoons baking soda	temperature
1 teaspoon baking powder	1¼ cups buttermilk
¾ cup sugar	2 eggs, separated
½ cup brown sugar	1 teaspoon vanilla extract
⅓ cup creamy peanut butter (don't use a natural or fresh-ground type)	

FROSTING

¼ cup butter, at room temperature	½ cup evaporated milk
1 cup sugar	1 cup creamy peanut butter (don't use a natural or fresh-ground type)
½ cup brown sugar	

Serves 12

Preheat the oven to 350° F. Grease and flour two 9-inch round cake pans. Cut waxed paper or parchment circles to fit the pans, place them in the pans, and grease again.

In a medium-size bowl, sift together the flour, baking soda, and baking powder, and set the mixture aside.

With an electric mixer, cream together the sugars, peanut butter, and butter. Add the sifted dry ingredients in batches, alternating with the buttermilk, egg yolks, and vanilla, and beat with a mixer.

With the mixer, beat the egg whites until very foamy. Fold the whites into the batter by hand.

Pour the batter into the prepared pans. Bake for 30 to 35 minutes, or until a toothpick inserted in the center comes out clean. Cool the layers for about 5 minutes before removing them from the pans. Cool the layers on cake racks.

Prepare the frosting after the cake is cool, since the frosting thickens quickly. In a heavy saucepan, melt the butter over medium heat. Add the remaining ingredients, except the peanut butter, and bring to a boil over high heat. Boil for 5 minutes. Remove from the heat and immediately stir in the peanut butter, mixing well.

To assemble the cake, place one layer of the cake on a decorative serving platter. Spread just the top of the layer with half of the frosting. Add the second cake layer and repeat the process, again frosting just the top. The cake is best served the day it's made, but if tightly covered, leftovers will remain moist for another day.

South Georgia Pound Cake

Pound cake made its first American appearance in colonial Virginia about the same time as barbecue. It spread from there to other states, which often developed treasured local variations. This sour cream rendition was influenced by an heirloom Georgia recipe.

3 cups all-purpose flour	⅔ cup sour cream
¼ teaspoon salt	1 tablespoon vanilla extract
1 pound butter, at room temperature	½ teaspoon lemon extract
2 cups sugar	5 eggs

Serves 8 to 10

Preheat the oven to 350° F. Grease and flour a 10-inch Bundt pan or tube pan.

Sift together the flour and salt and set the mixture aside.

With an electric mixer, cream together the butter and sugar. When well blended, mix in the sour cream and

The Barbecue Championship of Nebraska is always a neck-and-neck competition, staged each September at the Omaha race track.

the vanilla and lemon extracts. Beat in the eggs one at a time, alternating them with the flour.

Spoon the batter into the prepared pan. Bake for 60 to 65 minutes, or until the cake is golden and a toothpick inserted in the center comes out clean. Let the cake sit for 10 minutes, then invert onto a cake rack to finish cooling. Serve warm or at room temperature.

☆**Serving Suggestion:** In honor of the cake's origin, top it with fresh peaches or our Bourbon Peaches.

Becky's Pineapple Cake

The bubbly hostess at the Glenmar Plantation Bed & Breakfast near Springfield, Kentucky, Becky Mandell often serves a cake similar to this for afternoon snacking. It's as simple as it is scrumptious.

CAKE

2 cups all-purpose flour	1 cup chopped pecans
2 cups sugar	1½ teaspoons vanilla extract
2 eggs	¼ teaspoon salt
2 teaspoons baking soda	
20-ounce can crushed pineapple with juice or syrup	

FROSTING

8 ounces cream cheese, at room temperature	2 cups powdered sugar
8 tablespoons butter, at room temperature	1½ teaspoons vanilla extract

Serves 8

Preheat the oven to 350° F. Grease a 9-by-13-inch baking pan.

In a large bowl, mix together all the cake ingredients. Pour the batter into the prepared pan. Bake for 35 min-

Two cousins from Louisiana—Foster and Woody Phillips—compete against each other in a pair of popular barbecue stands in the same Los Angeles neighborhood. The cousins are close friends, but the patrons at Phillips—Foster's place—will argue barbecue all night with a loyal customer of Woody's.

utes, or until a toothpick inserted in the center comes out clean.

With an electric mixer, beat together the cream cheese and butter. Mix in the powdered sugar and vanilla and beat until smooth. Spread the cake with the frosting. The cake can be frosted warm or cool. It keeps well for 2 days, refrigerated. Bring to room temperature before serving.

Black Walnut Cake

From the Carolinas to Kansas City, black walnuts are prized for their rich pungency. They're worth seeking out, but if you can't find them, substitute the more common English variety. The inspiration for this cake comes from an old recipe included in Beth Tartan's classic North Carolina and Old Salem Cookery (*University of North Carolina Press*), *in print for some forty years.*

CAKE

3 cups all-purpose flour
1½ teaspoons ground ginger
1 teaspoon baking soda
½ teaspoon ground cinnamon
½ teaspoon salt
1 cup cane syrup or ½ cup dark molasses and ½ cup light corn syrup

1 cup butter, at room temperature
3 eggs
1 cup buttermilk
1 teaspoon vanilla extract

FROSTING

1 cup sugar
1 cup brown sugar
½ cup buttermilk
¼ cup butter, at room temperature

1 cup black walnut pieces
¾ cup dried currants or chopped raisins
1½ teaspoons vanilla extract

Serves 12

Bozo's is a legendary name in Tennessee barbecue, founded in 1923 by Thomas J. "Bozo" Williams. Located in the small town of Mason, the restaurant features pork plates and sandwiches that are good enough to draw fans from Memphis, which has a hundred or so joints of its own and calls itself the "Pork Barbecue Capital of the World."

Preheat the oven to 350° F. Grease and flour two 9-inch round cake pans. Cut waxed paper or parchment into circles to fit the pans, place in the pans, and grease again.

In a medium-size bowl, sift together the flour, ginger, baking soda, cinnamon, and salt; set the mixture aside.

With an electric mixer, cream together the syrup and butter. Beat in the eggs. Add the sifted dry ingredients in batches, alternating with the buttermilk and vanilla, and continue beating until well mixed.

Pour the batter into the prepared pans. Bake the cakes for 25 to 30 minutes, or until a toothpick inserted in the center comes out clean. Cool the layers for about 5 minutes before removing them from the pans. Cool the layers on cake racks.

To prepare the frosting, combine the sugar, brown sugar, buttermilk, and butter in a heavy saucepan. Bring the mixture to a boil and boil for several minutes, until thickened. Remove from the heat and mix in the walnuts, currants, and vanilla.

To assemble the cake, place one layer of the cake on a decorative serving platter. Spread just the top of the layer with half of the frosting. Add the second cake layer and repeat the process, again frosting just the top. The cake is best served the day it's made, but if tightly covered, leftovers will remain moist for another day.

☆**Serving Suggestion:** Because of the cake's density and richness, it's best after a lighter barbecue meal, perhaps Kingly Salmon or Mint Trout.

Candy Bar Cheesecake

The only dessert offered in many Bar-B-Q joints is candy from a rack near the door. Here's a way to replicate that taste—at least for a Mounds bar—in a classier dessert form.

CRUST

5 to 6 ounces chocolate wafer cookies
1 cup shredded sweetened coconut

2 tablespoons sugar
¼ cup butter, melted

FILLING

1 pound cream cheese, at room temperature
¾ cup canned cream of coconut
½ cup shredded sweetened coconut

3 eggs
½ teaspoon vanilla extract

TOPPING

8 ounces bittersweet or dark sweet chocolate
2 tablespoons butter

2 tablespoons canned cream of coconut

Serves 10 to 12

Preheat the oven to 350° F.

In a food processor, combine the cookies, coconut, and sugar, and process until crumbly. Pour in the butter and process just to combine.

Pat the mixture into the bottom of a 9-inch springform pan. Bake the crust for 10 minutes, until lightly set. Put the crust aside to cool.

Reduce the oven temperature to 300° F.

In a food processor or electric mixer, combine the cream cheese, cream of coconut, and coconut. By hand, stir in the eggs, one at a time until fully incorporated, and then add the vanilla. Pour the filling into the crust. Fill a baking pan or dish with water and place it on the

The post-barbecue candy of choice in many Southern states is actually a kind of cake that is called a pie—a Moon Pie. Made solely by the Chattanooga Bakery in Chattanooga, Tennessee, it's a gooey fistful of marshmallow sandwiched between graham cracker–style cookies coated in chocolate or other flavorings. They likely took their name from an early salesman's comment about them being "as big as the moon." If you aren't lucky enough to live in Tennessee, Arkansas, Mississippi, or another Moon Pie stronghold, you can order them by the case directly from the bakery at 800-251-3404.

lowest rack in the oven. Bake the cheesecake on the center rack for 1 hour, or until lightly set. Let the cake sit at room temperature for about 15 minutes, then cover it and chill for at least 1 hour.

Remove the cheesecake from the refrigerator. In a small heavy saucepan, melt together the topping ingredients. Remove the mixture from the heat and spread it gently over the top of the cheesecake. Return the cheesecake to the refrigerator for at least 3 more hours or overnight.

Before serving, allow the cheesecake to sit for 10 to 15 minutes at room temperature. Remove the springform sides from the pan. Slice the cheesecake with a warm knife, to cut through the chocolate topping most easily, and serve.

Sweet Potato Pudding

If you've ever had a sweet potato pie, you won't be surprised that the spuds also make a superb pudding, topped here with a praline crunch.

PRALINE

½ cup chopped pecans
¼ cup chopped crystallized ginger

¼ cup brown sugar
2 tablespoons butter, at room temperature

PUDDING

2½ cups baked sweet potatoes (about 3 medium potatoes), scooped from the skin
½ cup brown sugar
4 eggs
⅓ cup milk
2 tablespoons butter, melted

2 tablespoons vanilla extract
1 tablespoon cane syrup or dark corn syrup
1 tablespoon rum
½ teaspoon salt
½ teaspoon ground cinnamon
½ teaspoon ground ginger

Serves 6 to 8

reheat the oven to 350° F. Grease a 1½-quart baking dish.

In a small bowl, combine the pecans, ginger, brown sugar, and butter. Reserve the mixture.

With an electric mixer, beat together all the pudding ingredients until smooth and light. Pour the pudding into the baking dish.

Bake for 25 minutes. Sprinkle the reserved praline mixture over the pudding and bake for an additional 20 to 25 minutes, until the pudding is set and slightly puffed. The top will sink as the pudding cools. Serve warm or at room temperature.

☆**Serving Suggestion:** Serve the pudding as the finale for a Thanksgiving feast featuring Worth-the-Wait Turkey and all the trimmings.

'Nana Pudding

PUDDING

1 cup sugar	2½ cups whole milk, heated
2 tablespoons cornstarch	2 teaspoons vanilla extract
Pinch of salt	12-ounce box vanilla wafers
6 egg yolks	5 to 6 bananas

MERINGUE

6 egg whites	Pinch of salt
⅛ teaspoon cream of tartar	3 tablespoons sugar

Serves 6 to 8

o make the pudding, stir together the sugar, cornstarch, and salt in the top of a double boiler. Mix in the egg yolks and place the pan over its simmering water bath. Pour in the warm milk gradually, stirring constantly. Continue to stir frequently as the pudding

The sign at the entrance to Rosedale Barbeque, near downtown Kansas City, proudly announces that the restaurant was born on July 4, 1934. Anthony Rieke founded the lunchroom-cum-bar and designed his own pits, including a rotisserie smoker for ribs that he tested first by riding in it himself.

cooks. It will gradually thicken, usually in about 15 to 20 minutes, but don't rush it. The pudding is done when it coats a spoon and slides off slowly. Remove the pan from the heat and stir in the vanilla.

Preheat the oven to 350° F.

While the pudding cools, arrange a layer of vanilla wafers at the bottom of a shallow, 1½-quart baking dish. Slice the bananas thin and layer half over the cookies. Spoon half of the pudding over the banana slices. Repeat with the remaining cookies and pudding. Tuck more cookies in around the sides of the dish as well. We normally use only about two-thirds of the box of cookies, but some people manage more.

To make the meringue topping, beat the egg whites with an electric mixer. When the egg whites begin to froth, add the cream of tartar and salt. Gradually beat in the sugar and continue beating until the whites form a stiff-peaked meringue.

Crown the assembled pudding with the meringue, heaping it high in the center. Bake for 15 to 18 minutes, or until the meringue is firm and golden brown.

Cool for 30 minutes before serving. Refrigerate the pudding if you plan to hold it longer than that. Leftovers can be kept for another day, although the bananas will darken somewhat.

Santa Fe Capirotada

Most versions of bread pudding come from the New Orleans tradition, which involves a liberal use of eggs and cream. This version hails from farther west, in New Mexico, and it gets its richness from butter and cheese. A similar version is offered by the Santa Fe School of Cooking in some of its classes.

½ cup raisins
½ cup brandy
10 to 12 slices white bread, torn in small pieces and toasted
½ cup chopped pecans, toasted
1 cup grated cheddar or Monterey jack cheese (4 ounces)
4 tablespoons butter
1 tart apple, peeled and chopped

2 cups sugar
2½ cups hot water
1 cup apple cider
2 teaspoons vanilla extract
1 teaspoon *canela* (Mexican cinnamon) or ground cinnamon
½ teaspoon ground nutmeg
Pinch of cloves

Whipped cream, for garnish (optional)

Serves 8

Place the raisins in a small bowl and pour the brandy over them. Set aside to soften for at least 20 minutes.

Preheat the oven to 350° F. Butter a 9-by-13-inch baking dish. Arrange the bread in the baking dish. Top the bread with the pecans and the cheese, mixing both in lightly. Scatter the raisins over the cheese and add any brandy not absorbed by the fruit.

In a small skillet, warm 2 tablespoons of the butter. Add the apple and sauté until softened. Spoon the apple over the raisins.

Pour the sugar into a large, heavy saucepan. Warm it over medium-high heat until the sugar melts and turns a deep golden brown, 8 to 10 minutes. Stir occasionally to assure even melting. Using caution, pour the water

In Denver they name streets after their best pitmasters. The section of 34th Avenue outside Daddy Bruce's Bar-B-Q is now officially Bruce Randolph Avenue, in honor of the man who brought real barbecue to the city and helped to feed the needy each Thanksgiving.

into the melted sugar. Stand back from the pan because steam will rise as the water hits the sugar. The mixture will partially solidify. Continue cooking it until the sugar becomes liquid again, stirring occasionally. Add the cider, vanilla, spices, and remaining 2 tablespoons of butter to the syrup.

Ladle the syrup over the bread carefully. (Should you get any caramel syrup on you, immediately rinse the spot with cold water.) The syrup should be about equal in level to the bread itself. Push the bread into the syrup if any isn't already coated.

Bake the pudding for 20 to 25 minutes, or until the syrup has been absorbed and the cheese has melted into the pudding. Serve hot, topped with whipped cream if you wish.

☆**Serving Suggestion:** Serve the bread pudding following a barbecue of Southwestern Cabrito.

Booker's Bourbon Mint Ice Cream

This is a little like a creamy, frozen mint julep. We named it after Booker Noe, grandson of Jim Beam and Master Distiller today at the big family business in Clermont, Kentucky.

6 tablespoons bourbon	¾ cup sugar
¼ cup minced fresh mint	5 egg yolks
1 pint half-and-half	1 tablespoon vanilla extract
1 cup whipping cream	

Serves 4 to 6 (makes 1 quart)

In a small saucepan, warm the bourbon with the mint over medium heat. Remove the bourbon from the heat and allow it to steep 15 minutes. Strain the bourbon into the top pan of a double boiler. Add the remain-

Booker Noe's company, Jim Beam, is the oldest continuing business in Kentucky, founded by farmer Jacob Beam shortly after he moved to the frontier territory in 1788. We don't know for sure, but it's likely that Jacob liked barbecue as much as his bourbon and that he preferred both to ice cream.

ing ingredients and place the pan over simmering water. Warm the custard mixture, whisking until well blended. Continue heating, frequently stirring up from the bottom, until the mixture thickens. Expect the process to take about 15 minutes. Do not boil the custard. Remove the pan from the heat and strain the custard.

Transfer the custard to an ice cream maker and process according to the manufacturer's directions. Freeze it until serving time. The ice cream is best eaten within several days.

☆**Serving Suggestion:** Serve the ice cream over South Georgia Pound Cake and garnish with fresh mint.

The Best Cure for a Southern Summer

As much as we love the previous desserts, we're not sure that any of them beat cold watermelons, so naturally sweet that they were once processed into sugar. Ice down a big melon and forget heat, humidity, and your air-conditioning bill.

1   watermelon

Serves 8 or more

Chill the melon in the refrigerator or iced down in a tub. Slice and serve.
Save the leftover watermelon rind to turn into watermelon pickles.

LC's in Kansas City advertises the old-fashioned way. Everything is cooked in a pit that sits directly on a street corner along a busy boulevard. Even speeders can't miss the smoke.

382

Cool and Cheery
☆ Drinks ☆

It can get pretty damn hot cooking outside. You're contending with the sun, the wood or charcoal fire, the smoke, and maybe even a lot of hot air from some expert helper, like your spouse. If it doesn't drive you to drink, you probably haven't met enough good temptations in your life. Try these.

Bloody Bud

Beer is the beverage of choice for most pitmasters, particularly light-bodied American brews, such as Budweiser. To keep up with the crowd at a barbecue cook-off, you start bending your elbow about the time you light your fire in the morning. If that sounds too early, or if your cranium is still complaining about the night before, drink your first beer like a Bloody Mary. It may not exactly cure a hangover, but it'll at least shock that sucker into submission.

12 ounces ice-cold beer
12 ounces tomato or V8 juice, chilled
1 tablespoon Worcestershire sauce
Several splashes of Tabasco or other hot pepper sauce

½ teaspoon celery salt
½ teaspoon barbecue dry rub, preferably a spicy one such as Southwest Heat (page 39)

Serves 2

Pour half of the beer, tomato juice, Worcestershire sauce, and Tabasco into each of two tall iced tea glasses. Top each glass with half of the celery salt and the dry rub. Drink, don't sip.

☆**Serving Suggestion:** A full hangover cure includes some Up and At 'Em Lamb Sausage and Buttermilk Biscuits.

On a hot day at the barbecue pit, our thirst sometimes reminds us of an old Prohibition politician, the one who promised voters that he would make their state so dry the residents would have to prime their mouths to spit.

386

The origin of the mint julep is obscure, but Kentucky has claimed credit for the invention since the early nineteenth century. Old lore about the drink suggests many secrets for success, such as picking the mint in the dewy cool of the early morning, using cold spring water "pure as angels are," and, most important, serving the julep in a silver goblet.

Derby Day Mint Julep

Mint juleps have been the traditional drink of the Kentucky Derby since the founder of Churchill Downs, Colonel Meriwether Lewis Clark, started the race in 1875. On Derby Day, special bars at the track sell about eighty thousand juleps to the 125,000 spectators. Some people think the concoction is too sweet, some say it's too strong, but you'll always find a julep in the winner's circle in the bluegrass and bourbon state.

1 cup sugar	Kentucky bourbon
1 cup water	Mint sprigs, for garnish
1 cup loosely packed fresh mint leaves	

Serves 10 to 20

In a saucepan, bring the sugar and the water to a boil for 5 minutes, without stirring. Allow the syrup to cool for several minutes.

Place the mint loosely in a jar and cover it with the syrup. Cap the jar and refrigerate the mixture overnight or for a full day. Remove the mint and discard it. The mint syrup will keep refrigerated for 2 to 3 weeks.

Make juleps individually. For each serving, fill an 8-ounce glass with crushed ice. Add a half-tablespoon of mint syrup—or as much as a full tablespoon if you like your juleps on the sweet side—and 2 ounces of bourbon. Stir gently to frost the glass, garnish with a sprig of mint, and serve at once.

☆**Serving Suggestion:** No Derby Day party is complete without a bowl of Kentucky Burgoo.

Lynchburg Cooler

Kentucky may be the home of bourbon, but Tennessee also produces its share of good whiskey, including the Jack Daniel made in the small burg of Lynchburg.

2 ounces Jack Daniel or similar
  whiskey
1 ounce brandy
1 ounce rum

1 ounce water
1½ teaspoons sugar
4 twists of lemon peel

Serves 2

In a cocktail shaker or lidded jar, combine all ingredients except the lemon peel and shake until the sugar dissolves.

Pour over ice cubes in old-fashioned glasses. Top with the lemon peel. Serve immediately.

Jack Daniel hosts one of the most prestigious barbecue cook-offs each fall in Lynchburg. You must be invited to enter the competition, and you won't get that honor without winning other contests. In 1992, thirty thousand spectators descended on the village (population 361). It's a good thing they came for a taste of something other than whiskey because Lynchburg is in a dry county.

V.W.

Nothing tastes better than watermelon in the summertime, even in a beverage.

3 ounces vodka
2 cups watermelon juice
  (made from puréed
  watermelon)

Powdered sugar (optional)

Serves 2

Half-fill two tall 10-ounce to 12-ounce glasses with ice. Pour in the vodka and the juice. Stir and taste. If the watermelon wasn't particularly sweet, you may want to add a touch of powdered sugar. Mix in the sugar, if needed, and serve immediately.

☆**Serving Suggestion:** The perfect appetizer to eat with a V.W. is Mouthwatering Watermelon Morsel.

The next time you're in Luling, Texas, for the annual summer Watermelon Thump, have lunch downtown at the old City Market. The pitmasters fix such juicy brisket and links that you might find yourself wanting to enter the watermelon seed–spitting contest. If you can reach 69 feet in the sport, you'll break the world record, currently held by a Luling pro.

Firewater

Some major American chefs, including Paul Prudhomme and Mark Miller, offer variations on this theme under different names at pretty steep prices. You can make your own, and earn your own fame, for a much lower cost.

1 liter decent vodka
3 to 4 fresh serranos or
   jalapeños, split

Twists of lime peel and/or green
   olives, preferably jalapeño-
   stuffed, for garnish

Serves a party

In a bottle or jar, combine the vodka and chiles and cover. Let the mixture steep at room temperature for a minimum of 3 days.

Transfer the vodka to the freezer and allow it to chill thoroughly. (It won't freeze.) Serve straight up or over ice, garnished with a twist of lime or olive, martini style.

☆**Serving Suggestion:** To soothe your throat, munch on smoked cheese, such as Can't Wait Queso or Unholy Swiss Cheese.

Yankee Shooter

The barbecue contest circuit is full of colorful characters, but none is more entertaining than Obie Obermark, the lean, tall Texan who invented the Yankee Shooter. To fix the Shooter right, you have to use Yankee Blaster, one of seventeen barbecue spice mixes that Obie makes and sells. Our suggestion for a substitute works in a pinch, but it's not the genuine article.

Shot of high-quality tequila
Yankee Blaster spice mix (or an equal combination of cayenne and
    crushed chile de árbol)

Serves 1

Add 1 to 7 shakes of Yankee Blaster to the tequila or the same number of TINY pinches of the substitute spice mix. Yankee Blaster is named for its heat level, so beware. Obie takes a full 7 shakes but doesn't recommend it to anyone who isn't a veteran of jalapeño-eating contests.

Cover the glass with your hand and shake it vigorously, one shake per dose of the dry spices. Gulp the contents immediately and completely, trying to remain upright.

In addition to being a champion pitmaster, Obie Obermark writes for several barbecue publications and provides dynamic leadership for the International Barbecue Cookers Association, the second largest membership organization of its kind after the Kansas City Barbeque Society. If you can't find Obie's Yankee Blaster and other spice mixes locally, write P.O. Box 226124, Dallas, Texas 75222-6124, or call 214-943-9974 for ordering information.

Turquoise Margarita

This is a festive take on the margarita, perfect for a barbecue party.

Salt
Lime wedge
1½ ounces high-quality tequila

1 ounce blue Curaçao
¾ ounce fresh lime juice

Serves 1

The Jack Daniel Distillery sponsors a barbecue cook-off team headed by Mike "Fish" Fisher, a technician at the whiskey plant. Cooking on a huge smoker in the shape of a Jack Daniel bottle, the group took up their hobby with genuine enthusiasm after they were invited to barbecue for a bikini contest in Nashville.

Place a thin layer of salt onto a saucer. Rub the rim of an 8-ounce glass with the lime wedge and immediately dip the rim into the salt. Set aside.

Pour the tequila, Curaçao, and lime juice into a cocktail shaker or lidded jar, add several pieces of cracked ice, and shake to blend. Pour into the prepared glass and serve.

☆**Serving Suggestion:** Little Devils are made to match any tequila drink.

Apricorita

Another specialty margarita, this is a frozen version with a fruity tang.

2 ounces high-quality tequila
1 ounce apricot brandy
¾ ounce fresh lime juice

1 tablespoon honey, or more
to taste
1½ cups cracked ice

1 fresh apricot, halved, for garnish (optional)

Serves 2

In a blender, combine the tequila, brandy, lime juice, and honey and blend until well combined. Add the ice and blend until smooth. Pour into tulip-shaped champagne glasses and garnish with apricot halves, if you wish. Serve immediately.

Sangrita Maria

In Mexico, bartenders often serve shots of tequila with a side glass of sangrita, a zippy tomato and citrus mixture. We're too lazy to wash two glasses when one will do, so we just combine the ingredients into a south-of-the-border Bloody Mary.

2 cups tomato juice
½ cup fresh orange juice
2 tablespoons fresh lime juice
1 tablespoon chopped onion
2 teaspoons Worcestershire sauce
1 fresh serrano or jalapeño, chopped

4 ounces high-quality tequila
Sprinkle of celery salt
Dry rub, such as Wild Willy's Number One-derful Rub (page 36) or Southwest Heat (page 39) (optional)
Whole serranos and lime wedges, for garnish

Serves 4

Combine the juices, onion, Worcestershire sauce, chile, and tequila in a blender. Blend the mixture briefly until well combined. Pour it into tall glasses filled with ice cubes. Shake a little celery salt over each drink and, if you wish, a bit of dry rub, too. Garnish with a serrano chile attached by a toothpick to the lime wedge.

The Delta Jubilee Barbecue Cooking Contest in Clarksdale, Mississippi, gives awards for two related achievements. If you win the "Party 'til ya Oink" trophy, you'll probably want to be pretty tight the next morning with the folks who take the prize for the best Bloody Mary.

Iced Sunshine

2 tablespoons simple syrup, or more to taste
2 cups pink grapefruit juice (from about 4 large grapefruit)

¼ cup high-quality tequila, preferably silver
Splash of grenadine

Serves 2

In a cocktail shaker or lidded jar, combine the simple syrup, fruit juice, and tequila. Pour the mixture over ice in tall glasses. Add a splash of grenadine to the top of each drink and serve.

To make simple syrup, combine equal amounts of sugar and water and bring the mixture to a boil until the sugar dissolves. Cool. The syrup keeps indefinitely.

392

Maui Mai Tai

A couple of these and you'll feel as balmy as a Hawaiian breeze.

1½ teaspoons simple syrup
1   ounce dark rum
1   ounce light rum
1   ounce fresh lemon juice
½   ounce Curaçao or other
    orange-flavored liqueur

1½ teaspoons orgeat syrup
    (an almond-flavored syrup
    available at well-stocked
    liquor stores)

Fresh pineapple spear, lime wedge, and fresh mint sprig,
    for garnish
Little paper parasol, to make your friends giggle (optional)

Serves 1

Combine the simple syrup, rums, lemon juice, Curaçao, and orgeat syrup in a cocktail shaker or lidded jar and shake well. Pour the drink over ice in a double old-fashioned glass. Garnish it as desired and serve.

☆**Serving Suggestion:** Mai Tais go great before a Hawaiian seafood dinner, such as Kohala Tuna Steaks or Jungle Prince Scallops.

Barbecue, beer, and blues form a soulful trio at Kansas City's Grand Emporium. "Amazing" Grace Harris cooks the 'Q' and serves it six nights a week with some of the hottest licks in town.

Peachy Daiquiri

Here's the best use for canned peaches we've ever found.

16-ounce can peaches in heavy
   syrup, undrained
1 cup light rum

Juice of 1 to 2 limes
2 cups cracked ice
Lime slices, for garnish

Serves 4

Combine the peaches, rum, lime juice, and ice in a blender and blend until smooth. Pour the drink into tulip-shaped champagne glasses, garnish with lime slices, and serve.

Plumb Loco Coco Punch

1 cup dark rum
½ cup canned cream of coconut
¼ cup Mint Syrup (page 395)

¼ cup milk or half-and-half
1 tablespoon vanilla extract
4 cups cracked ice

Mint sprigs, for garnish

Serves 4

Place the rum, cream of coconut, syrup, milk, vanilla, and ice in a blender and blend until the mixture is smooth. Pour the drink into tall glasses, garnish with mint, and serve. Sip slowly, or you'll find yourself as loco as the punch.

Fort Worth is a Texas-size party town, home to Billy Bob's Texas ("the world's largest honky tonk") and to Angelo's, a barn of a joint where the barbecue, beer, and brouhaha seem as natural together as a pig and a pit.

Mint Syrup

1 cup sugar
1 cup water

½ cup mint leaves

In a saucepan, bring the sugar, water, and the mint to a boil, and boil the mixture until the sugar is dissolved and the liquid is clear. Set the syrup aside to steep as it cools. Strain before using. The syrup keeps, refrigerated, for several weeks.

When you belly-up to the bar at the Bar-B-Q Shop in Memphis, you find yourself facing a former Catholic confessional. The elaborately carved backdrop looks splendid, but it may not whet your appetite for demon rum.

Cold Buttered Rum

Here's an ice cream alternative to the winter favorite, filling enough to replace dessert.

1½ ounces dark rum
1 large scoop butter pecan
   ice cream
½ cup cracked ice

Dash of bitters
Sprinkle of nutmeg
Orange slice, for garnish

Serves 1

In a blender, combine the rum, ice cream, ice, and bitters and blend until smooth. Pour the drink into a balloon-shaped wine glass. Sprinkle it with nutmeg, garnish with the orange slice, and serve immediately.

☆**Serving Suggestion:** With any spicy barbecue meal, Cold Buttered Rum makes a refreshing after-dinner drink.

Cham-gria

Nothing says summer like sangria, or sangaree, as it's sometimes known in parts of the South. Spanish in origin, the wine concoction seeped into the country through Florida and Texas. This version uses a bit of the bubbly in the blend.

3 oranges, sliced and halved
3 limes, sliced and halved
2 lemons, sliced and halved
1 cup sugar
1½-liter bottle fruity red wine
1 cup apricot brandy

½ cup triple sec or other
    orange-flavored liqueur
Juice of 2 limes
750-milliliter bottle inexpensive
    champagne or sparkling wine

Makes about 1 gallon

Place the fruit in a pitcher or large bowl. Cover the fruit with the sugar and let the mixture sit at room temperature for about 1 hour.

Pour the wine, brandy, triple sec, and lime juice over the fruit and stir to dissolve the sugar. Chill the mixture for at least 30 minutes and up to several hours.

Just before serving, mix in the champagne and add enough ice cubes to make the drink really frosty. Serve the sangria over more ice, adding a few fruit slices to each serving. *Salud.*

Some things people do while barbecuing: drink beer, lie like a politician, play with children, pop another top, curse work, laugh loud, lose the church key, recollect younger years, dip a chip, and down more cold ones. Some things you don't do: pay bills, mow the grass, watch TV, or use a freeway to go get more ice. Vote for the party of your choice.

Mango-Lime Spritzer

A refreshingly light cooler, this is good as a nonalcoholic beverage, too. Just replace the wine with more club soda or carbonated mineral water.

1 large ripe mango, peeled and cut in chunks
Juice of 1 lime

Lime slices, for garnish

1 cup white wine
½ cup club soda or carbonated mineral water

Serves 2

Combine the mango and lime juice in a blender and purée. Add the wine and club soda and blend thoroughly. Pour the mixture through a strainer into 2 tall glasses. Add ice, garnish with the limes, and serve.

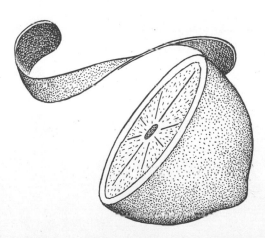

Sunny Sweet Tea

Set this outside in the sun with you while you barbecue and you'll have great iced tea by lunch time. You can substitute artificial sweetener for the sugar, but a venerable rule of barbecue etiquette requires some kind of sweetening.

6 tea bags
1 quart cold water
Sugar, a lot of it

Ice
Lemon wedges, for garnish

Serves 2

Put the tea bags and cold water in a large jar, setting it out in the sun to soak up some rays. You'll have tea in a couple of hours, but give it at least twice that long for the fullest flavor. Add sugar to taste, traditionally until your teeth ache.

Let the tea stand at room temperature until needed or pour immediately over ice. Use a good quantity of cubes, but don't overdo it. Serve the tea in barrel-size plastic glasses for the most authentic touch. Add a hefty wedge of lemon per glass. Always offer refills. Iced tea tastes best the day it's made.

Bar-B-Q joints sell plenty of sweetened tea, but they are often big on soft drinks as well. If you want to evoke the right feeling at home, serve R.C. Cola instead of Coke or track down a carton of Big Reds, a popular barbecue drink in central Texas.

The Lipton Tea Brewers and Bar-B-Quers work for a Lipton plant in Independence, Missouri. At contests the team barbecues in a giant tea kettle, once used at the plant to make instant tea. When the 'Q' is done, the pitmaster blows the kettle's whistle.

Acknowledgments

Every cook in the world is indebted to scores or even hundreds of other people who've taught him or her tricks of the craft. We're more indebted than most, maybe because we're slow learners, but also because there are so many wonderful people in the world of barbecue eager to share anything from their food and beer to their secrets.

Our first teachers, who go back to childhood, were the pitmasters in Bar-B-Q joints across the country, especially in Kansas City, Memphis, and Texas. They taught us what barbecue should taste like and they continue to inspire our aspirations. From the time when Bill was a teenage soda jerk in Dallas in the 1950s, he recalls one grizzled old-timer in particular at a neighborhood joint—the name of the guy and the place long forgotten but not the sawdust floors and the superb sandwiches.

Among contemporary mentors, Wayne and PJ Whitworth stand out as delightful friends and savvy down-home cooks. They introduced us to the marvels of log-burning pits and provided the joy of their company over numerous hours of barbecuing and partying. Just as expert at the same pleasures, Jim and Donna Quessenberry graciously took us in as Arkansas Trav'lers team members at the Memphis in May World Championship Barbecue Contest. We'll always cherish the great time we had with them, Arthur, Brian, Crayton, Dan, Tammy, and the rest of the reveling crew.

All the good folks at the Kansas City Barbeque Society have been helpful, particularly Carolyn Wells and Bunny Tuttle. We've visited their fair city often over the years to do some smoking and eating with Bob and Lynn Pierle and Henry and Madelyn Moran, dear friends who love the 'Q' as much as we do.

Back at home, another group of friends has always been ready to join us in a barbecue blow-out. The front line of critiquers and consumers includes Ed Reid, Ellen Bradbury, John Loehr, Sally Martin, Gayther and Susie Gonzales, Bob and Lisa Wade, Shirley and Richard Jones, Cindy and Jim Turner, Susan and David Curtis, Rob and Mary Coffland, Deborah Madison, Patrick McFarlin, Terry Melton, Jana Edmondson, Lenore Tapia, and Heather Jamison. Our masterful meat-cutter, Seva Dubuar, joins us occasionally and provides invaluable advice all the time, as do her colleagues, Art "Nobody Beats Art's Meat" Pacheco and Paula Garcia Jones.

Obie and Pat Obermark bring spirit to any occasion, some of it in the form of the tequila in their Yankee Shooters. Obie's barbecue writing adds color and humor to several newsletters, and John Thorne's two newsletters—*Simple Cooking* and *Cookbook*—are full of wit and solid information when he deals with barbecue or any other subject. Among cookbook authors and other food writers, we're particularly indebted in this project to Rich Davis and Shifra Stein, Nathalie Dupree, Linda West Eckhardt, John Egerton, Greg Johnson and Vince Staten, Jacqueline Higuera McMahan, Chris Schlesinger and John Willoughby, Phillip Stephen Schulz, Bobby Seale, Jane and Michael Stern, Jonathan St. Laurent, Beth Tartan, Jeanne Voltz, Maggie Waldron, and Carolyn Wells.

Executives at a number of companies and organizations volunteered help beyond the call of duty. They include Lloyd Davenport at Oklahoma Joe's, Donna Ellis at Cookshack, Stan Williams at Brinkmann, Pat Wilson at C.M. International, Betty A. Hughes at Weber-Stephen Products, Mike Dietert at New Braunfels Smokehouse, Ron Snider at the New Braunfels Smoker Company, Don Burnett at Smokemaster, and Theresa Harden at the National Barbecue Association.

Most of all, perhaps, we need to thank the folks who made our ramblings and recipes into a book. Bruce Shaw, Dan Rosenberg, Chris Blau, Andrea Chesman, Lois Ellen Frank, and Eric Kampmann actually put money and other support behind this pig-out. Eric, the distributor, deserves special commendation for his energetic dedication, maintained even after he turned fifty last year.

People, Places, and Products Index

☆

Recipe and BBQ Tips Index

☆

Other Cookbooks from The Harvard Common Press

The following titles can all be ordered directly from the publisher. Please enclose payment with your order and include $3.00 for postage and handling (add $.50 per additional book). Massachusetts residents please add 5% sales tax. All orders can be mailed to The Harvard Common Press, 535 Albany Street, Boston, MA 02118.

BY CHERYL AND BILL JAMISON

The Border Cookbook: Authentic Home Cooking of the American Southwest and Northern Mexico
$14.95 paper   1-55832-103-9
$29.95 cloth   1-55832-102-0
512 pages
From the Gulf of Mexico to the Pacific, from Sonora north to Sonoma, the border region is the source of a boundless variety of spectacular food. *The Border Cookbook* celebrates the simple pleasures of Southwestern and Northern Mexican home-style cooking with more than 300 tantalizing, easy-to-prepare dishes, for special occasions and for soul-satisfying everyday eating.

Texas Home Cooking
$16.95 paper   1-55832-059-8
$29.95 cloth   1-55832-058-X
592 pages
If the splendor of American cooking lies in the variety of cooking styles, each faithful to tradition but open to creative new blends, then Texas cooking surely is a national

treasure. Anglo, Mexican, Cajun, German, Czech, and other influences combine to make Texas cooking vibrant, colorful, and delectable. In over 400 mouth-watering recipes and with a wagonload of anecdotes and tales, Cheryl and Bill Jamison celebrate the breadth and bounty of true Texas cooking.

The Rancho de Chimayó Cookbook: The Traditional Cooking of New Mexico
$10.95 paper   1-55832-035-0
144 pages
The Rancho de Chimayó Cookbook celebrates the traditional New Mexican fare served at one of the nation's most acclaimed eateries, nestled 30 miles north of Santa Fe in the mountain village of Chimayó. These recipes represent the best examples of a distinct Southwestern cuisine.

BY OTHER AUTHORS

Cold Soups
by Linda Ziedrich
$10.95 paper   1-55832-078-4
$19.95 cloth   1-55832-077-6
144 pages
Here are eighty cool, easy-to-prepare recipes — sumptuous starters, hearty one-dish meals, refreshing snacks, and delightful, fruity desserts. Favored by chefs for their elegance, and by home cooks because they can be made ahead with no last-minute work, cold soups are the perfect way to make use of seasonal produce from grocery or garden.

The Book of Chowder

by Richard J. Hooker

$10.95   paper   0-916782-10-7

144 pages

"Joy to chowder heads . . . Hooker has unearthed some fascinating lore and recipes that make reading his book as much fun as cooking the chowders. *The Book of Chowder* impressed and enchanted me, as I'm sure it will any chowder lover. The recipes, the headnotes, and the illustrations are a delight." — James Beard

J. Bildner & Sons Cookbook: Casual Feasts, Food on the Run, and Special Celebrations

by Jim Bildner

$12.95   paper   1-55832-064-4

256 pages

From the gourmet food experts at the sophisticated J. Bildner & Sons grocery stores come imaginative recipes to enhance all the ordinary and extraordinary occasions in your busy life. Here is a collection of casual feasts for family and friends, terrific food for the daily whirl, delicious picnic fare, and perfect make-ahead dinners.

Chris Sprague's Newcastle Inn Cookbook: Recipes and Menus from a Celebrated New England Inn

by Chris Sprague

$10.95   paper   1-55832-049-0

$18.95   cloth   1-55832-050-4

176 pages

The culinary craft and wide-ranging repertoire of chef Chris Sprague have earned her a loyal following. Her Continental creations lean toward the Mediterranean and southern European, featuring the lighter and healthier sauces typical of those cuisines, and there is plenty of homey, hearty American cooking as well. Whether on their own or combined in one

of Ms. Sprague's menus, these are recipes that will make cooking the pleasure it is supposed to be.

The Blue Strawbery Cookbook: Cooking (Brilliantly) Without Recipes

by James Haller

$8.95   paper   0-916782-05-0

160 pages

Chef James Haller, one of the founders of the world-famous Blue Strawbery restaurant, lets us in on the secret of his brilliantly imaginative American high cuisine — no recipes! Simple food, simple tools, and the basic "roadmap" to creative cooking from soups to sherbets provide even the inexperienced cook with the ingredients of success.

Another Blue Strawbery: More Brilliant Cooking Without Recipes

by James Haller

$8.95   paper   0-916782-46-8

$14.95   cloth   0-916782-47-6

176 pages

In his sequel to *The Blue Strawbery Cookbook,* James Haller remains as committed as ever to the principles of freshness and wholesomeness of food for the body, and innovative combinations of flavors and textures for the spirit. In addition to new starters, main dishes, and desserts, he has added new chapters devoted to making your own flavored butters, vinegars, and oils.

The Gardner Museum Café Cookbook

by Lois Conroy

$9.95   paper   0-916782-71-9

160 pages

Lois McKitchen Conroy's spectacular treats — Chilled Nectarine Soup with Champagne; Roquefort and Apple Quiche; Salmon Pie; Baby Lamb Chops with

Cilantro Butter; Peppers Stuffed with Rice, Pine Nuts, and Currants; Mandarin Orange, Walnut, and Papaya Salad; and more — from this elegant museum café in Boston are all collected here.

The Abbey Cookbook: Inspired Recipes from the Great Atlanta Restaurant
by Hans Bertram
$10.95 paper   0-916782-26-3
$15.95 cloth   0-916782-23-9
224 pages
The Abbey Cookbook compiles 155 gourmet recipes from this prize-winning Atlanta restaurant where the food is continental, eclectic, and classical — all with a dash of nouvelle. Bring the food from this great restaurant to your dinner table with a cookbook the *Los Angeles Times* calls "heroic and uncompromising."

The Pillar House Cookbook
by David Paul Larousse and Alan R. Gibson
$14.95 paper   1-55832-005-9
248 pages
The informative cooking tips and highlights following each delectable recipe will encourage even the novice to try Pillar House specialties like Salmon Tortellini in Vodka Cream, Lobster Stew with Mussels, Roast Nantucket Duckling with Raspberry Ginger Sauce, or Praline and Peach Cheesecake.

The Plimoth Plantation New England Cookery Book
by Malabar Hornblower
$12.95 paper   1-55832-027-X
224 pages
With help from the staff of the famous Plimoth Plantation, Malabar Hornblower has artfully combined authentic 17th-century dishes with recipes that represent the best modern adaptations of traditional New England cuisine, in this culinary tribute to one of the country's leading outdoor museums.

A Taste for All Seasons: A Celebration of American Food
by the chefs of ARA Fine Dining in association with David Paul Larousse
$24.95 cloth   1-55832-020-2
224 pages
Discover the philosophy, techniques, and regional delicacies of the ARA Fine Dining Division in this treasury of seasonal fare that reflects the chefs' finest and most requested recipes, including Iowa Blue Cheese Tart, Oyster and Spinach Strudel, Veal Roulades, and Cherry Cobbler.

Starting a Small Restaurant, Revised Edition
by Daniel Miller
$11.95 paper   0-916782-37-9
224 pages
Daniel Miller, founder of a successful small restaurant in Cambria, California, outlines everything you'll need to know to break into this alluring business. He offers advice and information concerning location, menus, income forecasts, equipment, regulations, design and decor, personnel management, suppliers, maintenance, advertising and public relations, pricing and profits, emergencies, and computer systems.

Buller's Professional Course in Bartending for Home Study
by Jon Buller
$7.95   paper   0-916782-33-6
128 pages
A complete home-study course for professional bartending, this guide includes recipes for the 30 basic cocktails (as well as 150 other drinks), and tips on how to get started as a bartender, dealing with problem customers, legal liabilities, and more.